'Would you think m
have a shower, too?'
see, the facilities in
Within minutes, hi
and I sprayed him wi
way into my bedroon
'Now, I'm going to ... innermost secrets,' I warned him.
'I took an oath, when I became a member of The Magic Circle, that I would never divulge to anybody the secrets of our magic,' Merlin informed me.
'There are other secrets which I find more interesting,' I replied, as I pulled his towel off and contemplated his naked body. I leaned across, pulled him onto the bed and started to caress his chest and strong, hairy shoulders . . .

By the same author

The Happy Hooker
Letters to the Happy Hooker
Xaviera!
The Best Part of a Man
Xaviera's Supersex
Xaviera Goes Wild!
Xaviera Meets Marilyn Chambers (with Marilyn Chambers)
Knights in the Garden of Spain
Xaviera's Magic Mushrooms
Madame l'Ambassadrice
The Inner Circle
Lucinda, My Lovely

XAVIERA HOLLANDER

Fiesta of the Flesh

This edition published 1995
by Diamond Books
77–85 Fulham Palace Road
Hammersmith, London W6 8JB

First published by Panther Books 1984

ISBN 0 261 66640 1

Printed and bound in Great Britain

Set in Baskerville

Contents

1

Marbella

'Life is full of chances and changes.'

Aristotle

Every year I spend some months during the summer in Spain. I am no longer a mere tourist since I own a comfortable apartment in Marbella which is, for me, home from home. In an earlier book, I have described how I came to settle in Spain – that is as far as a gipsy like me can ever be said to have settled.

This year, I was accompanied by my faithful Franny. Readers of such books of mine as XAVIERA'S MAGIC MUSHROOMS and THE INNER CIRCLE will remember that I have described Franny as being a son, a daughter and a slave to me. Her personality changes like the weather. There are times when she is happy and apparently uncomplicated, almost like a child at play. This is Franny relaxed, perhaps when she is playing tennis or helping me with odd jobs around the house. Then I am contented also, and I show her affection to which she responds eagerly. At other times, it as though clouds have obscured the sunny side of Franny's temperament. She is nervy and awkward, difficult and critical, driving me into such a rage that I will strike her with my hand or with her whip or paddle, satisfying my own deep seated sadism and her ardent masochism. One thing never alters with Franny: that is her unfailing devotion to me, no matter how mean I am to her. So, she is an ideal companion to me since she can be relied on when I go through some bout of loneliness or moodiness on one of those days when nothing goes right. And when life is fun, Franny can let her hair down with the best of them. No matter how much we may argue or how cruel may be our sessions together, the love-hate bond that ties us is unbreakable and each year it seems to get stronger.

'So, what goes on in this Marbella?' Franny asked, as we sat on the balcony of my flat, enjoying the sunshine, warm as a lover's embrace. She had just carried our suitcases and all the other parcels and packages which we had brought from Amsterdam up from the car, and we were recovering from the last leg of the gruelling drive across Europe. 'Are the beaches good?'

'They're alright,' I answered. 'I've seen better with whiter sand or less polluted water. But, you know, once you have been on a few of the famous beaches in Bali, Java, Australia, Mexico, Argentina or Rio or St Tropez, you don't get so excited by the sight of one stretch of coast or another. The climate here is lovely, and of course, we'll go on the beach and get a good, deep sun tan. I have a lot of friends also who have villas with pools, and we can call on some of them and sunbathe away from the tourist crowds. The sunshine is one of the few things about Marbella which has not changed during the five years I have been coming here.'

'What did change?' Franny slipped off her shirt as she put the question to me.

'Well, for instance, what you are doing now,' I told her. 'Going topless was unheard of when I first came here, not that long after the death of Franco. Spain was a typical Catholic country, modest to the point of prudishness. I think that I can claim the honour to be the first woman who brought topless sunbathing to Spain though I never received an official citation. Now, there are even some secluded beaches which are totally nudist, but naked sunbathers are expected to cover up when, on a Sunday afternoon, their deserted beach is invaded by Papa, Momma and all the little niños with their picnic baskets, blankets, rubber balls and inflatable rafts.'

'So, the country has become more tolerant, more liberated?'

'Yes, in some ways, but there is still of lot of humbug. A policeman who may make trouble for you if you are guilty of what he calls indecent exposure and offending public morality will drool over the photos of the chicks in "Penthouse". Of course, in Madrid, or even more so in Barcelona, you will find sophisticated sex shows, but in places which are a bit off the beaten track, sexy entertainment is a hell of a lot more crude. Porno pulp magazines, pictures of women with tits so large they could not stand upright - even women with three tits, in case you were so short sighted you did not notice the first pair.'

'But here, in Marbella,' Franny wanted to know, 'it can't be that backward. After all, this is an international resort, even the locals must have become more sophisticated.'

'You'd be surprised at the things I have seen,' I retorted. 'I've seen the respectable Spanish citizen sitting on a topless beach beside his decently covered wife, looking at his newspaper and ignoring the spectacle of soft, seductive female flesh. It's only when you get close, that you see that the stern and sober señor has bored a couple of peepholes in his paper so that he can play at being the unseen voyeur.'

'I guess I had better put my shirt back on,' Franny said. 'If things are as puritanical as that; we can be seen from other apartments and even from the road on this balcony.'

'I think that you will be OK here,' I smiled, gazing at Franny's small, firm and creamy white boobs. 'A couple of years ago, I gave my neighbours and some passers-by quite a display.'

I had a guy here who was a bit slow off the mark. I felt horny and to get him along, I gave a great strip tease show, slow, slinky and seductive, just over there in front of the window.'

'Did you have the curtains closed?' Franny asked.

'Hell no!' I laughed. 'It was so hot, the window was wide open, and with the lights on in the room, I was as visible as if I were on a stage.'

'And your lover, did he react?'

'You bet, Franny. He got wild, lust sweating out of every

pore; so much so, that he chased me on to the balcony. I played a tantalizing cock teasing game with him which ended with him cornering me over there, at the edge of the balcony, and as I held on to the balustrade, he speared me on his lance - and carried me in triumph until we both came and collapsed, exhausted.'

'And you're going to tell me that all this was seen by somebody outside?' Franny was anxious, as though the scene was still being enacted before her eyes.

I nodded.

'And did somebody call the police?'

'Not on your life. There must have been quite an audience, not just one, solitary peeping tom. We were applauded - clapping, whistling and cheers; they did everything to show their appreciation, short of sending flowers. That's Spain. It's moved so quickly from the straitjacket mentality to the most outrageous displays that you find the two moralities, side by side.'

'So what else has changed?' Franny demanded.

'The people. When I first came here, Marbella was a rather snobbish resort for the ultra rich Europeans. You would find up in the hills, luxurious villas owned by German industrialists, English lords, French bankers. Now, the Arabs have taken over. The aristocrats from Morocco always knew Marbella - after all, it's not far away. One night, the first year I was here, you could not walk through the Port - you'll see the Port later; it's about eight miles from here. There were police everywhere because Hassan, the King of Morocco, had come over to have dinner in one of the fashionable restaurants. But now, we have the oil sheiks, Saudis and their sidekicks from the Gulf states. They have brought all the choice property, the Marbella Club, the hotel which Prince Alfonso von Hohenlohe founded and managed and which started the cult of Marbella, and Puente Romano, the most beautiful as well as the most expensive development on the whole coast, and a few others.

They have also bought up villas as if they were a dime a dozen instead of millions of dollars each. The Arab community is so important that they are even building a mosque. It should be completed about the same time as the new synagogue. Of course, with that sort of money about, everything has become wildly expensive and you should see the scene at the Casino! Some of those guys will lose millions in one night and think nothing of it.'

'So are we going to meet some fabulously wealthy sheik?'

'Wait and see. With me in Marbella, anything can happen. What brings me back here, year after year, is the fun I get from meeting my old pals, but I'm always ready to make new friends. Every time I have stayed here, I've come across some fresh faces - and bodies. Stick around and see what turns up.'

'Sounds as if Marbella gets better every year.'

'I wish it did,' I sighed. 'Sure, I find new friends each year, but there are always old ones who go away. And if the place has become more permissive, which is fine with me, it's also come up to date in a more disagreeable way.'

Franny raised her eyebrows and gave me a questioning look.

'Crime and violence, honey,' I explained. 'Political troubles in Spain have got as far as Andalucia. Most of the trouble is in the big cities - Madrid and Barcelona and in the Basque country, right the other side of Spain. But there have been a few bombs here, aimed at disrupting the tourist trade. That sort of thing does not happen often. What is more worrying for us is the big increase in robbery, vandalism, housebreaking, that sort of thing.'

'Sounds like back home in New York,' Franny mused.

It was getting late and we had a lot of unpacking and arranging the apartment to do before going out for dinner. As we set about getting the place in order, I reflected on how Spain had changed, and not always for the better. Still, the country had a charm for me. I could be sure that there were new adventures awaiting me, new lovers, new conquests! What would this year bring in the way of Señores in the sunshine?

2

From Torremolinos to Churriana

'The ornament of a house is the friends who frequent it.'
Emerson

Marbella on a Saturday morning. Cars, buses and motor bikes crawl through the main street or block the narrow roads leading to the sea front. Housewives, doing their weekend shopping, jostle the hordes of tourists and the families from Madrid, snatching a couple of days leisure. The traffic police merely add to the hold ups and the confusion and no Spanish street scene would be complete without the stray dogs which seem to come from nowhere to bring their own touch of chaos. All in all, a good place to be out of!

'Let's get the hell out of here,' I called to Franny.

'Where can we go?' she asked.

'Torremolinos.'

'Torremolinos!' she exclaimed. 'Why that's insane! If this place is crowded, there must be ten times as many people there. I saw it as we drove through coming here. Talk about a concrete jungle!'

'We're not going to wander around the streets, stupid, nor the beach. While you were still sleeping, I put in a few phone calls and we are going to spend the afternoon at the house of a friend of mine, Herman. He has a lovely garden and a pleasant pool.'

'Great!' Franny was enthusiastic. 'I'll just go and collect my bikini.'

'Take a few other things as well,' I called, 'We won't be coming home this evening. I've arranged with Ben, another old pal, that we shall spend the night at his place in Churriana, a little village up in the hills. It's quite close to Torremolinos, yet it is remote and no tourist even ventures there.'

'Nice and quiet,' smiled Franny.

'I never said that,' I replied. 'You will be able to judge for yourself. Now get moving; the sooner we're away from the Marbella mob, the better.'

'So, who are these guys we're going to see?' Franny demanded, as we drove out of town.

She listened as I described Herman and Momir, his Yugoslav lover. Herman, a shade under six feet, was a macho looking man, with a forest of curly, dark blonde hair all over his chest and shoulders and even on his back. His broad, round face bore an expression of perpetual surprise because of the way his bushy moustache turned up at the ends. His large, round glasses were of the type which were tinted and changed their colour in accordance with the amount of light. He was something of a dandy, always wearing some heavy gold rings, in one of which was set an ostentatious diamond, on his meticulously manicured hands. But he was no pansy. His jewellery reminded me of the years that Herman had spent as a diamond dealer.

By contrast, Momir who spent his time painting naïve canvases was slightly built with a hairless body and thick, grey hair. He was well read, cultured and refined but a quiet, retiring man. Before he left Yugoslavia, Momir had written poems, some of which had been published. However, although he had spent twelve years in Holland, he still spoke Dutch falteringly. Strangely enough, when he was with Momir, Herman, who was normally boisterous and articulate, began to speak in the same manner as if he had caught some vocal disease from his partner.

The one thing which sometimes displeased me about the menage which we were about to visit was Herman's bossiness. He would order people about, snapping his fingers as though he was an old style colonial plantation owner. True, I would order Franny about, but there was love which tempered our relationships and made it acceptable.

We drove on until we reached Herman's place. He and

Momir welcomed us warmly and showed us over the house into which they had only recently moved. We came into an entrance hall which led, on one side, to a spacious, crescent shaped living room in which stood a comfortable, horseshoe shaped, grey sofa in a velvet material in front of an enormous open fireplace.

Opposite the living room was the master bedroom with twin beds and an adjoining bathroom. We walked out into the back garden where we saw there was a separate, self-contained annexe to the house comprising three small bedrooms and a kitchen. We settled ourselves by the kidney shaped pool, while Herman went back into the house to get us drinks from the big, well fitted kitchen which looked out on to an open patio with dining room table and pleasant, wooden chairs.

'It's a lovely place you have here,' I said to Herman.

'What I like most are the picture all over the place,' Franny observed.

She was right. There were some striking portraits, including one of Herman's son (he had been married for seven years before finally realizing that he was gay and divorcing his wife) and a number of pictures painted on glass in the primitive Slav manner.

'How long is it since you saw your son, Herman?' I asked.

'Eight years now. I miss him, you know. I tried to keep him but my ex-wife has remarried and the courts did not approve of leaving the kid with a gay father.'

'Well, if she has remarried, you don't have to pay child support.'

'That's no real comfort, Xaviera. I am sure that you know that.'

'By the way,' I said, 'you are all invited this evening to Churriana to call on my friend, Ben the Baker.'

'We've never met him,' protested Momir.

'No matter,' I replied. 'Ben is the most generous man I have ever met, and he has given me carte blanche to come up to his place whenever I like and to bring whomever I please. I called him from Marbella, so we are expected.'

We spent a lazy afternoon. Franny swam for a bit, but I was content to lie in the sun and gossip with my old friend, Herman.

Why don't you tell us something about Ben while we get ready to go up to Churriana?' Herman asked, as the evening drew nearer. 'Like why do you call him Ben the Baker?'

As we trooped in from the pool, I told them the story of Ben.

3

Ben the Baker

'Love is sweet, but tastes best with bread.'
Yiddish Proverb

'I first met Ben in July, 1977 at Lester Sullivan's. Lester has a splendid villa in Mijas, perched in the hills above Torremolinos and the coastal plain.' I started to tell my story as we climbed into my car, and I set out on the tortuous drive up to Churriana.

Lester was something of a local celebrity, since every Saturday he organized a baseball game in the fields surrounding his house. A sizeable contingent of the American colony would turn up to play or watch, along with a number of Spaniards who were intrigued and baffled by the antics of the players.

There were quite a number of Americans and Canadians who lived in the area and who formed a sort of club-like community, visiting each other, playing games together and generally keeping each other in touch with what was going on back in the States. Some of the man lived a bachelor existence or formed temporary alliances but many were married, almost without exception to American wives. This was not surprising, since they tended to keep to their own national clique and few of them had formed close friendships among the Spaniards.

They were a pretty healthy bunch, living an open air life, playing tennis, often under the expert tuition of Lew Hoad whose tennis school at Mijas was one of the attractions of the place, or going horse riding or swimming or playing golf - and, once a week, baseball at Lester's.

Most of the men drank quite heavily, but strangely enough, they were also into health foods and obsessed with absorbing their daily quota of vitamins. They had no confidence in the food available locally and would make expeditions to the US Navy base near Cadiz, where they were able to gain access to the PX and stock up with such necessities as Skippy peanut butter, pecan pie, sourdough buns for their hamburgers, Riceroni, and genuine American, English muffins.

Lester, a heavily built, attractive, grey haired man in his mid fifties, kept himself in magnificent physical condition, and he and his friends took the Saturday afternoon ritual very seriously, playing hard and fast. And Lester did not only play hard and fast with bat and ball; he was quite a playboy, a real 'Jock', whose indoor hobby was screwing Penthouse Pets and Playboy Bunnies, regardless of vintage. I had met him a few times and knew his reputation, so when he invited me to stay up at his place, I accepted out of curiosity. What sort of man was this sexual connoisseur, I wondered. As for me, I had never aimed at being a centre spread in a glossy girlie magazine, but as a regular contributor to 'Penthouse', I suppose I would qualify for his favours and I was in better shape than some of the more venerable models whom he had bedded.

But there was another side to Lester's character, quite different from the image of the sporty, raunchy playboy, as I was to discover.

Next to Lester's house, there was a small bungalow in which lived his mother. Although she must have been about eighty, she was as sprightly and alert as his seventeen year old daughter who, together with her fifteen year old brother, was also staying there. With his family, Lester was kind-hearted and considerate, a regular, cuddly, Jewish father and dutiful son.

Lester was very proud of his house, equipped with all the newest gadgets. Almost as soon as I arrived, he showed me into his gigantic bathroom which featured a pink, heart-shaped bathtub and pink bathrobes and towels. An army of cologne and bathoil bottles was drawn up for my inspection, and I had my choice from a dozen silk morning gowns in all the colours of the rainbow. I was presented with a new toothbrush, still wrapped in cellophane, and then the tour inevitably led to the bedroom.

Of course, the bed was enormous, larger than king size – emperor size, you might call it. I had to lie in it, so that he could demonstrate his vibrating mattress. I believe that Lester thought that I would be shaken into submission by this seduction special, but it merely made me giggle. Undeterred, he switched on his TV, video recorder and record player in succession by means of a remote control which he kept at the bedside. All that was harmless enough, but when he pulled out of a drawer in his bedside table a half dozen assorted dildoes and vibrators, intended to excite me, I considered that the time had come for action. So, I pulled him to me and, curling my lips around his ready and eager cock, gave him what was probably the blow job of his life. When, at last, I spat out his bitter come, I knew that the lion had been tamed for a while and I would be spared further displays of modern technology. I explained my simple tastes and persuaded him to give me a separate bedroom with less sophisticated fittings for the rest of my stay.

There were a lot of other guests in the house, and the following night, we were lounging on Lester's terrace after a substantial meal of spicy, barbecued steaks, admiring the view across to the sea, flanked by the rugged, moonlit hills and, in front of the terrace, an incongruous relic of Lester's past, burnt out remains of his private plane which had crashed on the runway at Malaga. Lester had miraculously escaped.

Suddenly a human tornado burst in, shattering the calm and rudely waking up those of us who had overeaten and were dozing in the heat. In marched Ben the Baker, carrying about half a dozen loaves in his arms. Ten o'clock at night is an unusual hour for a delivery of bread, but as I was to discover, Ben was an unusual man. Tall, muscular, with shoulders of a professional footballer and a broad chest, sprouting a huge crop of black hair, only partly hidden by his faded, red T-shirt, Ben exuded boisterous, cheerful virility.

Ben came straight over to me, a great grin stretching from ear to ear, dumping his bread on the table and ignoring everybody else. Lester was particularly irritated since he had just at that moment introduced me to another of his guests who had marked me down as the night's selected victim.

'I heard that you were staying up at Lester's, so I had to come over and see you,' Ben bubbled over. 'I jumped on my scooter – that's why my hair is such a mess – and brought the bread myself instead of waiting for one of the boys to make a delivery in the morning. I've read quite a few of your books. I love reading and I have a big collection of books up at the house in Churriana where I live. I hope that you will find time to get over and see them while you are around. Now, what was I saying? Ah, yes, about your books. I remember in one of them you quote an old Yiddish proverb – 'Love like butter goes well with bread.' That was in THE HAPPY HOOKER, so I thought that you would not mind meeting your Jewish baker. I hope that the bread will be to your liking and, who knows, could be taken with some love?'

Ben rolled his bright, brown eyes and I melted in the radiance of his smile. I found his spontaneity and openness overwhelming and far more appealing than either Lester's electronic toys or the man he had intended should be my lover for the night.

'If you are going to stay in this part of the world for a while, Xaviera, I would love to show you around. I've lived in these hills for the past ten years. The country is gorgeous and I certainly know my way about.'

'I have a place in Marbella,' I said.

'Marbella!' he echoed. 'Oh, but that's terrible! It's such a snooty hole. That means if I come over to visit you some time, I'll have to dress up – long pants and proper shoes. But do call me.'

And with that, Ben scribbled down his phone number on a scrap of paper, strode over and kissed me smack on my nose.

'I hope to see you real soon,' he beamed. 'Meanwhile, have a nice evening and enjoy the bread.'

With a cheery wave and a nod to the rest of the company, he hurried out and we heard the noise of his motor scooter drive off into the night.

'Where's Ben come from?' I asked Lester. 'He sounds American but not like the regular New York crowd I usually see here.'

'No, he was from Philadelphia before he came to Spain. He is a great guy; nothing is too much trouble for him and he is so handy - he can fix anything. It was Ben who fitted up all my gadgets, and if you ever need anything installed or mended, I am sure that he would be only too pleased to oblige. I think that you made quite an impression on him.'

'He seemed to me to be a truly warm human being. The sort of person you can confide in and who will talk to you straight from the heart,' I told Lester.

'It appears that he made a big impression on you as well,' Lester commented with a touch of bitterness. 'He is gauche and noisy, yet he can talk his way into and out of anything. He has chatted two girl friends away from me and now it looks as though you are going to be number three. That's what you get from a lawyer.'

'Lawyer?' I was mystified. 'He said that he was a baker.'

'So he is,' grinned Lester. 'Lawyer turned baker.'

'These other girls he captivated. Were they your regular Pets and Bunnies?'

'No, they were mature women, like you, in their thirties. To be truthful they were simply friends of friends who happened to be passing through.'

Immediately after my return to Marbella, I decided to call Ben. He was delighted and offered to pick me up the following weekend and drive me to his place, but I preferred to take my own car and find my way to Churriana.

Ben had given me instruction on how to find his house. Although the village was tucked away in the hills, it was very close to the end of the main runway of Malaga airport so that the idyllic peace would be torn apart from time to time by the scream of the jets. The streets were narrow, but as Ben had told me, if I missed the road, I had only to ask anybody in the street for 'Panederia Estranjera,' (The foreign bakery).

'Come whenever you like,' Ben had said when I called him. 'If you get here during daylight we can go up on the roof and watch the planes coming in and taking off. And at night time, I go up and watch the stars. The air is so clear that you feel that you could stretch your hand up and touch them. I have put a telescope up there so that I can pull them even closer.'

'Is there anything that you would like me to bring?' I asked.

'Well, you might bring some records. I'm crazy about music, and I put a lot of records on to tapes.'

'Anything in particular?'

'I leave the choice to you. I'm sure that I will like anything which is to your taste, and I can let you have tapes of some of my favourites. You are a woman after my own heart, and I know that your music will be alright with me. Come soon.'

He hung up and I felt a tingling throughout my body. I was horny for this man, and I was alone in Marbella with no guests or visitors so that I could look forward to my weekend without any distraction.

I had no difficulty in recognizing Ben's house since there were several bread delivery trucks parked outside together with Ben's battered Citroen Deux Chevaux and his old Vespa scooter. I was to see later, in his garage, lovingly serviced and polished till it gleamed, a powerful, ancient Harley Davidson motor bike which Ben would only parade before other Harley Davidson enthusiasts. The house was small and cozy and oddly shaped. At the entrance was his miniature office where Ben would deal with his correspondence and the bills. Behind that stood a space which he used as a laundry and behind that a dining area, complete with a large, round table and about a dozen chairs. At the back of this room was a stove, an old fashioned sink and racks of herbs and spices. From the wall, hung kitchen knives and other implements. Ben offered me a cold drink and led me to the patio behind the house. A grey parrot in a big cage whistled at me and chattered to itself. Dazzling white cotton sheets hung from a couple of clothes lines, and the place was dominated by two enormous refrigerators, one of which was working.

'You see, Xaviera,' Ben said, as he poured my drink, 'a fridge is always a problem in Spain. It's sure to break down and then getting the damned thing repaired is one long hassle. So, I have two. In fact, there's a third, a small one on the roof terrace. I keep ice and soft drinks up there; I hardly ever touch alcohol.'

'Like me,' I smiled. 'I never drink or smoke tobacco, though I do take the occasional joint.'

'Well, now we know that we dislike the same things. Do we like the same things as well?'

'We'll have to see, won't we,' I smiled mischievously.

'I know that you like music,' Ben said, 'so that's one interest we share.'

'Looks as if photography is another,' I commented as we walked back into the house and I pointed to the rows of photographs, neatly framed and displayed on the walls.

'That's right,' Ben was delighted, 'and I told you about my books. This house is only one of my libraries; I keep books in all sorts of places. Whenever I go to the States or to big cities in Europe with English bookshops, I buy new books until I have no more space to carry them. Around here, you can't find much in the way of English books, and I am afraid that foreign languages are not one of my strong points.'

On the way up to the roof, Ben waved at the first floor space which was one enormous room, pleasantly furnished with a big couch and pretty lamps.

'This is the floor which my ex-girl friend still uses from time to time.'

'Your ex-girl friend! Is she still here sometimes?' I asked warily.

'Come on up to the roof and I'll tell you all about it. We have plenty of time and I promise you that we won't get bored.'

Ben's roof was tiled and with a handsome marble table and rattan chairs. There was an inviting, swinging two seater garden chair with brightly coloured cushions. Ben's third fridge stood under a thatched roof which covered part of the space. All around stretched a fantastic view; a few white clouds were dotted about in the vivid blue sky and the gaunt, sun parched hills shone in the bright sunlight.

The first time a plane came in to land, the din was deafening, but as time went on, I became accustomed to these interruptions and they no longer troubled me.

I took off my sandals and nestled against his sturdy shoulders. I savoured the strong, manly odour of his body.

'Now, there's nobody to interrupt us, so tell me the story of Ben the Baker,' I demanded.

He needed no encouragement.

'I come from a wealthy upper class, Jewish family in Philadelphia. Of course, one of my brothers became a doctor and another a university professor, while my sister married a banker. As for me, I became a nice, respectable lawyer. But, you know what, Xaviera, it was all so much the perfect American dream, my parents' house straight from "Home and Garden", the profitable law practice; I was bored out of my mind. So, ten years ago, I decided to come and see Europe and look for my roots, as it were. In fact, my family came from Russia, but I had a great-aunt living in Paris so I could go there for a start.

I told you that I am not any good at languages, and I speak no French at all. In Paris, I felt like an idiot and I wanted to move on and get away from the big cities. I bought a scooter and rode. That's how I found Churriana.'

'But what about your job and your family?' I asked.

'Just before I left, I quit my firm and told them I was not sure whether I would be coming back. To my parents, I said merely that I was taking an extended vacation. I took with me a large bag full of books, which I had picked up for a few dollars at second-hand book stalls. As it happened, one of the books was called HOW TO BAKE YOUR OWN BREAD, a very old textbook with lots of illustrations. It was a new world to me; I didn't know how to even boil an egg. In fact, I'm still not too sure.'

'I see,' I pounced on him, 'so that's where your ex-girl friend came in, huh?'

Ben burst out laughing. 'She is more helpless than I am. No, the cook around here is my housemaid, Maria.'

'And this Maria, she only does the cooking?' I asked sarcastically.

'That's right. She has been with me for nine years, and she is quite a character - plump, about my age and very fierce to women she does not like. She has scared off quite a few of my girl friends. I don't sleep with her, but she is so protective and jealous that you might think that she is either my wife or my mother. But, you know, I think Maria will like you, Xaviera.'

'I hope so. And your ex-girl friend, did Maria like her?'

'No way!' Ben laughed. 'But I'll tell you about her in a minute. I had got as far as explaining how I had picked up this book on bread making and taken off on my scooter. I did not get any further than Churriana because that is where my money ran out. I had to stop somewhere and I fell in love with the place. I had picked up a few phrases in Spanish - hard work for me but I kept at it and I read up my baker's handbook. Then I went around to the local baker and got a job.'

'Just like that?' I asked in astonishment.

'That's right. The baker was a nice guy and as long as he spoke slowly, I was able to understand him. But after a few months, I began to get fed up; the work was very monotonous and humdrum. So I asked the baker if he would like to sell me the business. He said I could have the whole thing, lock, stock and barrel including the goodwill for no more than seven thousand dollars. Peanuts! So I cabled home for the money.'

'And your folks sent it so that you could become a baker?'

I found Ben's story incredible. What sane, Jewish, middle class poppa and momma would send money for their lawyer son, who had walked out on his sane conventional life, to become a baker in an unheard of village in the mountains of Spain?

Ben chuckled. 'They must have thought that I was crazy, but as long as I was well and happy, they were certain that sooner or later I would come to my senses. I became the foreign baker of Churriana. But it was a year before I realized that I had bought this house along with the bakery and the business. I was flabbergasted.'

'Do you mean to tell me that you, a lawyer, signed a contract without knowing what you were buying?' I stared at Ben in disbelief.

'Well,' he confessed, blushing, 'the contract was in Spanish, and I told you that languages were not my strongest point. And perhaps I was not the smartest of lawyers. I specialized in divorce.'

'I don't think I would trust you with my divorce; I would probably end up a bigamist,' I commented. 'Did you meet your girl friend when you moved in here?'

'No. First, Maria came into my life. She had no job and was supporting an illegitimate daughter. When I had this house, she offered to come and work for me.'

Ben paused in his narrative. He leaned across and pressed a kiss on my forehead and caressed my bare shoulders. His hands moved down my body, but I was not prepared to let him get off so easily.

'Ben, whenever I ask about your girl friend, who, you say still has rights in this house, and for all I know might walk in any minute, you change the subject. You tell me how you became a baker, how you brought this place, and how your domestic help arrived. I would say that, as an old lawyer, you are evading the issue.'

Ben stopped tickling my feet, straightened up and gave me a sad smile. I could see that it cost him a great effort to face up to discussing the woman in his life.

'She is a Danish girl I met on the beach about eight years ago,' he sighed. 'She is pretty. No, she is more than that; she looks terrific. Tall, slender with long blonde hair, much the same colour as yours. She was very spoiled and was bumming around town, being kept by the wealthy boys who were about.'

'By town, you mean Torremolinos?' I asked.

'Eight years ago, Torremolinos was not the cheap, tourist resort it is now. It was a pleasant little place with cozy bars and a hell of a different clientele from the package tour crowds. Anyway, to cut a long story short, we fell in love. Perhaps, now, looking back, I should say that I fell in love with her. She was glad to move in and we had a good time together. I did everything I could to make her happy. Then, several years later, I had to go back to the States to see my folks. When I got back I found that she had moved my things up to the roof and fitted up what had been a spare room as my bedroom!'

'But hadn't you been sleeping together?' I wanted to know.

'Hardly at all by then. She had a certain coldness. I thought that it was perhaps because she was Scandinavian, coming from a cold country, you know.'

'Ben, you are naïve! How come, the supposedly frigid Danes have all those sex shows and sex shops in Copenhagen?'

'Yes, I know, but I had been making excuses for her to myself. But now that I was back from the States, she was hardly ever at home, and I found Maria was always giving me pitying glances. Eventually I found out that she had been having an affair for more than a year with a playboy, the son of a rich Spanish industrialist. She had even brought him home and fucked in my bed where she had been caught by Maria one morning.'

'And then?' I asked.

'That's all,' Ben admitted in a low voice. 'It's just as I told you. She lives her own life and is off somewhere now. When she wants to come back, she lives on the first floor.'

'And you are exiled in your own house to living on the roof?' I questioned.

'Oh, I like the roof. I have everything I need here. I have put in a toilet and a shower.'

'And you, you idiot, you let her stay here after that?'

'We had shared eight years of our lives together,' he protested. 'I could not very well simply throw her out.'

'Why not? That's the way millions of people end their relationships. But it is fantastic. You, confined to the roof, while she has the run of the house and is kept by you.'

Our discussion was ended by the arrival of Maria to tell us that she had prepared a delicious paella which was waiting for us downstairs. After we had eaten, we went up to the roof again and watched the sun sink below the brooding hills, and the stars came out. There was a chill in the air after nightfall so we pulled together the twin single beds, and under the covers, we cuddled close and made love.

Ben was clumsy but eager. Suddenly I fired at him, 'What about those girls you seduced from Lester?'

'Oh, I never made love to them. I took them up into the mountains and tried talking to them, but they were too dumb. You know there is an art in listening and they didn't have it.'

I knew he was telling the truth. There was a simplicity and directness about Ben which defied deceit.

He kissed the back of my neck, hitting just the right spot. I felt goose pimples all over my body, and I kissed him first on his neck, then slid my tongue over his warm shoulders and nuzzled his hairy armpits. We had showered immediately before going to bed, but in the warmth of our nest, I relished the salty tang of his fresh sweat. His cock was big and hard with a nicely shaped head and his balls were large and full of sperm.

'I can't remember the last time I had sex,' Ben whispered. 'Please forgive me if I don't do things very well, but it is like learning all over again.'

'Don't worry, dear, everything is fine. Relax, it'll be alright,' I reassured him.

I guided his head towards my moist vagina; he kissed well and his tongue was long and quick. He gave a little groan and thrust his shoulders beneath my buttocks, lifting my Venus Hill over his face. I was practically flat on my feet as I pushed my crotch deeper on his questing tongue. Every now and then, his big, dark eyes would gaze up at me for approval. He was getting me along nicely, and I could feel my nerves tautening. I gripped his head between my thighs, and with one scream, I let go and came in an orgasm which convulsed every fibre of my being. Then, he drove into my thirsting pussy, his heavy body leaning on his elbows while his knees moved with the rhythm of the waves of the ocean. What had started as a shy encounter with an inexperienced partner ended in a fantastic, passionate session; Ben was surely a quick learner and for the next couple of days, he kept my oven hot and ready.

Next day, I enjoyed the sense of approval from Maria. She was even more friendly when I spoke to her with a few words of Spanish. A woman who could make her beloved master so gloriously happy, was OK by Maria.

We went up in the mountains, and Ben showed me what he called his hidden diamonds, tiny villages which nestled, diamond shaped among the hills, and then led me to a crystal clear spring which rushed into a big, secluded pool among the trees, where we undressed and swam. Here, Ben made love to me again, our bodies half submerged as we leaned against the green, moss covered boulders. Love on the rocks!

It was the next weekend that Ben phoned me to say that he had given his ex-girl friend enough money to pay a year's rent on a small apartment and told her to leave.

'As soon as she has finished taking her things out,' he said, 'I'm going to buy a new bed, a big bed for us to make love in. It'll be there when you next come and stay. Meanwhile, I took a photo of you which has come out really cute, and I have enlarged it and framed it. I have it over my bed with the text, 'DECLARATION OF INDEPENDENCE.'

By now, we had arrived at Churriana, so I turned to my companions and said, 'That's the story of Ben. Now you can judge the man for yourselves.'

Ben greeted me with a bear-like hug, and when, at last I got free, I introduced him to the group who had descended upon him. He was, as ever, the warm-hearted and generous host, and Maria had surpassed herself in the kitchen. We sat down to a veritable feast of 'Gallina en Pepitoria', chicken cooked with garlic and saffron sauce, salad and, to end, 'Polverones Sevillanos', a sort of sweet cinnamon cookie.

We were taking our ease after the meal with a drink in our hands on the terrace when Eva, a German friend of Ben's and her Spanish husband arrived. Eva was totally devoted to her husband, yet I somehow envied her the easy relationship which she had with Ben all the year round. She was a ball of fire and had a trendy boutique in Torremolinos. Her husband had never learned one word of German or English, but he seemed to keep up with her somehow.

Herman was full of the fashion show which he was arranging for the following weekend for a famous Dutch couturier, Guus Harms, who habitually spent his summers in the neighbourhood.

'You must come along, darling,' he pleaded with Eva who had found in him a kindred spirit. 'All of you,' Herman insisted, 'you must get over to see it. I promise it will be fabulous. Xaviera, you will come I know, and Ben, how about you?'

'Me?' Ben threw back his head and laughed, 'Could you imagine me with all those fairies? No, Xaviera can go and tell me all about it.'

'And I'm afraid I won't be able to make it either,' Eva said. 'Saturday is the busiest day of the week in the boutique, and the only assistant I had has left me to spend her time carrying drinks for some beach boy who has got her pregnant, so I am alone.'

'What a shame,' Herman cried, 'but we must get together again, all of us and I will cook you a meal which you will remember.'

Momir turned to Herman with a yawn, 'I guess that it is about time we made our way back.'

'But honey,' Herman growled, 'it's so early. Let's go to The Bronx.'

Momir, who liked to get a full night's sleep, refused, and when Herman invited everybody to go along with him, he was disappointed to find nobody accepted. When he could not remain the centre of attention, Herman could get a bit bad tempered so I soothed him.

'I've heard of The Bronx; that's the gay disco not far from your place, isn't it? Maybe another time. Franny and I could stay over at your house, but tonight we are Ben's guests and it's only right that we should spend a little time with him, don't you think? It's months since I last saw him – not since last year.'

'Oh very well, have it your own way,' Herman growled.

'I'll drop Momir off at the house; the poor sweetie is tired out, but I'm hot to trot. Xaviera, I'll call you in Marbella.'

Eva and her husband left while Herman and Momir were thanking Ben for his hospitality. Ben called for a taxi for them and while we were waiting, Herman said to me, 'That Ben is a lovely man. I really like him. Bring him over to our place - any time you like.'

'Oh,' I smiled, 'I thought that you were taken by Eva.'

'Not on your life!' Herman sneered. 'She's just a pretty little thing, but has no depth. Not like you, sweetheart!'

Alone at last, Ben and I pulled some mattresses together on the roof and made love under the stars. The night was warm and sweet with the fragrant scent of the trees and bushes. The months of our separation melted away in our passionate embrace, and our bodies were united in the rhythm of love. The great honey coloured moon looked down and smiled.

4

After the Fashion Show

'Certainly nothing is unnatural that is not physically impossible.'

Richard Brinsley Sheridan

Herman did not want me to forget his fashion show. Every morning he would remind me and when the great day came, I turned up at his house with Franny and a new acquaintance, Bill.

Bill, a strikingly handsome Englishman in his mid-twenties, had moved in with me. Typical of the guys who hung about the Coast, Bill was idle and a drifter. His Dutch wife, tired of his laziness, had thrown him out in favour of a macho Spaniard who would give her the occasional spanking. I had seen her, tall, blonde and aggressive, when Bill had taken me to the beach bar which her new mate ran where he had gone to discuss details of their separation. Without anywhere of his own, Bill hung about Frank's Beach Bar, where his good looks would attract some lady with a bed. Bill would stay with her, enjoying her hospitality and bestowing his favours on her until, bored out of his mind, he was incapable of faking another orgasm. His lady would then return him to stock, as it were, on the beach which had become a regular meat market for the predominantly English speaking section of the population. Bill's seductive powers had been increased rather than diminished by his breaking an ankle when attempting to enter the bedroom of a Swedish girl by means of the window in preference to the more conventional method through the door. Elderly women doted on him, changing his bandages, ferrying him to the hospital, washing his dirty clothes and generally fussing over the partly helpless man. I willingly took a turn at entertaining him. Although his lovemaking was too relaxed, not entirely due to his foot being in plaster, it was still a pleasure to mount his sturdy cock and ride him to orgasm. He was not much into kissing or oral sex, but was ready enough to come in my mouth.

I need variety in my life. Ben lavished on me all I required in the way of deep, emotional love; from Bill I got cool, uninvolved sex. He was also agreeable company, inoffensive, undemanding and sufficiently intelligent to provide me with a flow of easy conversation which I could not obtain from Franny. With my dividing my attention between the two men, she felt more and more excluded and became increasingly moody. She would lie in misery, listening to my moans and cries of pleasure as I fucked in the next bedroom, every sound carrying clearly through the paper thin walls. Many times, I had heard her nervous cough after I had come to an orgasm, and leaping out of bed, I would catch her standing outside the door, trembling, her eyes pleading to be beaten. Bill, like other lovers before and after him, was astonished when I seized her roughly by the leather dog collar which she always wears in my presence, tightened it until the marks showed on her delicate neck, and fastened it to a long metal chain. Then, after securing her hands and feet with special straps and manacles, I would whip her, strike her with a hard, leather paddle and hurl insults at her. Instead of finishing her off myself, I would command her to masturbate before us.

To give her a break, I would allow Franny, a horny, little thing, to take a nap with me during the afternoons when Bill would sit in the living room, reading a book or listening to my music. I would feel her leg, artfully pulled around my thigh and pressing ever tighter. As she squeezed, I would feel her body shudder and I knew that she was approaching orgasm. Then, I would suddenly turn on her, the instant before she was going to peak, smack her face and yell at her that I was not a live dildo. However, there were times when I would allow her to kiss and caress me, and we would engage in mutual cunnilingus, her clitoris swelling in my mouth and her raging excitement driving me to a frenzied climax myself.

Another day, when I was in a hurry and had other things on my mind, I ordered Franny to come within ten seconds or to forget it. I counted rapidly and she went crazy, jerking spasmodically like a creature possessed. She came.

The afternoon before the fashion show, I wanted to stay in bed with Bill which meant that Franny would be deprived of her customary nap with me. So, rather than have her sulk for the rest of the day, I brought her into bed with the two of us. But before we could make love as a threesome, I had to tie her down and beat her with a bamboo stick I had found on the beach. She appreciated being included and not being left in the corner like a naughty child while the grown-ups got on with their adult games. For to me, although she is in her early thirties, Franny, with her awkward adolescent walk and youthful chatter, was both a mischievous little boy or a shy, young girl, according to her mood.

When we arrived, the gay boys looked Bill over approvingly as he limped in on his crutches. I had foreseen that they would be interested, and so had he. Consequently, he was reluctant to come, but I had promised to protect him from their advances and so persuaded him. I think that his immobility made him feel that he would be a sitting target, and like Ben, he had always been straight and was uncomfortable in the presence of homosexuals. The house and garden had been decorated for the show with coloured lights and masses of flowers. A wooden catwalk had been erected over the pool along which the models had to tread their precarious way. The place was packed with people waiting for the show to start.

I found the fashion designer, fidgetting with the dresses which he was fitting on the mannequins, pinning, stitching and tugging into shape the shiny, glittering materials of his creations. There were four lovely models working furiously to get themselves to their glamorous best. Three of them were women, the fourth and most feminine, a sexy, gay Spanish boy with long, soft hair, delicate, dusky skin and long, heavy, black eyelashes, looked as though he had walked off the cover of a glossy, fashion magazine.

In contrast with the meticulously dressed models, most of the guests were gay boys wearing scanty shorts, sarongs or tiny G-strings. Herman, who was rushing about in the kitchen, preparing food for after the show, informed me that when the mannequins had ended their parade, everybody could go naked. He had got special permission from Momir, who was rather prudish over such things and who would take his afternoon walk earlier than usual.

The noise of the crowd mounted as the sangria made its rounds. There was a lot of girlish giggling and when the show proper started, enthusiastic whistling and cheering. I had got a large mattress on which Franny, Bill and I were able to lie in comfort and watch the spectacle.

Herman bustled out of the house, sweating like a pig, as he dispensed more Sangria and plates of meat balls. I was amused to watch the other guests. Some were speaking Dutch among themselves while a group of Germans were endeavouring to pick up some Spanish boys, having to use sign language and wave their hands energetically and suggestively. Among the gay boys, there were a few, interesting women, one of whom, a Dutch friend of mine, nicknamed 'Ducky,' came over and joined us.

Ducky was in her early forties with a lean, youthful body extravagantly dressed but her face was somewhat wrinkled from spending so much time in the sun. She was living with a younger Indonesian. Ducky had a weakness for jealous, macho men and was more attracted by brawn than brains. She had one such escort, a handsome Spaniard, with her who would not let her out of his sight for a minute. Since most of the men were gay, the guy did not have much to worry about, but when she started talking to Bill, he immediately pushed his way between them.

'I love it when he gets possessive,' she shouted to me in Dutch. 'It makes me feel wanted and all-woman.'

'Speak Spanish,' growled her Romeo.

But my attention had been captured by another woman. A petite brunette with a sexy, well rounded figure and admirable boobs, she introduced herself to me and said that her name was Angelica.

'I am Swiss, but I have lived for several years in Holland,' Angelica told me in Dutch, speaking with an extraordinary Schwitzer-Deutsch accent.

Of all the men and women present, Angelica gave the impression of being the least attracted by Bill's good looks or even his physical helplessness. She told me in a low voice, so that none of the others could hear, that she was a lesbian.

Then, over came gay Herman, a big smile on his face. 'Do you know, Xaviera, I turned straight last week for Angelica. Now, isn't that something?'

It certainly seemed a bizarre combination to me. I shot an enquiring glance at Angelica who was blushing furiously, but said nothing.

'You see, I picked up this fellow – a great number on the beach. But guess what? He was straight. It shouldn't be allowed. Anyway, something had to be done, so I used Angelica as bait. She did a great job, cock teasing him, but she was not in the mood to be fucked by the guy. So we got into a nice, friendly huddle together, and it ended with my fucking Angelica while he sucked her. Then I bumfucked him and he was as good as gold, not a murmur, as long as he had Angelica to distract him. First woman I've fucked for years – I really am quite versatile.'

I turned to Angelica, 'So you are not all that lesbian?'

She laughed. 'Oh, you know Herman. He loves to tell a tall story.'

I was not convinced. There was something about Angelica which made me feel that I could not trust her. While she was chatting to Bill, I asked Ducky what she knew about her.

'Oh, she works in a peepshow and does a bit of hooking on the side,' she told me.

'Really! A bit unusual for a lesbian, wouldn't you say?'

'Lesbian?' hooted Ducky. 'Did that bitch tell you that she was a lesbian?'

I nodded.

'Well you just watch her with your boy friend there,' Ducky warned me. 'She is getting really pally with him,isn't she? Then she'll put on her lesbian act with you so as to get to bed with the two of you, and before you know what is happening, she will have a damned good try to get him away from you. That's the way she works. Lesbian! Why she's fucked more men than all that gang of gays put together!'

'Well,' I told her, 'Bill is not my boy friend. He is just a pleasant guy who is staying with me for a few days. He has too low a sex drive and is too passive for my taste.'

'He's not doing so badly now, is he?' Ducky tossed her head in Bill's direction. Angelica was gazing into his eyes and was practically rubbing her knee against his crotch.

'Listen, Xaviera,' Ducky continued. 'Even if he is not your regular boy friend, this Bill seems a nice guy, certainly too good for her. You see, I know all her tricks because she is staying with me. I knew her from Amsterdam and she had nowhere to live. Herman's house is full, there are always guests, so I have been landed with the little cunt. And she is making a pass at my guy. He is faithful – not the sort to fuck about. But she is always bumping into him after she has taken a shower and she runs about nude. Just how much temptation are you supposed to put before a man? No, Xaviera, make sure that she doesn't get her claws into Bill. She's frustrated with all these gay men around her – that's the real reason she fucked with Herman last week. Give her something to think about.'

I am not a jealous woman, but I decided that Ducky was right and Angelica needed putting in her place.

'Angelica,' I called in a sweet voice, 'I am so thirsty and I just hit my foot. Please, would you mind walking over and getting me a drink?'

While she was away, I moved the company around on the mattress so that when Angelica came back she found Franny on one side of Bill and me on the other. She was not pleased, but said nothing and was evidently going to stick around for another chance.

Herman came hurrying by again and I called him over. Quietly, I told him in Dutch that Angelica was becoming a pest and ought to be eliminated as soon as possible. He understood at once and promised to look after the matter.

The party was over and most of the guests had left. Only a few of Herman's closest friends remained, mostly gay boys who were splashing about in the pool and, of course, Angelica who was sticking to our party like a leech. Not far away, Ducky was watching developments.

'Come on, Angelica, be sociable!' I called to her. 'We girls can swim while Bill looks on like a Roman emperor.'

Franny and I pulled our cripple to the edge of the pool where he could trail his sound leg in the water. Meanwhile, Herman had taken off his clothes and gestured to us to follow suit. Angelica needed no encouragement, and Franny and I slipped out of our bikinis. We had a bit of a job, coaxing Bill out of his bathing suit, but lying down without his crutches, he was virtually helpless. Franny brought our lame pasha whatever he wanted to eat and drink before she joined Angelica and me in the water.

Herman came to sit with Bill and to take some photos of the three of us, frolicking in the pool. Then, he dived into the water, and Bill took over on the camera while Herman lifted Angelica and me on his powerful shoulders. We could see that by now Herman had sprouted a formidable hard-on. It might have been for me, but Angelica, bearing in mind her exploit of the previous week, doubtless thought that she was the object of his desire. She knew how to tease, that girl, and, confident that she had Herman good and hot, turned away from him to swim across to where Bill's leg dangled invitingly in the water. But Herman was too quick for her. Pushing her roughly aside, he swam over to Bill, levered himself half out of the pool and started to caress Bill's limp cock.

Bill was taken by surprise and, sprawling back with a drink in one hand and a cigarette in the other, was not in much of a position to defend himself against Herman's advances. Embarrassed, he gazed at the three naked women in the pool, and the sight of us triggered his cock which grew rigid and eager. Seizing his opportunity, Herman pulled himself out of the water and gently placed his lips around Bill's member, all the time darting glances over his shoulder to make sure that Momir had not returned from his walk. The coast was clear and Herman resumed sucking delicately at Bill's cock. The cigarette fell from Bill's hand, and he gasped and shuddered while Herman threw back his head and swallowed theatrically.

'I've had my vitamins for the day,' he laughed.

The only person not to be amused by Herman's adroit performance was, naturally enough, Angelica. She had wanted Bill's sperm in her hungry mouth or her pussy and was sore at being outsmarted by Herman. I later found out that Ducky had secretly preserved the scene for posterity with her camera, and she presented the pictures to Herman as a tribute to his talent. What a man; even I could learn a trick or two from him!

Shortly afterwards, Ducky and Angelica left. Before going, Angelica suggested that we all meet later that evening at The Bronx. If she had missed out on Bill for lunch perhaps she would be luckier for supper?

'Good idea,' Herman agreed heartily. 'You'll come, won't you, Xaviera? But a disco won't be any fun for Bill.'

'I don't mind staying home and waiting for you,' Bill offered.

'Well, Franny can keep you company,' I put in.

Franny, who was never a great one for late nights, agreed readily enough.

That was the end of Angelica's designs on Bill for the day, and we saw to it that she never got another chance.

5
The Bronx

'Morality is simply the attitude we adopt towards people whom we personally dislike.'

Oscar Wilde

I never could understand why Torremolinos became the gay centre of the Costa del Sol. Sitting with Herman at a supposedly Italian ice cream parlour at one of the central terraces, we were surrounded by ugly, cheap people in an overcrowded, garish town which lacked any trace of class. A few gay spots had begun to open up in staid Marbella, and there was a transvestite bar in Puerto Banus which was flourishing, but it was sordid Torremolinos which had become the magnet for Herman and his kind.

Shortly after midnight, the two of us made our way to The Bronx. There were a couple of macho boys on the gate, but Herman talked us inside without our having to pay. All the waiters knew Herman; he was a gentleman who tipped well.

Downstairs, the music was deafening. Conversation was impossible, but clearly, the clientele of The Bronx did not drop in for a quiet chat. They were cruising, flirting, dancing, drinking and getting stoned. Taking drugs was forbidden by the management, but it was widespread and I saw plenty of kids who were drunk, plenty who were stoned, and even more who were 'stunk' – both stoned and drunk!

We sat at a table and Herman brought me an orange juice. For a while, we watched the crowd of gay men. Some greeted each other with a warm embrace, others were strutting by with their noses in the air. There were the occasional couples who shook hands, most hugged and kissed or indulged in a friendly pinch of the buttocks. Herman was peering into the mass of moving bodies, obviously looking for somebody.

'There's this divine kid,' he screamed to me over the

earsplitting racket. 'I had him when Momir was away for a few days, and next week he has to go into the army so I must find him tonight. He was superb and he has been looking out for me, but with all the preparations for the fashion show, I haven't had a chance to get hold of him.'

I realized now why Herman had been so insistent that I come along. He had no car, and provided he found his boy, my roomy BMW would come in useful. I did not resent this; it would give me an opportunity to repay some of his hospitality. After all, what are friends for?

Despite the air conditioning, the heat was intense and I was happy enough to sit back and watch Herman, as he sauntered around the floor. He towered above most of the rather feminine boys who tried to flirt with him. Suddenly, he darted through the throng and clutched, in a rapturous embrace, a young man.

The boy was definitely good looking. He had a delicate appearance, with brown eyes, big as saucers. He was dressed all in white with baggy pants and an open Indian style shirt which revealed his suntanned, hairless chest. When I saw his angelic face and long, flowing, black hair, I was sorely tempted to take upon myself the pleasurable task of converting the young homosexual, even if only for one night.

For a while, the two men danced together, folded in each other's arms, hardly moving but swaying amorously to the beat of the music. Later, I danced with the boy for a bit. Although we were not hugging each other like the men, I brushed against his body which felt good, slender yet firm, and with quite an acceptable hard-on. I became aware that he was also stoned out of his mind, his pupils dilated, his speech slurred. I warned Herman, who drank little and did not use any dope at all, that I thought that his lover was on some sort of trip, probably LSD.

Herman seized the kid and marched him over to the bar. He was not too good at walking or even standing upright, and Herman forced some orange juice down his throat. The boy demanded a whisky, but Herman was adamant.

'No more alcohol,' he ordered. 'What have you been taking?'

'Nada, 'the kid mumbled.

'Nada! What do you mean, nothing?' Herman howled in fury, 'Un poco morphine or snow?'

The boy just stared at Herman, who now in a thoroughly bad temper, told him that we should all leave and that he was to come back with us to Herman's house in my car.

Suddenly, the music stopped in the middle of a number, and all the lights were switched on. Confusion broke out and I turned to Herman.

'What the hell is going on?' I wanted to know.

Before he could answer, the shout went up from the part of the crowd nearest the door, 'Police, police, it's a raid.'

'Oh, my God, ' cried Herman, 'that's all I need. What the hell do these bloody Spaniards want from us?'

'Shut up, you idiot,' hissed some of his friends who were huddled by the bar. 'Don't you know when to keep your big mouth closed?'

A line of grim-faced, uniformed Guardia Civil were filing down the staircase, guns at the ready. Some were also holding flashlights, although the place was as bright as daylight, while others clutched handcuffs. A few of the panic stricken kids tried to scamper away, they were caught and they, together with any who were foolish enough to scuffle with the police, were immediately picked up and bundled out of the disco.

Herman and I froze. Even his spaced out lover was sobered up sufficiently to stay motionless and silent. My mind flashed back to the months I had spent in South Africa when the police would invade even the most discreet gay bars in Johannesburg, arresting everybody in sight. The raids were given the maximum publicity, and the names of everybody involved were splashed in the newspapers, ruining careers and destroying marriages. Were the same things going to happen in Spain, the new permissive, post-Franco Spain?

A second wave of police arrived, more brutal than the first. They were armed with clubs and riot sticks and beat savagely some of the cowering, gay boys. I was frightened by this naked barbarism.

Herman muttered a few words to the bartender, and at a sign from him, the three of us joined him behind the bar and then ducked with him below the high bar counter where we lay, not making a sound, for the next half hour.

At last, the uproar subsided and we peeped out of our hiding place. The place was practically deserted and had been turned into a shambles. Everywhere there were smashed glasses, overturned tables, broken barstools. Herman gave a handsome tip to the bartender who had given us refuge, and we picked our way through the debris. The police had departed; they had done their work - the disco had been closed.

We hurried into my car where, to my amazement, Herman told me that he was horny and asked me to put on the interior light so that I could see what he would do with the boy on the back seat. I could not understand how anybody could feel like sex after such an experience, and I felt awkward, as though I was intruding in some private scene between them. However, Herman insisted, so I watched.

It was miserable. The boy was so scared that he could not get an erection either when Herman masturbated him with his bejewelled fingers or when he sucked him. The kid was tense and wide eyed, like a hunted animal. Herman, annoyed, pulled his own cock out of his tight fitting pants and forced the boy to suck him. That was no better. Herman furiously pushed the kid's head lower until he nearly gagged. He pulled his cock away and stuck his finger in the boy's mouth.

'Here, suck that,' he said scornfully. 'When you can

manage a finger, I'll teach you know to suck cock.'

Maybe the kid revolted against Herman's harshness or, more likely, he suffered some sort of cramp in his jaw, but he bit Herman's finger. Herman screamed with pain and with his other hand, slammed the boy in the face so that he fell forward, blood spurting from his nose. He released Herman's finger and started to cry. The sadistic little drama was too sordid for me. I started the engine, turned off the inside light and drove back to Herman's house in silence.

Without saying a word, I went upstairs to my bedroom. Franny was lying asleep, making soft noises, and I cuddled up to her warm, sweet body.

'I missed you,' she whispered, her eyes tight closed.

'Go back to sleep,' I said.

I hugged her and in minutes we were asleep, me, holding her spoon fashion to me, my hands enclosing her rosebud breasts.

Next day, several of the gay boys were on the beach, showing off their bruises, bandaged limbs and black eyes. There were complaints to the authorities as a result of some of the men who had been harassed and beaten up, protesting through their consulates, but the story never hit the Spanish national press. During the next few weeks, I heard of a number of similar raids by the police on foreign owned gay bars along the coast, but I never heard of any action being taken against the police, those zealous guardians of the nation's morals.

6

You Are Never Too Old To Learn

'A stander-by may sometimes, perhaps, see more of the game than he that plays it.'

Jonathan Swift

We enjoyed a lazy Sunday morning, that is all of us except Momir who excused himself and hurried back to his studio. He explained that the fashion show and the preparations for it had completely disorganized the household and he needed to catch up with his work. Herman never mentioned the trouble of the night before, and I did not ask him how and when he had left his little friend.

Herman had not forgotten Ben's hospitality the previous weekend, and he suggested that we invite Ben to join us for brunch. The place livened up after Ben had burst in, full of energy like a big, affectionate dog, practically wagging his tail with pleasure at the company and greeting me with a touching tenderness.

Momir made a brief appearance for the meal and disappeared again the moment he had finished eating. The rest of us, Franny, Bill, Ben and I joined Herman on the terrace.

I recounted to the others what had happened the night before at the Bronx, tactfully omitting any reference to what took place subsequently in my car.

'The boy you were with got away alright?' Franny asked Herman anxiously.

'Julio?' That was the first time I had heard Herman mention the kid's name. 'Yes, he managed. As a matter of fact, I arranged to meet him in town at our favourite cafe this afternoon.'

As he spoke, Herman cast an anxious glance at the doorway as if to make sure that Momir was safely out of the way. 'You know,' Herman continued in an earnest voice, 'that boy shows me so much warmth, so much love.'

'He seemed a bit cool last night,' I commented drily. Secretly, I was astonished that Julio would be ready to see Herman again so soon after he had undergone such brutality.

'Oh, last night he was not himself,' Herman assured me airily. 'He was upset by all the fuss, you know. Normally, he will kiss and cuddle me - can't keep his hands off me. It makes me feel good. It's as though I am the only person in his life. All the other boys on the beach, my buddies, are terribly envious.'

'From what I have seen in The Bronx and in Amsterdam, you gays live in a superficial world of your own,' I said. 'You are all so damned fickle.'

'No more than the straights,' Herman protested. 'I know gay couples who have lived together for years.'

'Sure,' I argued, 'but they are not the ones you see cruising on the beach or at The Bronx.'

'Even the most faithful wants a break once in a while,' Herman said. 'In a heterosexual marriage, one or perhaps both of the partners, will have the odd affair or go on a sidekick. Why should we be any different?'

'All you guys seem to think about is getting your rocks off,' Bill put in. I guess that he was still feeling a trifle insecure from the way Herman had blown him the afternoon before.

Ben joined in the attack, 'Why do you gay guys exaggerate everything? The way you walk, talk, dance, dress - everything is so affected, as if to draw attention to yourselves. Some friends took me to a beach at Torremolinos and there were a whole mob of gay types, chattering about who fucked whom. Jack had picked up John, but John had slept with Dieter and that had upset Dick, who had gone off and fucked Tom. But Tom had been with José and so on. Who gives a damn who slept with whom or how big was the last cock up somebody's bum?'

'Be fair,' Herman pleaded. 'In any bar, you can hear men

discussing girls, even when they haven't been able to get them into bed. What's the difference?'

'True enough,' I conceded, 'but you fellows do seem to go on about your affairs more than most straight guys. Even you, Herman, can't stop talking about your Julio although you are living with Momir.'

'OK,' Herman flared up. 'So I need a bit of affection in my life! Someone to love me. Love, love,' he repeated savagely. 'Don't you know what it means to crave love?'

'But don't you get love from Momir?' Franny asked.

'Momir!' Herman laughed bitterly. 'Of course, but all he really cares about is his work. Oh, and I nearly forget, yes, he loves his cat. I tell you he shows more affection for that animal than he does for me. When he is away, I miss having him around. But as soon as he gets back, we have a ritual. I fuck him. Without saying a word, we go into our bedroom. He drops his pants and pushes his rump in the air. In I go and, bang, in less than five minutes we have got that over and done with. What sort of love is that?'

'You mean no foreplay at all?' I demanded.

'He will hardly even say hello.' Herman's tone was bitter. 'He makes me feel as though I am fucking a whore. And it's me who does all the shopping and the cooking and the entertaining—'

'And it's Momir who pays for everything,' I interrupted.

'Yes. But can't even you, Xaviera, understand what it is to want to hear the words, "I love you" and to be treated with feeling, not like a piece of furniture?'

I could see the pain in Herman's eyes. I read there his inner loneliness beneath the outward show of good humour and swaggering sadism. I went over to him, put my arms around him and kissed him.

'Come on, Herman, cheer up.'

There were tears in his eyes as Herman looked up at me. He could feel that, from me at any rate, there was the sincere warmth for which he thirsted. He smiled gratefully and planted a big kiss on my lips.

'Let's have a swim before I meet Julio,' Herman called out. 'Don't bother with your trunks, Ben; we're all friends here.'

'Promise you won't rape me,' Ben laughed.

'Wouldn't dream of it,' Herman said seriously, at the same time reaching for a pair of binoculars which he kept handy near the pool.

'Where are you going with Julio?' I asked, as I took off my clothes.

'Well to tell the truth, I was thinking of asking Ben if he would let us come back to his place. We could use the bedroom on the first floor, if it's OK by him.'

'I don't mind,' Ben said. 'You can do whatever you like, and as it is Maria's day off, nobody will disturb you. The rest of us will keep out of your way.'

'Good, old Ben! You are a real friend,' Herman said, training his binoculars on Ben's muscular, and now naked, body.

'Franny, you can play some tennis if you like while Herman is up to whatever tricks he pleases in the bedroom,' Ben called to the girl. 'I'd invite you to a doubles game, but I can't see Bill rushing back for my lobs. Here goes.' With that he dived into the pool and shouted to us to come and join him.

'I'll wait a bit and watch,' Herman murmured. I don't think that Ben noticed the binoculars focused full on him.

'And talking about watching, Xaviera,' Herman spoke softly so that I alone could hear. 'When I am making it with Julio, I'll leave the door ajar, so that you can see what we do. It'll give me an extra thrill to know that we are being watched without Julio knowing it.'

'Oh, I don't know, Herman. After last night in the car, I don't fancy playing the voyeur.'

'But, don't you see, Xaviera, because that was such a bad time, I want to show you what it can be like. It's important for me.'

'Well, if it means so much to you. But I'll either have to explain to Ben or make some excuse for keeping out of his way while you are performing. You know how he likes me to stay close to him.'

'Better still,' Herman grinned, 'get him to come and watch as well.'

'You're out of your mind, Herman. Ben is as straight as a flagpole. He'd never agree to spy on you and Julio in order to satisfy your exhibitionism.'

'But that's the point, Xaviera. He should never know that I arranged the show. You pretend that the two of you are peeping without my knowledge. It'll be twice as much fun. Go on, you can talk him into it.'

I could not resist the mischievous gleam in Herman's eyes, so I promised that I would do my best to persuade Ben to join me outside the bedroom door.

'Isn't anyone going to swim with me?' Ben called.

'Coming,' I shouted and jumped into the water.

Bill and Franny were lying in the shade, so our sole spectator was Herman who went on discreetly peering through his binoculars. And there was plenty to see. Ben swam over to me with a magnificent erection. He made a gallant attempt at an underwater fuck, but the resistance of the water seemed to hinder penetration, so we contented ourselves with swimming about like a pair of eccentrically joined Siamese twins.

Afterwards, we dried ourselves off and rubbed suntan lotion into our glowing bodies. Herman announced that he was going to take a short walk over to the gay beach to see how his friends, who had been beaten up at The Bronx, were. So, while the other two dozed in the shade, Ben and I slid together and fucked in undisturbed peace.

It was just before four, that we piled into my car and drove into town to pick up Julio. Going back to Ben's place, the six of us were pretty cramped, and Bill's crutches kept getting in everybody's way. Julio was wearing a light purple, Moroccan jellaba which showed his suntan to perfection. I understood the satisfaction that Herman got from the boy's unaffected love, as they embraced passionately in the middle of the town square, shocking some of the straight passers by.

At Ben's house, Franny and Bill took themselves off to the roof. The sun was not so intense, and they were able to bask with cold drinks by their sides. Herman and Julio went to take a shower. Ben was about to go up on the roof, to leave the lovers with the whole first floor to themselves, but I stopped him.

'Wait here, Ben,' I said. 'It's cooler and I've had enough sun for today. Besides, I am curious to see how Herman makes out. Let's stay and watch.'

'What?' Ben was startled. 'We can't do that. It would embarrass them.'

'You must be joking,' I scoffed. 'There's not much that would embarrass Herman. He would probably be excited if he knew. I was thinking that we could hide behind the door, but if you would rather, I'll ask him if we can look. We could sit by the bed or even join in.'

'No, no,' cried Ben, 'I couldn't bear that. If we watch, they must never know.'

I wonder what Ben would have said if he had known that the whole scene had been pre-arranged for his benefit.

'Why are you so uptight?' I asked. 'Herman watches me make out with both men and women in his garden, and he enjoys it. I'll tell him that we are going to sit in.'

'No, Xaviera, don't do that. He would probably put on an act.' Ben's voice was excited and I knew that I was getting through to him. 'We can stand outside the door as you said. But, first of all, let's go downstairs as if we are getting drinks from the kitchen. Then, when they are in the bedroom, we can tiptoe back here, without their knowing.'

'Not bad thinking for an innocent baker,' I smiled. 'Are you sure that you do not make a habit of spying on lovers?'

'Good God, no! I swear to you that I've never done anything like that in the whole of my life,' Ben exclaimed.

'But you are looking forward to it now, aren't you?' I smiled knowingly. I could read Ben who was an unsubtle soul.

Ben pointed guiltily to his bulging erection. 'See how hard my cock is! That is for you, but the thought of those two has got my imagination working. Quick, downstairs! They're coming out of the bathroom.'

We scampered down the stairs like a pair of naughty children. We heard the bathroom door closing and then a lot of giggling. I put my finger to my lips and led Ben back upstairs.

'That's a bit of luck,' he whispered. 'They have left the bedroom door open. If we stand in the angle here, we can see everything without ourselves being seen.'

Luck like that does not just happen, I thought; it is arranged, but Ben suspected nothing.

Herman had laid Julio on his stomach and was slowly massaging his shoulders and tenderly kissing his back. Neither man had bothered to towel himself thoroughly after the shower, and their naked bodies glistened in the bright sunlight. The boy had lifted his body slightly, so that he was crouching on his knees, swaying gently with Herman's rhythmic movements. We saw Herman slide one hand under Julio's belly and start to caress his balls and penis. The youth's cock was by now rock hard, but we only had an occasional glimpse of it because of the position of his body. As his excitement grew, Julio heaved his feminine, rounded ass higher, and Herman knelt behind him and gratefully accepted the boy's buttocks, first with his mouth and then with his fingers. All the time, the two of them whispered sweet words of love and endearment in Spanish to each other. For a few moments, Herman turned the boy around and hugged him so tight that he must have squeezed the breath out of his body. Then, realizing that he was a heavy weight on his lover's frail, delicate body, he lifted himself on to his knees and elbows, while he covered Julio's face with passionate kisses. I saw a tiny diamond glint in the boy's ear, probably a present from Herman, as the older man nibbled it.

'Oh, mi amor, te quiero!' I heard Julio pant, but I could not catch what Herman muttered into the boy's ear.

By now, both of them were thoroughly aroused, their bodies, soaked in perspiration, making squishy noises as they rubbed frenziedly against each other. Then, Herman pushed his stiff penis into the boy's eager mouth. As he approached a climax, Herman jumped back and withdrew swiftly.

The effect of this display on Ben was electrifying. His breathing was as heavy as that of the participants in the room, his eyes were popping out of his head, and his whole body was shaking with excitement. He pulled up my flimsy dress and thrust his own straining cock against my ass. He was pushing his burning body against my back, one hand fingering my breast and the other seeking my already dripping cunt.

Perhaps Herman could sense the drama which was being played out in the corridor and that made him more horny and more provocative. He and Julio had now adopted the 69 position. Faster and faster, they sucked at each other until with a gasp, they fell apart, Herman shooting his thick, white juice all over Julio's face while receiving in his eyes, nose and mouth, the boy's spurting sperm. At the same moment, I felt Ben burst into orgasm within me, and I came as well, shaking and pulsating. It was with an effort that we avoided falling into the bedroom, but we managed to creep away into the living room, with Ben's come, slowly dripping down my legs.

However, the entertainment was not yet over. Herman, I knew, had remarkable powers of recuperation, and within a few minutes, Ben and I were back at our post, watching a repeat performance. This time, Herman spat on his hands to lubricate his ever willing cock and slip it into Julio's inviting ass. As Herman fucked Julio, he also masturbated the kneeling boy. Once more, we spied on the gradual acceleration of their sinuous, intertwined bodies until, with a harsh cry from Herman and a groan from Julio, they came, Herman driving his load deep inside Julio and, a moment later, the boy's wet, sticky seed splashed into Herman's hands.

The two men were still getting their breath back in their room, and Ben and I were in a similar state when Franny burst into the living room. 'Anyone for tennis?' she called.

By an odd coincidence, the very next day after Ben had received his invitation into the world of homosexual love and so soon after the seduction of straight Bill, I received a letter addressed to me at 'Penthouse' which seemed to me to be so appropriate that I have decided to print it here in full.

Dear Ms Hollander:

Having just recently tied the matrimonial knot, I find myself, like everybody else, having to adjust my personal lifestyle to accommodate another person. And, while I am married to a sweet young lady, I do have second thoughts about the life of relative freedom I wound up kissing goodbye. I am twenty-three, completed my education just before marrying, and took a job as high school teacher while my wife completes her final year of study. Quite naturally, she is much more dependent upon me than vice-versa, my being the bread winner and what-have-you. But lately, some things have happened in my private life that make me wonder if I should have given up celibacy.

Unlike myself, my wife is not much of a beer drinker, and she definitely has no use for even light stuff like marijuana. To accommodate her straight laced approach to life, I usually smoke a joint or take a few bong hits well before she gets home from school. By that time, I'm lit enough to not mind throwing together supper, the whole bit. One evening around Christmas, I was sitting alone listening to my stereo rig and taking some bong hits of great stuff when the doorbell rang. Unthinking, I quickly opened the door to our apartment, only to find our paper boy standing there in a cloud of marijuana smoke that breezed out the door when I swung it open. 'I'm here to collect,' he grinned broadly, 'but payment doesn't have to be in money.'

Realizing that the youth wanted to get turned on to my supply, I invited him in. Kevin is only sixteen, so I did feel a little uncomfortable letting him partake of the goods. I wondered just how my wife would take it if she walked in on the two of us getting high. After only a few bong hits, Kevin's throat was dry and he asked if I had a beer. I offered him one on the condition he swore not to tell where he got it. 'I drink brew all the time,' he boyishly boasted.

Within an hour, Kevin and I had smoked a good deal of my bag and polished off a six-pack. He awkwardly thumbed through old issues on the coffee table of - guess - 'Penthouse.' Ogling the pictures, he said to me, 'This stuff gets me hornier than hell. I ought to go to your bathroom and whip off!'

'Go to the bedroom and beat it if you want,' I joked.

'Only if you'll come with me, dude,' he snickered, to my surprise.

'For what, Kevin?' I stammered.

'Whatever comes up,' he answered.

Quite honestly, I had never in my lifetime engaged in any activity that was even remotely homosexual, though I had sometimes wondered about how many people really did prefer and practice it. The high from the grass and brew, the general curiosity about a gay experience, and Kevin's beautiful looks prompted my inner self to respond, 'Okay, let's go. We've got about an hour before my wife's here.'

The minute we got to the bedroom, Kevin stripped to the buff, revealing a rather huge cock for such a tall and lean boy. He stretched out on my bed and watched as I unclothed, taking a whiff with each nostril from a tiny bottle. 'What's that?' I asked.

'Butyl nitrite, poppers,' he replied. 'They get you worked up and help get you off.'

I crawled on to the bed and took two snorts from Kevin's vial. Instantly, my heart was sent pounding, my breathing deepened, and I felt the compulsion to get it on with hot, raw sexual activity. I fell upon Kevin and we began to French kiss, my mind wondering if it was a dream or a reality. After probing each other's mouths with curious tongues, Kevin and I assumed the sixty-nine position and we began to lick and suck each other's cocks. As I licked the length of his young and probably virginal organ, working my way down to his musky smelling balls, I thought to myself that homosexuality - at least the variety I was now engaging in - wasn't all that bad.

He followed my every move, and I figured that he had to be relatively inexperienced. I grasped the taut buttocks in my hands and found myself licking his asshole while he did the same to me. Xaviera, I have to truthfully admit that this had to be the most intriguing, zestful sex I had ever experienced in my life. Since Kevin is no sissy at all, very cute, and built nicely, I found myself pondering just why I had not tried such delights much earlier. Sure, our experience was carnal, but it was gentle and satisfying.

The real surprise came when Kevin emptied his cock into my mouth. I took the full load as if I were accustomed to doing it all the time - and it wasn't as unpalatable as I had imagined. As his cock throbbed, sending small, thick jets into my mouth, I hungrily sucked to obtain every drop.

'You didn't come,' Kevin noted. 'Why don't you fuck me?'

Without questioning, I reached for the Intensive Care lotion my wife had by the bedside, and I lubricated his ass and my cock liberally. Kevin assumed a squatting position on his knees with his back to me. 'Drill me, stud,' he sighed, such talking making me all the more delirious.

I slowly entered the lad's tight ass, waiting until his muscles eased and allowed fully entry; not knowing his background, I didn't want to rush things. As he relaxed, he pushed his ass back and consumed the length of my cock. We both took hits from his poppers and I believe I performed the best fucking I've ever attempted. In no time, I was shooting my load deep within his rump, my right hand working his firm cock. Kevin came again within seconds of me and we both fell to the bed in a sweating, heaving heap, our act of lust completed.

Funky smelling, we took a shower together, and Kevin was just walking out the door of our apartment as my wife came in, loaded down with books. 'Did you tip Kevin?' she asked me.

'Sure,' Kevin replied. 'Your husband's very generous,' Kevin grinned sneakily. Of course, I myself felt a bit awkward.

Since that eventful afternoon, Kevin and I have 'tricked' two other times and he has even told me that he thinks he's falling in love with me. Xaviera, I do love my wife, but I'm developing an attachment to this guy. So enamored is he with me that he even offers to wash my car, give me free newspapers, etc. Do you think it's possible for me to continue seeing Kevin on the sly, or should I give up such cavorting and chalk it up to an 'experience?' I might add, however, that he knows better than my dear wife how to 'work a guy' in the rack.

It's true! You are never too old to learn.

7

Peter From Poona

'Nowhere can man find a quieter or more untroubled retreat than in his own soul.'

Marcus Aurelius

After my hectic weekend with Herman and Ben, I was pleased to be back in my own place. I had the good fortune to meet a nervous, American woman who lived in the same building as me. Her boy friend had walked out and she felt insecure without a man about the house. It was a relief to be able to pass on Bill, crutches and all, to this grateful recipient. It was time for his next move, and although she was a bit skinny and uptight, his new guardian angel had a car, which Bill obviously took into account. I would bump into him from time to time over the next few days, but he soon moved on to the next lady who could find a spot in her heart and home for him and I lost contact with him.

Franny and I were amused to witness the daily routine of the English 'playboys' of Marbella. Their day would start on Hank's Beach, where they would try to pick up young girls from every imaginable country who paraded there with the express intention of being picked up. The playboys found this thirsty work, and by the end of the afternoon, many of them were too drunk to see straight, walk straight, or think straight. They would totter off to dine with their newly acquired escorts who would be sure to choose the most expensive restaurants. Then, to the 'in-place', which at that time was Oscars, a discotheque owned by racing car driver, James Hunt. Before going back to his place together, each man's lecherous objective, they would look in for a last drink at the oldest and still the most crowded of Marbella's discos, Pepe Moreno. While the aging playboys would swap yarns about their deals, the girls, neglected by their great white hunters, flirted with the sexy Spanish waiters, sober, virile and available. So, when the playboys staggered out, ready for home and bed, they found that the playgirls had already taken off and the whole day's chase was wasted. The boozy, blundering idiots made the same stupid mistake, day after day, and ended up declaiming how deceitful were the bloody women who exploited them for all they were worth. I had no respect for the girls, who cheapened themselves and let the men treat them as whores or trophies to be collected. But I had even less sympathy with the men who got no worse than they deserved.

Sometimes, for a change, we would go up to La Florida, a private club, a short distance from Marbella, in the hills, which boasted a very pleasant swimming pool where we could go topless, and an outdoor bar and restaurant. I would play the odd game of backgammon, although I never aspired to the skill of the regular tournament players who congregated there.

Most of the crowd who patronized La Florida were dreadful snobs and worse gossips than the inhabitants of Peyton Place. Quite a number were members of the cliques who frequented Hank's Beach. Indeed, during the evenings, Hank himself was always there, since he had the concession to run the bar which his pals looked after in the daytime when Hank was usually occupied on the beach. Hank was a boisterous Englishman who, when polluted, which happened frequently, would play such pranks as pouring champagne over the bare breasts of women sunbathers during his occasional afternoon visits. It was while he was well tanked up one evening, that Hank fell clumsily into the pool, breaking his hip. After that experience, he stayed sober for several weeks.

Once a week, Hank would organize a barbecue at La Florida which would be attended by all the fashionable folk and the regular layabouts, like Bill, as well as those tourists who had heard about the event by word of mouth. I would go with my own circle of friends, which included an intelligent, handsome man, named Peter.

I liked Peter and found him a well educated and kindly person. He had spent three months in Poona and had come back to Spain, a changed man, after sitting at the feet of the most celebrated guru, Bagwan.

Before his pilgrimage, Peter had devoted his time to chasing petite brunettès with gigantic tits. Whenever the stock of women in his environment lacked any of that pattern, Peter would go without sex, rather than break out of his set behaviour. His wife, a brunette with gigantic tits had left him, taking their three year old son with her, and this had left Peter, cold and bitter. He would also be repelled by the least contact with a man, even if it were completely devoid of any sexual significance.

The new Peter was a soft, gentle men who wore silky, orange clothes, and would express his love of humanity by putting his arms around men, as well as women, and kissing their foreheads. He would even be charming to women who were not brunettes with gigantic tits!

So, one night during the barbecue, Peter and I were sharing a chaise longue and smoking a hidden joint, a little wày apart from the rest of the crowd, and I took the opportunity to ask him how Bagwan had changed his way of life.

'Tell me, Peter,' I demanded. 'Of course, I have read articles about it and I must admit I am a bit critical of the set up and the influence it seems to exert over people.'

'You have misjudged it,' he replied. 'The beginning is tough because they aim at crushing your ego. It's as though they have to destroy you before they can rebuild you, purified. Then, after a few weeks, it is a wonderful experience. That's when I leaned to become sexually liberated.'

'You mean that, thanks to Bagwan, you are free from your fixation for big-boobed brunettes?' I asked sarcastically. 'How did they work that miracle?'

Peter smiled at me patiently and patted my arm. 'I had heard about Poona being a permissive place where everybody could fuck anybody, anywhere,' Peter said, 'but the place must have changed a lot since I found that everything was well controlled.'

'Is that why you went, for promiscuous sex?'

'No, Xaviera,' Peter rebuked me. 'It was a decision I made after the breakup of my marriage. Let me tell you what happened.

'My wife left me after six years during which I was practically totally faithful. I guess she left because my laziness eventually got on her nerves.'

'What about the brunettes?' I asked.

'Well, yes, I used to flirt like mad, but, as I said, I didn't actually cheat with any other woman. However, while I was taking life easy, my wife went and fell in love with an energetic and highly successful Spanish lawyer. I still see her sometimes but her life style has certainly changed. Talk about from rags to riches! She used to be such a natural person, never wore make-up or fancy clothes, but was content, living the primitive life up in the mountains, doing her daily yoga exercises. Now, she is so sophisticated, eating in the fanciest restaurants, gambling at the casino. You would not think it could be the same woman.'

'And is she happy with this new life?'

'Yes, Xaviera, she seems to be doing fine,' Peter answered. His voice was tinged with regret. Then, he added, 'God, how I loved that woman!'

'And still do,' I remarked.

'And how do you know that?' Peter shook himself out of the reverie into which he had fallen, recollecting his lost happiness.

'It's written all over your face. But you should not be bitter. Surely, if you love her, you will want her to be happy?'

'That's one of the things I learned at Poona,' Peter

replied. 'And the experience convinced me that I had to change my life. Cut out the drink and find some purpose in living. That is why I went to Poona.'

'So what did you do there?'

'All sorts of things to heighten my awareness. But the most important was the way we were trained in our relations with other human beings.

'One day, I was with a group, sitting in a large, bare room around one of our masters. We sat, lotus position, on the floor, unmindful of our aching backs, silent and motionless. Then the master picked me out and ordered me to sit in the middle of the circle. He told me to select a woman from the other students, somebody of a type which I did not find physically attractive. I had no idea what was in store for me, and I chose a heavy, German blonde in her mid twenties with a fat, podgy face. Then the master told me to pick another woman, also somebody very different from my usual taste. So I took a big, impassive looking, black woman. Not unattractive, but I have never felt like fucking a black girl: they simply do not appeal to me. The three of us had to sit, very close to each other with our eyes closed, and stroke and fondle each other's bodies.

'It was a curious sensation. At first, I was conscious of the German girl's layers of fat which revolted me, but then I became aware of the softness and smoothness of her skin. The black girl's thighs rubbed against mine, and I could feel the difference in her skin texture, tauter, harder, a trifle rougher but without a trace of a wrinkle. "Now move around each other, explore every part of your bodies," the master instructed us. By the way, did I mention that we were all naked?'

'I had assumed that,' I replied, amused.

'I eased my finger tips over the black girl's slight breasts, caressing her tiny nipples and then moved down to her finely moulded ass while, with my other hand, I rippled the folds of the German girl's creamy flesh. All the time, I could feel their hands, seeking out my body, inquisitive yet tender. "Now, open your eyes," we were commanded.

'There was subdued, Indian music in the background, and the room was dimly lit. The extraordinary thing was, when we gazed at each other, the serenity on our faces and those of everybody in the room. People were kissing and fondling each other, and sex seemed the most natural thing in the world without a trace of guilt, shame, or self consciousness. I found that I had a massive erection, and the black girl leaned forward, and closed her beautiful, full lips around the tip of my cock, while the German girl lowered her body over mine, so that her great, lush breasts were offered to my mouth. She engulfed me and I had to fight against a feeling of helplessness, but then, holding her body as if it were a precious thing, I was able to suck her swollen nipples. She moaned softly, and the other girl took her mouth away from my cock, which she now softly stroked with her fingers, while she sought out the German girl's clitoris with her tongue.

'I have never liked oral sex, but the sight of the calm pleasure that the two of them gave each other affected me deeply and I had to participate. I buried my head deep between the black girl's thighs and took her strikingly pink clitoris in my mouth.

'At the end of this daisy chain, the German took over my cock and finally sucked me off, while her partner sat on my face, drenching me with her strong smelling, tangy juices. All three of us were perspiring and we drank in the smell and taste of each other's bodies. In an ecstasy, I came in the blonde's face and she lapped up every drop of my sperm. A short time later, when I had recovered somewhat, we were told to get into a fucking position, and I enjoyed a second, superb orgasm with the German riding me while I clutched her hips and the black girl continued on my face.'

'Sounds great!' I mused. 'I feel horny, just hearing about it.'

Peter stroked my hair and said softly, 'Maybe if we had

not become such firm friends over the years, Xaviera, we might have had a wonderful time together. When I see how loving is your relationship with your young friend, Franny, I feel moved and want to be part of it.'

I gave way to a sudden urge to kiss Peter, and our lips met for what seemed an eternity, in a passionate embrace. His sensuous tongue savored the sweetness of my mouth, and I thrust my own against his strong, white teeth and on into the depths of his own mouth. That kiss was as fulfilling as an orgasm. I closed my eyes in bliss.

'Look at me, Xaviera,' Peter said quietly. 'Look at my face in the moonlight and then look at the stars.'

He held my face in his hands, and I gazed at his green eyes and the golden beard, which wreathed his angelic face, in the silvery light of the full moon. I stroked the bulge in his pants, and we lay back, next to each other, enjoying the knowledge of each other's body.

I never had the urge to go to Poona. I found that I could appreciate the joy of touching, the true knowledge of a body, without having to attend classes or sessions with any guru. As for Peter, we never made love in the accepted sense, but that night, we both delighted in mental orgasms.

8

Rule Britannia!

'England is the paradise of individuality, eccentricity, heresy, anomalies, hobbies, and humours.

George Santayana

Soon afterwards I took Franny on a short trip to Portugal in my BMW. My old friend David and I had invested in a chic new disco, the Silver Screen, in Albufeira. He wanted my advice and support at the official opening, which was performed by Miss World, Gina Swainson. I drove Franny wild with jealousy by sampling some of the local cocks. I had to give her a severe beating as a result.

On David's advice we took a short cut on the way home to Marbella. I was able to cut more than an hour off my journey by taking a more obscure road which twisted and turned through the mountains to the old town of Ronda, a picturesque fortress dominating the only route across a dizzy ravine. When I had first come to Spain, Ronda was practically isolated from the coast, the road with thousands of hairpin bends and a broken, stony surface was so dangerous. For most of the thirty miles to San Pedro de Alcántara, there was a sheer drop on one side and a mountain wall on the other. Now, the road had been extensively modernised, and in the afternoon sunshine, it was an easy run down to where we could see the Mediterranean, sparkling and inviting, in the heat haze.

'Let's stop in San Pedro for a snack,' I said to Franny.

It had been a long and tiring drive, and it was late to go shopping. A break would be welcome, especially as I did not have anything to eat and drink in the apartment. I found a spot to park in the middle of the little town, and both of us were grateful for the opportunity to stretch our legs.

Siesta time in San Pedro tended to go on till five, and the streets were deserted. Rather than sit in the heat on one of the terraces on the main road, I led Franny into a narrow shaded, pedestrian street where, among the local shops selling food or clothes, we came across Daphne's Book Bar.

I knew Daphne's as a spot where The English colony would swap yarns over a gin and tonic or a genteel pot of tea. More than half of the space was taken up by a lending library of English novels, mostly sentimental romances, very popular with the middle-aged spinsters who eyed any newly arrived men without a great deal of hope and found inspiration for their fantasy lives in tales of demure virgins being wooed by handsome, wealthy aristocrats. I never found a copy of THE HAPPY HOOKER or any of my subsequent books on Daphne's shelves.

Daphne's had not long been open for the evening and the place was nearly empty. Franny and I took a table and studied the menu. It seemed ages since we had eaten and we ordered a selection of 'tapas' - typical Spanish light snacks which the English clientele of Daphne's had taken up with enthusiasm.

Daphne, herself, took our orders. She was a formidable, big bosomed, matron of severe appearance, and she ruled her establishment with the dignity and authority of a latter day Queen Victoria. Everything about Daphne suggested that this was a lady who would stand no nonsense. Frivolity and indecency would be frowned upon, and any outsider, guilty of the crime of bad taste, would be studiously ignored and frozen out.

Daphne's was very different from the other restaurants, cafes or bars which I frequented, but that afternoon, the calm, quiet, atmosphere was welcome. Not one of the half dozen people already sitting at the bar or at tables when we arrived gave Franny or me a second glance - or so I thought. Most of them were talking to each other in upper class, drawling accents, and their eyes spelled out the message clearly enough that they were members of the club and that we were not. The exception was a small, blond man, sitting alone at the bar, sipping a whisky.

We had only been sitting there for about five minutes and were still waiting for our food, when in walked one of my favourite Englishmen.

Arthur was an impressive looking man, tall, with a powerful physique. Now in his sixties, his face was rugged, with long, wispy, grey hair and wise, knowing grey-blue eyes. His complexion tended to be florid and his nose was heavy, almost Cyrano-like in its splendour. It was not until after I had met Arthur several times that I discovered that he was a member of the British House of Lords; he never used his title in the free and easy Marbella bars and cafes which he patronized.

'Why, Xaviera, fancy finding you here! What a pleasant surprise. May I join you?'

I motioned to Arthur to take a chair at our table and introduced him to Franny. Then, his eyes caught those of the lone man at the bar, and Arthur called out to him, 'God bless my soul, Stephen Noble! A bit early for you to be out, isn't it? I'd have thought that you would still be at home, sleeping off last night's tipple. Have you met Xaviera Hollander?'

'Not yet, but I would certainly like to,' replied Stephen with a broad smile. He slipped off his stool to come over to take my hand, and I was surprised at how short he was. He spotted my expression and chuckled to me, 'You're absolutely right. I am one of the few men who is taller sitting down than standing up. Allow me to present myself – the Magic Midget.'

He gave us an exaggerated bow.

'I heard the Poisonous Dwarf,' Arthur retorted.

'Ah,' replied Stephen, 'you must have been talking to one of my girl friends.'

The two men continued their good natured banter for a few moments, but they were too polite to carry on a conversation from which Franny and I were excluded. In answer to an enquiry from Arthur, I told him about the opening of the discotheque in Portugal.

'Capital country, Portugal,' he commented. 'Some of the oldest and most respectable English families live there, mostly in the north, around Oporto. But tell me, what does your friend do? Franny, did you call her? What an unusual name!'

He beamed at her, encouraging her to open her mouth.

Franny gave me a despairing glance as if to ask how she should deal with the question, but before I could intervene, she said, 'I am Xaviera's slave.'

Neither of the imperturbable Englishmen turned a hair.

'How jolly,' smiled Stephen. 'You should have been at school with me. The young boys, fags we called them, were flogged by their elders pretty regularly. You'd have had a lovely time, but in those days, there were no girls in the old Public Schools.'

'I think that Franny could very well have passed herself off as a boy,' Arthur commented. 'Have you ever wanted to be a boy, my dear?'

'Sure. Whenever Xaviera makes love to a man, I wish I were a big, virile man to please her.'

'Never mind about being big,' Stephen reprimanded her. 'Virility has nothing to do with size. I am about the same height as Napoleon and he managed alright. Aren't I right, Xaviera?'

Before I could reply, Daphne arrived with our food. She served us in silence. There, in front of Daphne, Franny and I were acutely conscious that we ought to be ashamed of ourselves for not being English. When she had left, I turned to Arthur and said, 'I am interested that you should have remarked how boyish Franny is as soon as you set eyes on her. I love her sexual ambiguity. I can see her as a boy or as a girl, according to her mood.'

'You must know how fascinated I am by that quality,' Arthur answered. 'After all, I was the first man on record to have married a transsexual.'

All Marbella knew Arthur's story, since it had been splashed in the British newspapers and was even news in the American and European press. He had married the man who became April Ashley, and subsequently he had taken a keen interest in other transsexuals, a number of whom had Arthur to thank for paying for their sex change operation.

'As a matter of fact,' Arthur continued, 'when I was a boy, I used to dream of being a woman, and I even went so far as to try and dress as one.'

'Why did you stop?' asked Franny.

Arthur laughed, 'I looked in the mirror. Do you think that I could ever look feminine?'

Burly, masculine Arthur was just about the last person one would expect to have transvestite inclinations.

'What is it about transsexuals or transvestites which gets to you so strongly?' Stephen wanted to know.

'Well, I'll tell you. I love women who are truly feminine, and with all due respect to the ladies present, I have never found any woman who can match a transsexual or a real transvestite in feminine sexuality. It's the way they talk, the way they walk or move their hands. They have a sensuous beauty which you can feel in their touch and see in the way they dress. I imagine that is why I wanted so much to be a transvestite myself.'

'You are the nearest thing possible to a male lesbian,' I told him.

'I suppose so,' Arthur agreed amiably, 'but you know, I have had and still do have love affairs with transvestites and I always play the male role.'

'Where do you find pretty transvestites around here?' I wanted to know.

'At Carmen's,' Arthur replied. 'You've been there, haven't you, Xaviera?'

I shook my head.

'Oh, well you must come. It's the best transvestite bar on

the Coast. It's only at Estepona, no distance from where you live. What are you doing tonight?'

'We've only just got in from Portugal, so I guess that we are going to take it easy.'

'Well, then, come with me tomorrow night. How about that? And bring Franny with you, of course.'

'That will be Franny's last night in Spain. The following day she is flying back to the States. Would you like to go to that bar on your last night?' I asked her.

'Yes, sure. Provided you spend the night alone with me and don't bring home one of the TV's.'

'OK, then, Arthur, it's a date,' I said.

'That'll be lovely,' Franny put it. 'To have my last night with you - perfect. The only thing I miss, is not being able to get in a game of tennis before leaving.'

'Well, now,' Stephen told us, 'perhaps you will let me complete Franny's vacation. I live in an "urbanizacion" - an estate, if you like, up in the hills not too far from here, called La Pacheca. It would give me great pleasure if you two ladies would be my guests tomorrow afternoon. We could have lunch, and along with a friend of mine, we could play tennis on our own courts. That would leave you plenty of time to come down in the evening to go to Arthur's dive in Estepona. What do you say?'

I had already decided that I liked the look of Stephen Noble although at that time I knew nothing about him. He had a merry twinkle in his eye, and I was sure that he could be great fun. Why not find out? So I accepted on behalf of Franny and myself.

I looked around and noticed that all the other occupants of the bar had stopped their conversations and were obviously listening to what was being said at our table.

'Do you think that all this talk about lesbians and transvestites is proper in this bar?' I asked Stephen. 'After all, I have the feeling that our English friends are just a bit conventional and on the square side, wouldn't you say?'

'Oh, don't worry about that,' Stephen replied in his loud, rasping voice. 'Everybody knows that there is a brothel upstairs.'

I gazed at him in disbelief.

'Graziella says so, and she should know. You've met Graziella?'

I nodded. Graziella was a big, busty American woman of fifty who came to Marbella every year on her husband's yacht with the express purpose of starting outrageous rumours. Graziella's husband was a Hungarian baron with a trace of Romanoff blood, so that meant that Graziella's rumours could be circulated among all the 'best' people.

'Graziella said,' Stephen continued at the top of his voice, making sure that his words could be heard by everybody, 'that she came along this street one evening at about eleven. You know that opposite here is a bar with a rather dubious reputation. Well, Graziella, virtuous woman that she is, turned her eyes away from the bar of ill repute, and in the window above Daphne's, she saw the form of a woman. Of course, there could only be one explanation – or so Graziella says. The place was a brothel.'

'You mean, seeing one woman in the window of what is almost certainly a bedroom at night, means that the place is a brothel?' I asked.

'You, my dear Xaviera, are not the first person to have had some doubts. So, Graziella came by, with a couple of her cronies from the boating crowd, at three one afternoon. 'I shall prove it,' she declared, and she picked up a stone and threw it through the window. A startled woman pushed her head out. "There you are," Graziella cried. "You see, she is only wearing a nightdress." Any house where the woman is wearing her nightdress at three in the afternoon is a brothel. Graziella says so.'

'But that's ridiculous,' Franny retorted. 'At three, people here take their siesta. Surely it is likely that the woman had got undressed before she went to sleep?'

'Why spoil a good slander with the truth?' Stephen asked. 'Anyway, Graziella said so and she is a baroness, so it must be true. Even the English cannot argue with a baroness.'

I saw the look in Daphne's eye.

'Come on Franny, I guess that we ought to be on our way,' I said hurriedly. 'Thank you for an entertaining time, and we'll see you tomorrow for tennis and TV.'

We fled. I haven't been back to Daphne's since.

9

Sports and Pastimes

'Love-thirty, love-forty, oh! weakness of joy,
The speed of a swallow, the grace of a boy,
With carefullest carelessness, gaily you won.'

Sir John Betjeman

La Pachecais a pretty development of apartments and houses, nestling in the hills at the entrance to the village of Benahavis, about eight miles from Marbella. The road, like that down from Ronda, twisted like a serpent in agony – certainly no place to drive if you were drunk, I commented to Franny.

Stephen's apartment, a split level, was not very large, but it had a certain elegance and I took an immediate liking to the furniture and the general decor. The Magic Midget was his exuberant self and gave us a hearty welcome, before introducing us to the remaining member of the mixed doubles.

'This,' Stephen announced pompously, 'is Eric the Rat.'

Franny blinked. She clearly thought that Stephen could have been a bit gentler on his friend. He surely did not look like a rat, with his blond, wavy hair, keen, slightly squinting eyes and athletic build. I would have put Eric the Rat's age at approaching forty: he looked a typical, upper class, English ex-Public School boy.

'So, who did you rat on?' Franny asked him.

'I fear that you are labouring under something of a misconception,' Eric replied in the same Oxford accent as Stephen's. 'This rather unfortunate soubriquet has been attached to me by Stephen and his ilk because I am, by occupation, a rodent operative.'

Franny gazed at me helplessly. 'What's he saying?' she pleaded.

'Don't be put off by the way he speaks,' Stephen

comforted us. 'The truth of the matter is that Eric is the local representative of the Pest Control outfit which disinfects buildings and deals with all sorts of problems arising from rodents and insects. He's quite a nice guy really, but he cultivates his olde worlde English way of speaking because it goes down well in the villas of the Marbella snob set.'

'Pleased to be of service,' smiled the Rat. 'Just let me know if you have any pests in your place which you require to have exterminated. No charge to you.'

'Thanks a million,' I answered, 'but all of my pests are of the two-legged variety and I can usually cope with them myself. At the moment, I am glad to say, I am trouble-free.'

Stephen had prepared a light luncheon for us, and he tactfully changed the subject as we sat down to a crisp, green salad, garnished with fresh shrimps.

We had hardly finished the last mouthful of our food, when Franny beamed at Stephen and asked earnestly, 'Can we play now?'

'I don't see why not,' he replied, 'but I am afraid that you may be disappointed.'

'The court looks fine,' I remarked.

'It's not the court that is the problem,' Stephen said with a grin, 'but you will find out soon enough.'

We trooped out into the bright sunshine into the neat gardens of La Pacheca, at the end of which stood a number of tennis courts. Nobody was playing: most people in that part of Spain prefer to play in the morning or the evening in order to avoid the worst of the heat. But Franny was too much of an enthusiast to wait a minute longer than necessary, and on her last day in Spain, nobody had the heart to disappoint her. All four of us were wearing shorts, and Franny was somewhat self conscious, since her legs were badly bruised as a result of our last night celebrations in Portugal. I saw the look of surprise in Stephen's eyes when he saw the marks, but he refrained from making any comment.

'I am afraid that I am not in very good shape,' Eric announced, 'so which of you ladies is willing to be my partner?'

'I am just as bad as you, maybe worse,' Stephen stated.

'I want to play with Xaviera,' Franny told them.

'But surely we play normal mixed doubles? The two of you against us two would not be fair,' Stephen pointed out.

'Never mind. I want Xaviera on my side. We girls will take you on even if the odds are against us.' Franny was adamant.

'On the contrary, it is you who will have the advantage,' Eric replied. 'But it does not matter. After all, it is only a game.'

'For Franny, tennis is a serious business,' I explained. 'She plays to win.'

The two men exchanged glances: Stephen shrugged his shoulders, and they walked very slowly on to the court.

'We'll knock up for service,' I called, as I picked up a ball.

'Nonsense!' Stephen protested. 'You are our guests. It would not be polite if we did not let you have first service.'

'Positively churlish,' Eric assented.

'Suit yourselves! Who am I to argue with English good manners?' I laughed. I prepared to serve, then changed my mind, tossing the ball to Franny.

'Here, this game is put on for your benefit. You might as well serve,' I said.

When she plays tennis, Franny is a different person. The rather awkward, shy kid is transformed into a purposeful, efficient athlete. Her clumsiness disappears and she moves with the ease and agility that comes from perfect fitness. I am physically stronger than her, but on the court, I am no match for the fearsome machine of mind and muscles which Franny becomes.

Franny screwed herself up and served. She had decided to dispense with the warming up process, and her first service was a full speed delivery aimed, with lethal intent, at

Stephen. It rocketed past him and bounced a foot out of court.

'Out!' I called.

'Thank God for that!' Stephen answered. Neither man had moved a foot.

'Serve slower until you are warmed up,' I ordered Franny.

Very deliberately, she placed her next service close to where Stephen was awaiting it. He shuffled towards it and got his racket to return it tamely over the net. I placed my return between the two men, neither of whom moved. Fifteen love.

Franny's next service was an ace. Thirty love. So was her next service. And the next for a love game. I was puzzled at the immobility of our adversaries.

Their game did not improve much when Eric served. He hit the ball hard and accurately, but whenever his service was returned, he and Stephen hobbled around the court like a couple of senior citizens, lining up for their pensions.

'Say, what's with you guys?' I called. 'I would have taken you for a pair of statues, if it were not for the sound effects.'

Whenever either of the men went for a shot, which they usually did if possible without moving their feet, they would emit heart rending groans, like souls in agony.

'I did warn you that it would not be fair if the two of you took us on,' Stephen answered. 'Both of us are black and blue with bruises - positively mutilated.'

'I fear that both our dexterity and our celerity have been impaired,' Eric commented.

At the end of the first set, 6–0, we took a breather. Neither Franny nor I were out of breath, but the male contingent needed a break, and Stephen explained to us how they came to be in so sorry a state.

'It's the Rat's fault,' he accused. 'You must have noticed that the road up here is not exactly what one might term straight? In fact, it resembles a corkscrew doing a rumba. Well, I am used to it. I can drink all night, and as long as I have not passed out, I can always drive that road like a gentleman. Never a problem. However, last night, Eric and I went down to Puerto Banus to a party in his car. We both had a skinful, and knowing that I have this peculiar talent for driving when pissed, I offered to take the wheel. But, Eric, being a stubborn bastard, insisted on driving. After all, he pointed out, it was his car and he was used to it. Well, he got to know it from a new angle last night when we landed upside down in the ditch.'

'Were you badly hurt?' Franny asked.

'Nothing serious, but you can see that it has ruined our tennis. It hurts to walk, and running is just a bad joke. But, if we don't have to move our feet, I think that we can give you a pretty fair game.'

I was prepared to abandon the game out of consideration for the specimens of suffering humanity who were limping around the court, but Franny had come to play tennis and she was going through with the game to the bitter end. She played with a grim determination and pitiless power, worthy of the centre court at Wimbledon. The final score was 6–0, 6–0; the men pointed out that there was no point in playing a third set, since we were mere women and might not be able to stand the pace.

Shortly after the end of the match, Eric the Rat's girl friend arrived. She was tall, blonde and with vivacious good looks. Also, she was French and her English was lisped with a charming and sexy sounding accent. Eric himself was taking a shower, and Stephen announced that he would rub Eric in with some sort of foul smelling horse liniment but, to the best of my knowledge, never carried out his threat. In fact, when Eric emerged, he was well scrubbed and smelt of a rather expensive cologne. He was wearing a shirt with coloured, horizontal stripes of a style very popular among the yachtsmen on the French Riviera, and a silk foulard, decorated with an Yves St Laurent print. Gone was the rather square, formal Englishman, and in his place we were faced by a suave, Gallic gallant. He presented Corinne as his fiancée, and chatted to her in French. To my amusement, I noticed that when he spoke to the rest of us in English, Eric, probably unconsciously, imitated Corinne's soft French accent and even the way he spoke was transformed. All his former fluency had vanished, and he made delicate patterns with his hands as he sought the words that now seemed to elude him. In a moment, he had become more French than his French companion. Even, Franny was startled.

'That's what love does for you,' I warned her.

The phone rang and Stephen answered it.

'It's for you,' he called to me. 'Arthur wants to talk to you.'

'Hello, Xaviera,' Arthur's rich, mellow voice boomed over the phone. 'How are you, my dear? Have you had a pleasant game of tennis?'

'I'm fine, thank you, Arthur. As for the tennis, let's say the game was a bit one-sided. We girls played the men.'

'That was not fair,' Arthur protested vehemently. 'They ought to have given you some points start and accepted a handicap. Dammit, they should act like gentlemen - it's not cricket! However, the reason I called was to ask you if you would mind our meeting this evening at a club in Estepona, called Scheherezade. Stephen can explain how to get there. I have a business meeting there, and I'm not quite sure when I shall be able to get away, so I would rather meet you there than have you waiting for me at Carmen's. We can go to Carmen's afterwards.'

'That's OK, Arthur,' I replied, 'but if you have a business meeting, perhaps you would prefer to see me another night.'

'No, not at all,' Arthur was emphatic. 'Besides, I remember it is Franny's last night here, and we should not disappoint her. But to tell you the truth, I would rather like you to meet my business associate and tell me what you think of him. He is considering, together with some friends, buying the Scheherezade, which needs a bit of money being put into it, and then installing me as manager. It's not general knowledge yet, but Stephen knows about it. I think that you are a far more businesslike person than I am, and I would value your opinion.'

'I'd be delighted,' I told him.

Arthur proposed that we meet at 11.30. I agreed and hung up. When I got back, Corinne was preparing to leave with Eric the Rat.

'Come, mon pauvre,' she said to her bruised lover. 'We go home and you rest yourself, yes? Do not exert yourself more by chasing the little ball. It is necessary that you relax yourself.'

'Assuredly,' Eric replied in his now halting English. 'Come, chérie, we take our leave.'

He shook Stephen's hand and kissed Franny and me on both cheeks. Then, with a little bow, Monsieur Eric and his petite amie, withdrew.

Alone, with Stephen and Franny, I recounted briefly what Arthur had told me. Stephen looked serious. 'I hope that it works out for him,' he said. 'Arthur is a good sort and deserves a break. You see, he is so good natured that a lot of the Spanish transvestites take advantage of him. He really has very little money, and they take him for every peseta. His genuine friends, people like Eric or me, will buy him a drink or stand him a meal, but those pretty bloodsuckers are only interested in what they can get out of him. I guess that he is very naïve for a man of his age.'

'Perhaps he enjoys it?' I ventured.

'Don't you believe it. He gets very depressed sometimes, and it is always the fault of some slut or other. Well, let's hope that this club will turn out well.'

Then, a mischievous smile once more on his lips, Stephen called to Franny and me, 'Come on, I'll take the two of you on, at backgammon and get my revenge for the undignified thrashing you gave me at tennis.'

Stephen did indeed beat us at backgammon, due largely

to our inability to concentrate as he told one anecdote after another, while the game was in progress. I have never met a man with more stories to tell than him, and as for the game, well we lost, laughing.

At last, the time came for us to leave, but not before I had arranged with Stephen for us to meet again. Although he was a little man, he would play a big part in my life during my stay in Spain.

Estepona is a quiet, small town with a sparkling new yacht marina on one side of the stately promenade, a scaled down imitation of the famous Promenade des Anglais of Cannes. Green lawns and sub-tropical trees made a charming setting for the shops, bars and restaurants - and the transvestite club, Scheherezade.

The club, like most night spots on the Coast, was very quiet before midnight, and when we arrived, there were only about half a dozen people, seated on the outside terrace. Arthur saw us arrive and he jumped to his feet, hurried across and opened the door for us. His manners were perfect and he welcomed us with a winning combination of warmth and courtesy.

'Xaviera, how kind of you to take the trouble to come. And Franny - it is good to see you again.'

Arthur escorted us to the table where he had been sitting with a short, stocky man, to whom he introduced us. 'This is my friend, Merlin Rees-Evans.'

'Are we interrupting a business discussion?' I asked.

'Not at all,' Merlin smiled, but I noticed that in front of him were spread several typewritten papers and some official looking forms and he was still gripping his pen. So I excused myself and walked across to the bar to buy Franny and myself a drink and to leave the men in peace to continue their business.

As I reached the bar, I felt somebody take hold of my elbow, gently but firmly. 'Now really, Miss Hollander, we can't have this.' Merlin nodded to the barman. 'In this place you are my guest, and you must grant me the privilege of buying you and your friend a drink. Also, I insist that you come back to the table immediately. Arthur and I have got about as far with our business as we can, and we had already resolved that we would stop as soon as you arrived. Come along now.'

Merlin had the same well bred voice as Arthur. I decided that they were both products of Eton, but later Arthur was to tell me that he was at school at Rugby and Merlin was educated at Shrewsbury. I was suitably impressed. Merlin was neither handsome nor ugly, but his heavily masculine features were striking, and he had the body of a wrestler. Yet another charming Englishman, I reflected. I realized that it was about time that I came across some good, sexy males. I liked the look of Stephen, and now there was Merlin who intrigued me.

As we sipped our drinks, I looked around me at the club. Even in the subdued light, I could see that the place needed smartening up, fabrics were worn, some of the furniture was stained, and I noticed that some mirrors were badly chipped. I wondered whether Arthur appreciated how much money would have to be spent to give the club the sort of glamour which would entice a new clientele through its doors.

Merlin did not have the appearance of a wealthy man. His shoes were of a good quality, but well worn and his suit was of an outmoded cut. He looked less untidy than Arthur, but his hair, though shorter, was badly styled. However, it was clear that neither of the men were of the conventional Marbella snob set and did not give a damn about being chic or trendy.

'Arthur and I would like you to see the show here tonight,' Merlin told me, 'but it does not start for another hour and a half. I propose that when you have finished your drinks, we go over to Carmen's, the bar where you were originally going to meet Arthur.'

'I've never been to Carmen's,' I confessed. 'You see, I tend to stick to the places in and around Marbella. But, if you think it would be fun, that's fine with me.'

'The fact that you are there will make sure that it is fun,' Merlin purred, and I felt the pressure of his knee against mine.

'Never mind me,' I told him. 'Think of me as just another Dutch girl on vacation. Tell me about yourself, instead. What do you do for a living?'

'This is not the time nor the place,' Merlin replied. 'But, some time, when we are together, just the two of us, somewhere quiet and peaceful, I'll satisfy your curiosity.'

I said nothing. I had the same strong impression that Merlin and I were destined to spend some time in each other's company, and till then, I was ready to leave him with the aura of mystery with which he had surrounded himself.

Carmen's turned out to be very much of a local bar, completely Spanish in its ambience with no pretensions as a spot for the tourist or jet sets. I found it cozy and the music was good. Carmen, himself, was a transvestite in his late forties and considerably older than the rest of the personnel, who were all transvestites also.

One of them was a divine looking, petite brunette who could have stepped out of a flamenco ballet, and it was clear that she was the great attraction for Arthur. In no time, she was nestling on his lap, whispering endearments in his ear. In her person, she summed up all that Arthur had told me he admired about transvestite femininity, the grace with which she moved her legs, the alluring glitter of her long, false eyelashes. Her hair, however, was her own, and it stretched far below her shoulders when she removed the heavy, decorative comb. It flowed, rich, black and glossy, as Arthur savoured its perfume and let his fingers play through its silkiness.

In response to some encouragement from Arthur, his love with a couple of her friends, performed a flamenco dance to music on a cassette recorder. She sang with a low, husky intense voice which throbbed with the warmth of a moonlit, summer night on the sierra, and when she danced, her red, polka dotted skirt whirled with the passion and the fury of a matador's cape. Her feet stamped ever louder and faster, until at the climax of her wild, savage dance, she threw herself on to Arthur's lap and he covered her face and arms with kisses. I got a tremendous glow of pleasure at the sight of his total enjoyment of the charms of the little, transvestite, bar-hooker.

Carmen's was meanwhile filling up, almost entirely with locals, mostly rather macho looking men with not one gay boy to be seen. However, it was time for us to return to Scheherezade for the cabaret. Regretfully, Arthur tore himself away, and we walked in silence back to the club.

After what we had witnessed at Carmen's, the show was, for me, an anti-climax. I have seen some very impressive transvestite shows, sexy and witty, like that of Michou in Paris for example, but this was stale and unenterprising by comparison. I suppose that it was different from what was generally available on the Coast at that time, so I made no criticism, but after a couple of acts, I felt that I had seen everything. I sensed also that Merlin and Arthur had things to discuss with the woman who owned the place, which they had politely let drop when I had arrived. So, at about half past two, I made our excuses, explaining that Franny had to be up early next morning to catch her plane.

As I made my way to the door, Merlin asked me, in a low voice if he could call me.

'Arthur will give you my number,' I answered. I was sure that he could read eagerness in my eyes, and for my part, I was certain that I would not have long to wait for his call.

10

The Constant Nymph

'Most woman are not so young as they are painted.'
Max Beerbohm

When I drove Franny to the airport, I was surprised and relieved to see that her body had practically healed from the battering I had given it in Portugal, and apart from a few heavy bruises and scratches, she appeared almost like any other young girl returning from a holiday in the sun and not, as I feared, like a Vietnam veteran.

'I'm OK,' she reassured me. 'If my parents do happen to notice the marks, I'll say that I fell down the stairs.'

'It would be an odd shaped staircase to give you bruises where you have them,' I commented.

We did not talk much before she kissed me goodbye and loped off through the passport control to make a few last minute purchases at the tax-free shop for her parents and friends. We both knew that it was time for us to part. If she had stayed any longer, the games would have become more violent, the strain upon us, intolerable. But, once back in the States, she would long for my presence - the more she suffered, the more she loved. And I knew that I would miss her and that although there was nobody on whom I had inflicted so much pain and anguish, there was also nobody for whom I felt the same tenderness. There are many ways of loving: who is to say that ours is less sincere and worthy than any other?

However, I am still young enough to look to the future rather than dwell on the past, and I had called Ben and arranged to pick him upon my way back from the airport. Ben had wanted to spend a few days with me, in my apartment in Marbella, and this seemed the ideal opportunity.

Ben was as affectionate as ever and made a fuss of me as

soon as I came through the door.

'It's great to see you again,' he cried excitedly, as he hugged me so tight that I could hardly breathe.

'I am so looking forward to being with you again,' Ben enthused. 'I even went so far as to buy myself a new pair of pants at the Corte Inglés.'

That really was something. Ben's wardrobe was not his strong point; indeed, he was a contender for the title of The Worst Dressed Man of the Year combining, as he did, the careless elegance of a New York Shopping Bag Lady with the sartorial splendour of a South Sea Island beachcomber. Ben, who was so generous in the way he threw his house open to me and my friends, became a penny-pinching miser when it came to buying new clothes. His purchase of a new pair of trousers at one of the most expensive shops in the area was therefore an event of the greatest significance.

'They were reduced in a clearance sale,' Ben explained as if he needed to apologize for his rashness.

'They are magnificent,' I told him. 'They show off your bow legs a treat. How about celebrating with a new pair of sandals?'

'No need,' Ben answered, 'there's plenty of wear left in these.' And he pointed to the faded, tattered slippers which hung dejectedly from his feet.

'No way can you wear those in Marbella, except on the beach,' I insisted. 'And to encourage you, tomorrow I'll take you shopping in Marbella and buy you a decent pair of swimming trunks. Wouldn't you like the girls by the sea to admire your great, sexy ass?'

'You always choose just the right presents for me,' he chuckled. 'That red toothbrush, shaped like a nude woman – terrific.'

'Well, stop talking about it and pack it into a case with whatever else you need to bring with you.'

'Oh, I'm ready. I had packed before you got here.' Ben pointed to a couple of plastic shopping bags into which he had crammed his possessions.

'God! What would the fashion magazines do without trendy guys like you?' I scoffed. 'Well, come along, my peacock.'

Ben and I had only been back at my apartment a few minutes before the phone rang. It was Louise, an American who lived with her husband, Bill, in a super house which they had designed themselves in the hills above Benahavis.

'Say, honey, how come I see nothing of you?' Louise came from Oklahoma, and her voice had never lost its soft, slow drawl.

'Oh, Louise, you know how it is. I've only just got back from a trip to Portugal.'

'Portugal,' she echoed. 'I thought that you would have been frittering away your time with all those Arabs. You can't stir a foot in Marbella without tripping over some sheikh or other. All that oil! All that money,' she added.

'Why, Louise, I would have thought that you would be the last person to object to either oil or money.' I knew that Louise's money had come from her family's ownership of one of the earliest of the Oklahoma pipeline companies. 'Anyway, my only companion right now is Ben.'

'Well now, why don't you two come on right up here? There's an exhibition of paintings by David Cradle opening this evening. And Horst will cook you a great meal. Anyway, I want to see you again. I've got something to show you.'

'And I'd like to see you too, Louise. Tell me, how are things working out between you and Bill?'

'That's to do with what I want to show you. Now don't you argue, young Xaviera. You and Ben just hop into your big, shiny automobile and get along here, as soon as you like.'

When I first got to know them, Bill and Louise were an odd, yet attractive couple. He was slow and ponderous, not unlike a larger than life version of Orson Welles, with a warm, booming bass voice. Good humour shone out of his broad, bearded face. He took great pleasure in entertaining in his fabulous house, which he had built around a big pool and under-water bar, and he delighted in cooking his own specialities for his guests. His wife, like him, in her early fifties, was one of the most natural people I have ever met. She wore no make-up on her lightly freckled skin, and her hair was brushed straight down in a simple fringe. Whenever I saw her, she had on a loose kaftan type dress, comfortable and cool, but completely unrevealing. Her dress sense equalled that of Ben. But they were so good-hearted that when one day, somebody had driven up to their isolated house in a taxi, under the impression that it was a hotel, they had invited him in and given him a meal.

But things had changed in their household, and I knew that their marriage was going through a crisis. First, there had been the arrival of Horst, a very butch, German, gay type who was a professional cook. People were always dropping in on Bill and Louise and hanging about for days or even weeks. Horst had stayed where he had dropped, and gradually, Bill relinquished the kitchen to him. More disruptive had been the presence of Virginia, an English writer who, I understood, was collaborating with Bill. Bill had once mentioned to me that he had an idea for a book which would be sensational, but he needed a bit of professional assistance. He never asked me directly to help, and I was far too busy to volunteer to get involved. I wondered how things had worked out as Ben and I drove along the winding road up to Benahavis.

The sound of my car, laboriously climbing up the gravel driveway to Bill's house, brought a host of cheering, waving men and women to the windows and balconies. As usual, there was a house full. Bill came to meet me and I was shocked at how bad he looked. He seemed to have shrunk: the skin hung loose upon his face and his belly was flabby and wasted.

'Well, now, Xaviera, good to see you.'

I wished I could have sincerely said the same thing about Bill, but before I could respond, Horst had grabbed me and welcomed me with a big kiss.

As Bill led the other guests out to the pool, I received my second shock.

'Xaviera, why let's have a look at you.' Louise ran downstairs and pulled me to one side. 'Well, tell me, what do you think?' she asked.

It was a new Louise who stood before me. She was wearing a sexy, canary yellow, wraparound dress, and in place of her sandals, she teetered on golden, spike heeled shoes. I found the black eyeliner and big, fluttering false eyelashes excessive. Her green eye make-up had been applied with more exuberance then expertise. Her light brown hair had been swept back into a sophisticated bouffant style and glinted with the highlights of a recent blonde rinse.

'Why, Louise, you're rejuvenated. You look as if you had walked straight off the cover of a fashion magazine.'

'That's what I wanted to show you,' she announced triumphantly.

'But, why? What's it all about?'

I could see that Louise wanted to talk to me on my own, so I sent Ben off to take a quick swim in the pool before lunch. We set together in the lounge, Louise in all her finery and me.

'That bitch, Virginia,' she mused. 'It all started because of her. Xaviera, do you know how much I love Bill? Christ, I would have laid down my life for that man! So what does he do about it, the big baboon? Gets that cow to stay here!'

'Wasn't she helping him with his book?' I asked.

'Don't make me laugh! Bill's book was going to be so epoch-making, so earth-shattering that it was going to topple the United States administration. More than that, it would revolutionize the whole of American society. Now, you know, honey, that takes an awful lot of book, and can you see my Bill as a cross between Karl Marx and Jesus Christ?'

'It does sound far-fetched, when you put it that way,' I agreed.

'Far-fetched! Horse feathers!' she snorted.

'I never knew how you got to know Virginia,' I said.

Louise laughed bitterly. 'Well now, you know what a big-hearted guy, my Bill is. I would sit at home while he would go down into Marbella or San Pedro. He'd do all the shopping and sit on the terraces of the bars with a coffee or a drink. When he met anybody he found sympathetic, he would invite them up to the house. Don't get me wrong, Xaviera, I am not complaining about that. I met a lot of very nice people that way, so I thought nothing of it when he brought back Virginia one day, along with her teenage daughter.'

'Were they living on the Coast?' I asked.

'No way. They were over from England on a short vacation and staying in one of the smaller hotels. I tell you, honey, I liked them. Virginia was fun. She spent a lot of time with me. As a matter of fact, it was she who showed me how to fix my hair - hairdressing was a hobby of hers. Bill was more interested in the daughter - or so I thought.'

'They were staying in a hotel, you say?'

'That's right. But there was only another week left of their holiday, and Bill suggested that they stay with us rather than go back to the hotel - it was very crowded and noisy.'

'So that's when the business of Bill's book started?'

'Sure. He found out that Virginia was a very competent secretary while she was up here, and he proposed that the two of them stay on. The daughter wanted to get back, so she took off, leaving her sweet, helpful mummy here, to work with Bill.'

'Didn't you think something might be wrong? I mean you weren't suspicious?' I had always found a streak of simplicity in Louise, but this seemed to be even more naïve than usual.

'No. You see, when her daughter was here, she was fine. Behaved like a real lady. And, as I said, she was a vivacious person who got on well with the two of us. I thought that she would liven things up a bit. Boy, how right I was.'

Louise paused to get herself a drink and brought me an orange juice.

'Once the daughter had gone, things changed pretty fast. She spent less and less of her time with me. Well, that was OK. I reckoned she and Bill were getting down to some serious work. But then she really started to drink. You know, Xaviera, Virginia was a young woman in the way she looked, and there were days when you would have taken her and her daughter as sisters. But when she got on the booze, she would put on twenty years in an afternoon.

'Virginia was going through the grand drama of her divorce, and she was upset, so that was why she took to the bottle,' Louise informed me sarcastically. 'She and Bill used to sit all the afternoon, her telling him her life story and the pair of them getting smashed. Boy, could they drink!'

'You are not above having a skinful yourself, now are you, Louise. Be fair.'

'Compared to those two beauties, you would have thought that I had taken the pledge. Anyway, then they would go off to Bill's room for their work for the day.'

I knew that Bill and Louise had separate bedrooms, at the opposite ends of the house.

'You know,' Louise continued with a dry laugh, 'I was so innocent, I suspected nothing until, one day, Horst said to me, "Louise, Bill and Virginia have been hard at work every day now for six weeks. Why don't you ask her to show you what they have managed to get through after all this time?"

'So I broke in. Virginia had a plastic folder which she told me contained all their precious work. Bill just looked embarrassed. She didn't want me to peep into that folder, but by now, I was curious. Before she could stop me, I whipped the folder out of her hand. And do you know how much of Bill's epic, they had finished? There were three typed sheets inside. I swear to you, Xaviera, that was the lot. Fast workers, don't you think?'

'I guess at that rate, it would have taken Tolstoy about three hundred years to get WAR AND PEACE out of his system.'

'I tell you, honey, I was boiling. After that, I started showing up unexpectedly. They were not very careful. The first couple of times, I just caught them kissing. But then – oh hell, do I have to tell you? I went straight out and bought her a one-way ticket to London. "Listen, you," I said to her in front of Bill, "either you use this ticket tomorrow, or I shall. And if it's me who goes, ask Big Bill where the money to run this place will be coming from, because it won't be from me any more."'

'She left?'

'She had to. That was one bluff that Bill dared not call.'

'So what now, Louise?'

'I'll tell you what.' Her voice quavered with emotion. 'I need that man's love, that's what, Xaviera; can you understand that, after all that he has done to me? I still love him. So I get around to thinking, perhaps it was not all his fault. If I had made myself more appetizing – taken a bit more trouble over my appearance, maybe he wouldn't have had to look at some other woman. Mind you, he can't be that horny. He hardly ever gets it up any more. But I want him back – the way it used to be.'

'And how does Bill react to your new look?'

'Oh he's so damned practical. I put on these shoes and I want him to admire my legs. Look, they are good – long, slim, young legs. They are, aren't they, Xaviera? Say they are good legs.'

'They're fine,' I said soothingly. She so badly needed praise and admiration: she must have been dreadfully unhappy.

'All he said was that I should leave them off before I fell over.'

There was a pause. I could see tears, glistening in the corners of her eyes. She brushed them away, and then with a twisted smile, she said to me, 'I think that while it's just the two of us sitting here, I'll kick them off for a few minutes. They are so tight, they hurt like hell and my feet are so hot.'

'Now, you know, Louise, I think that you ought to go easy with all that glamour stuff. You'll drive all the men insane. Even Horst will go straight - he's obviously crazy about you.' I hoped that by adopting a jokey tone I could cheer Louise up, but my effort misfired.

'God, I don't want to get any man - just my old idiot. Mind you, I get so frustrated that I have even considered seducing Horst, but I don't think that he would survive the shock.

'You know I was going over to the States. But, then I dared not make the trip.'

'Dared not?' I echoed. 'What were you afraid of?'

'Xaviera, I tell you that Bill was really hooked on that bitch, and she was so cunning! I overheard him on the phone to her one day, and I realized that if I left, he could fly her back into the house and get me for desertion.'

'Louise, dear, don't you realize that you are a lovely person because of who you are? You don't need all this tarting up. I prefer the old, natural, Louise to what you have made yourself. If Bill can't see you for the sweet, loving person you are, then the fault is with him. He's blind.'

'But Xaviera, what can I do?' Her unhappiness made her desperate. 'Hell, why do I eat my heart out with that man? No woman would be so cruel and cold. I must be able to stretch my hand out and touch some human being. Tell me, wouldn't I find some solace from a woman? It's not too late for me to try lesbianism, is it, Xaviera? And you are so understanding and sensuous. You are fond of me, aren't you, Xaivera? Would you make love to me?'

She pressed her urgent lips to mine. Every nerve in her

body was shrieking out for love. I hugged her and then, gently pushed her away.

'No, Louise, that's not the way out for you.'

'What's the matter with me? Am I too old, too ugly? Even you reject me!'

'No, it's nothing like that,' I comforted her. 'I know you too well. This is not what you really want. Afterwards, you would be ashamed; you are looking for a love that goes beyond mere kissing, hugging and orgasm. You want to be appreciated as a woman again. Of course, you feel sexually frustrated, but that would not be cured by some superficial affair whether with a man or a woman. With all that you and Bill have gone through, you have a psychological problem. If we were not in Spain, I would suggest that you go and see a shrink.'

'A shrink,' she repeated thoughtfully. 'You know I think that you may well be right. No, I could not find a decent shrink here, but you have made me see the situation from a different point of view. Our own chat has been better for me that what I could have got from some stranger. Thank you, Xaviera; whether you know it or not, you have been a great help. I have so few real friends, and I suspect that most of them know or guess that Bill was having that affair, so they are awkward with me. I guess that for a little, I lost my own self-respect: you have given it back to me.'

We were interrupted by the arrival of Horst to call us for lunch. Louise squeezed my hand, and I felt that a new courage was coursing through her veins.

Then we walked out on to the patio, where Horst had laid the tables. Louise walked over to her husband, put her arm through his and kissed him. For one moment, Bill looked surprised. Then, he took Louise in his arms and hugged her.

'Aren't they a lovely couple? And so happy,' smiled Ben as he took the seat beside me.

11

Ben Rises To The Occasion

'A hero is a man who does what he can.'

Romain Rolland

Much wine flowed during lunch, and after the meal, a siesta was the order of the day. Louise had assigned a comfortable guest-room to Ben and me. We took a shower and then made love, nice and easy. It had been some time since we were together, but it was as though we had never been apart. We knew each other's bodies so well, it was almost as if one was touching oneself. Our sex, that day, owed more to love than to passion and nothing to mere lust. After my recent stormy sessions with Franny, our quiet, uncomplicated lovemaking was more than welcome. It was good to snuggle up to Ben's hairy chest, and at last, exhausted, we both fell asleep.

The exhibition was not due to open formally until ten o'clock. Horst had prepared a delicious cold buffet, with a paté en croûte, worthy of one of the great chefs from Paris or Lyons. Most of the guests were going to the show. Ben had changed his shirt for the occasion. Now, he sported a pure white garment on which was printed the legend 'She is the Best' surmounted by a thick, black arrow, pointing to the right. He insisted that I walk beside him, on his right, naturally. This was extremely awkward, since the streets in Benahavis were narrow and crowded.

Ben and I made an early start and stopped to have a drink at what everybody along the Costa del Sol, called 'The Greek Restaurant'.

I had met Iris, the owner before she became a widow. Her husband had been a tall, spare Englishman of great charm and old world courtesy. His sudden death had left the family in a precarious financial position, with the restaurant still not fully established. But the family worked like beavers to keep the place going and the creditors at bay. And I am sure that it was the strong family feeling which attracted many of the Greeks' clientele. Even though they might quarrel or sulk, the widow and her three children - John, Catherine and Mary Rose - never, for a moment, lost that warmth such as that which I had come to love among so many Jewish families.

As Ben fought his way to the bar, I surveyed the scene. Catherine and her mother were rushing to and fro, carrying plates of steaming food to the tables out in the garden. The kitchen was working at full pressure: so was John behind the bar. Above the buzz of conversation, somebody was shouting my name, but the place was so crowded that I could not see who was calling. Then, Stephen appeared at my elbow.

'You can't stay away from me, can you, Xaviera?' he grinned.

'I might have guessed that you would be here,' I replied. 'Are you going on to the exhibition?'

'That building has a fatal attraction for Stephen, my dear.' The speaker was Mary Rose who had emerged from the kitchen to get some herbs which had been left to dry over the fireplace in the bar.

Stephen smiled uncomfortably.

'And ask him what he's doing with that Polaroid camera,' Mary Rose called, as she scurried back to her pots and pans.

'So what's all that about?' I demanded.

Ben had now rejoined us, and I introduced Stephen to him. Ben eyed him warily. He must have suspected that the diminutive Englishman would be a rival for my affection.

'I think that the Polaroid is a ploy which you may well appreciate, Xaviera.' Stephen was his old, unruffled self. 'How does a little fellow like me set about picking up an attractive girl in a bar? Your suntanned giants flex their muscles and puff their chests out like fighting cocks. I can make brilliant small talk and sweep the lady off her feet with my wit and charm. But how to break the ice - that's the question. I've found an infallible method is to take this camera with me and photograph the girl. Then I go up to her and, with a flourish, hand her the picture, telling her that she looked so stunning that I simply had to snap her. Works like a charm.'

'So the fact that you have your camera with you tonight means that you are on the look out for some poor, defenceless maiden to seduce,' I asked him, mockingly.

'Not at all,' Stephen replied without a moment's hesitation. 'I heard that you would be here, so I brought the Polaroid just for you.'

And with that, Stephen promptly took a picture of me.

Even Ben had to laugh at Stephen's charming flattery. It was strange being with the two of them. I was sure that Stephen was fond of me, although we had scarcely met. There was an indefinable attraction between us. At the same time, there was my loving Ben. They were so unlike and yet there was room in my heart for the two of them. And the rest of my body could accommodate them both as well.

Stephen did not stay long in the bar. He explained that he had made a date to meet Eric the Rat and Corinne at the exhibition, which was in the building opposite the restaurant. We had not yet finished our drinks, so I promised to join him in a few minutes.

However, before we left, Horst came into the restaurant. He adored Ouzo and this was the only place he could get a glass.

'Your old partner has just gone over to the exhibition,' John told Horst, as he served him.

Horst saw the enquiring look on my face. 'He means Stephen,' he told me by way of explanation.

'I never knew that you were partners.'

'Well, it never quite got to that,' Horst replied. 'It goes back to Stephen's romance with Mary Rose.'

'Tell me more.' I was intrigued.

'Well,' Horst narrated, 'Mary Rose is a rather pretty girl – or so I have been told by those who have an eye for that sort of thing. Men get a bit lonely up here at Benahavis, particularly in the winter, and there is a definite shortage of pretty girls – or even just girls. I suppose Stephen was bored – anyway he started to take notice of Mary Rose. You know what I mean? He would sit here and gaze soulfully.'

'So what became of the great romance?'

'Virtually nothing. Maybe they got tired of each other. Perhaps Stephen did not like the Arab who started courting Mary Rose. I think that she, and the rest of the family, got fed up with Stephen getting drunk.

'And, boy, did he get drunk! One night, Stephen was pretty far gone and got thrown out of here. So, still under the influence, next day, he bought the house opposite. It had been empty for months and Stephen, to get his own back, decided to turn the place into a restaurant in competition with the Greeks. It was all deadly secret, and I think that Iris didn't know anything about the deal for at least twenty minutes after it had been clinched. That was when Stephen got hold of me – he knew that I was a chef, but he wanted a Turkish restaurant to take on the Greeks. Of course, the whole thing came to nothing – like most of the big deals which are hatched in this village. I went up to Bill and Louise's place, and Stephen was lucky to get the place off his hands when David Cradle turned up and wanted a studio and exhibition gallery. Stephen still used to come in here for a drink, and the whole family made him feel as uncomfortable as possible, but by now, it has just become a poor joke.'

'Let's get over to the gallery and join the Magic Midget,' I proposed.

'Poisonous dwarf,' hissed Mary Rose, as we left.

The gallery was spacious and the exhibits well displayed. David Cradle was a sculptor who specialized in statues of animals. A stone shark contemplated a green frog, the work of David's girl friend, Rosy, and the central exhibit was a giant eagle, which was still behind wraps when we arrived. There were a number of smaller pieces, and it was gratifying to see that already quite a number had been sold. A lot of the Marbella upper crust had turned up. I brushed against a German baron, resplendent in his pure, white suit, immaculate and opulent. He was outranked by the English earl, who wore a crumpled, striped shirt and a navy blazer. I saw a discreet, Japanese businessman writing out a cheque. He had purchased a kangaroo.

'God, the Japs are annexing Australia,' Stephen commented as he moved to my side.

I was amused to notice a white robed Arab, surrounded by what was obviously a posse of bodyguards. His Highness's face was expressionless. After a few minutes, he turned on his heel and left. Perhaps he had hoped to find statues in solid gold.

There was no air conditioning and the ventilation was primitive. After a while, the place was as muggy as an equatorial jungle. There were a number of photographers who took the opportunity to get me to pose for some pictures with Rosy.

'They're better than your Polaroids,' I told Stephen.

'It's results that count,' he retorted.

Suddenly, things took an unforeseen and dramatic turn. The heat had become unbearable and the stars were hidden by heavy clouds. All at once, the storm broke. Torrents of rain cascaded down, and in minutes, the street outside the gallery was awash. Thunder rumbled and crashed like the opening drum rolls of an overture to some immense drama.

Suddenly, the door burst open, and a breathless, bedraggled girl stumbled in. She was gasping for breath and sobbing hysterically.

'Help. For God's sake, come quickly. There's a car fallen into the ravine. They'll all be dead. Please, come and get them out.'

Rosy ran and got the girl a glass of water and forced her to sit down.

'Now, tell us clearly,' she said. 'What's this about a car in the ravine? Tell us exactly where.'

'Oh, there's no time,' the distraught girl cried. 'My boy friend and I were driving into Benahavis when the storm broke. We were following another car, and at that great bend, just before the village, the other car went out of control. It skidded off the road and rolled over the edge. I saw it turn over twice. I could hear the smashing of the metal and the glass – and then nothing. They were friends of mine – three of them in the car,' she began to tremble and great sobs shook her dripping body. 'They may be dead or horribly injured. Please, will somebody come back with me to help?'

'Where's your boy friend?' Horst asked.

'He's stopped there to try and get to them. I hitched a lift. Please, don't stop and ask questions. Hurry.'

Nobody stirred. Then Ben shouted. 'What's the matter with the lot of you? Afraid of getting your hands dirty or soiling your beautfully laundered clothes? Don't you understand, there are people out there who need help. Xaviera, you'll drive us there?'

'Of course. Let's get going.' Then, turning to the shaking girl, I said, 'You had better come with us and guide us to the spot.'

As we made our way to the door, I found that we had been joined by Stephen and Horst. Without another word, we ran into the rainswept street and climbed into my car. Nobody else in that crowded building made a move to follow us.

'What a lot of creeps and phonies,' Ben commented in disgust.

I could not drive too fast for fear that the car would skid off the treacherously wet road, and we too would end up as victims of the savage storm. Gingerly, I felt my way around the bend to where I saw the girl's car, pulled off the road, and I slithered to a halt.

The young man who had stayed to help, eagerly ran up to us. As well as being soaked to the skin, I noticed that he was as white as a ghost. His girl friend fell into his arms.

'Are they dead?' she cried.

He shook his head. 'No, they have managed to climb out of the wreckage, but it's bad. I can see that Amy is injured. I think that the others are OK, but I can't get to them and I can't even hear what they say with the noise of the storm, no matter how loudly they shout. I've been passed by perhaps half a dozen cars, but none of them would stop. The bastards! They must have known that something was wrong.'

'Don't worry, son.' Ben automatically took charge, and his voice was strong and reassuring. 'The next one will stop alright.'

Even as he spoke, he saw the headlights of an approaching car. Ben strode out into the middle of the road and waved it down. The car came to a shuddering halt. Inside were three Spaniards who, as soon as they saw what had happened, were keen to help. What a contrast with the mob at David Cradle's party, I reflected.

Meanwhile, the girl had run to the edge of the road and was waving to her friends. Luckily, one of the Spaniards had a powerful electric torch, and with it and with the light of the car's headlights, I was able to make out the scene below.

The car had toppled into a ravine which dropped a hundred feet to the river bed, where the already swollen waters were frothing, as they rushed between the jagged rocks. But the fragile Citroen Deux Chevaux had not plunged headlong; it had lodged among some bushes which grew out of a narrow ledge, about twenty feet below us. I could see the two figures who were crouched against the car's upturned bonnet: the other injured girl was stretched, motionless in the bushes. They were exposed and must have been freezing and their position was precarious. A false move could send the wrecked car over the edge to where it would plummet down to the river bed, dragging them to their deaths, for they had no room on that tiny ledge to get out of the way of the falling vehicle.

Meanwhile, Ben had sent the Spaniard's car back to call an ambulance, but two of the occupants remained to help in the rescue.

'Have you got a rope in the car?' Ben asked me.

'I guess so, you had better look.' I had never found myself needing a tow, and I had only a rather vague idea of what was in my repair kit. Ben found a rope, but it was far too short to reach the trio, stranded beneath us.

'We must get to them quickly,' Ben snapped. 'I don't like the way their car is lying. It could over-balance any time.'

'I could probably climb down to them,' Stephen volunteered.

'What good would that do? No, I'll tell you what we must do. We'll form a human chain. Xaviera, bring your car as near to the edge as you can. I'll guide you from here.'

I obeyed Ben. When I stopped, he made me engage the hand brake as well as leaving the car in reverse gear. Then, he lashed the rope to the front fender of the heavy BMW.

'You stand beside the car, and if you see it slip an inch, you shout to us. But, at once – don't wait; we depend on you. OK?'

I nodded.

'Now,' Ben addressed the men, 'we're going to climb down that bank, holding on to the rope. Then, we form a chain, holding hands, and the last guy keeps hold of the rope for grim life. It'd better be one of you two,' he pointed to the Spaniards, 'since you are heavier than either Stephen or Horst and probably stronger.'

'But what about you, sẽnor?'

'I'll be the man at the other end. That girl will need some help.'

The rain had given over somewhat, and a watery moon peeped out from behind the clouds. Grabbing one end of the rope, Ben deliberately clambered over the edge of the ravine. I could hear his shoes scraping against the rock, as he searched for a footing. Gradually, he worked his way down until he was standing just a few feet above the wrecked car, at the end of the rope.

'Right,' he called. 'Next, Stephen, then Horst and lastly you, whatever your name is.'

Stephen followed down the rope. Lighter than Ben, he was able to move quicker. When he reached Ben, he took the end of the rope in one hand and extended the other to Ben, who edged his way further down. I watched my car. The springs seemed to groan, but maybe that was my imagination. We were all tense and nervous. Anyhow, the car did not budge and I sighed with relief. Now Horst was at the end of the rope, clutching the hand of Stephen who held on for dear life to Ben.

'We're nearly there,' Ben called encouragingly as he strained towards the man and two girls below. 'One more guy, and we'll make it.'

The Spaniards were ready. One after the other, they moved down the rope. I watched my car and then I saw the headlights of another vehicle tearing up the road at high speed. I was terrified. If it did not slow down, by the time the driver saw my parked car, he would be too late to stop and he would smash into the BMW, sending it spinning off the road into the void below and with it the human chain. I grabbed the flashlight, which had been left with me, and waved furiously at the oncoming motor, praying that he would brake before it was too late.

'Got her,' cried Ben in triumph. The elongated chain had enabled him to reach the first victim. 'No, leave the other girl for me,' he ordered. 'You climb up the chain and the rope. Down here, you are only in the way.' The second girl had crawled out of the bushes and was now standing up, against the car.

With the weight of the first victim added to the chain, I could hear the creaking of my car, but the brakes held. My attention was concentrated on the vehicle which was now almost on top of us. Suddenly, its brakes screeched and it slid to a stop, feet from where I was standing. Only then did I see that it was an ambulance.

By now, the first girl had reached the roadside, where the girl who had summoned us, hugged her and helped her to the ambulance. She could only use one leg and had been virtually manhandled up the rope.

'Is there nothing I can do?' her boy friend called.

'You did your bit by staying with them when they went over the edge,' I told him. 'The chain is long enough, and you would just be extra weight if you were in it.'

The man followed the girl and appeared uninjured apart from scratches, bruises and superficial cuts. But, Ben called that the remaining girl seemed to have broken her ankle.

We watched, breathlessly, as Ben, holding on to Stephen's hand for dear life, extended his other hand towards her.

'Hop or hobble, but get to my fingers,' he coaxed. Taking all her weight on her one sound foot, she inched her way forward, leaning against the car.

'For God's sake, don't put your weight on that car,' Ben cried. I saw the light shell of the Citroen sway, and with a little scream, the girl sprang back. As she jarred her injured ankle, she let out a gasp of pain.

'Come on, you can do it,' Ben called. 'Just once more.'

For what seemed an eternity, she made no move. Slowly she started to work her way forward again. The gap between her and Ben's outstretched hand closed until there could only have been a foot separating them. Then, she hopped with one despairing effort, at the same time, pushing against the shattered car with one hand while the other clawed in the air, seeking Ben's fingers.

Ben grabbed and seized her by the wrist. At the same instant, the car, against which she had thrust, lurched forward. It balanced for a moment on the tip of the ledge, then, slowly, as if in a dream, it tilted and disappeared into the abyss. There was total silence: then one great crash and the horrible sound of rending metal.

Meanwhile, Ben had dragged the girl upwards, and her grip had been transferred to Stephen who grunted with the exertion as he took the strain of her body. In seconds, she was clear and safe, and the men from the ambulance had her on a stretcher.

We had been so busy, concentrating on the injured girls that we had ignored the man who, Ben had assured us, was virtually unhurt. He had sat down at the roadside as soon as he had fought his way up the rope, but now got to his feet. I noticed that he was swaying, and I called over to him.

'Go easy. You've had a bad shock. Are you OK?'

'I can't see properly,' he answered. 'Everything is muzzy.'

'Let me have a look,' Stephen said. 'Xaviera, bring that torch across so I can see.'

I did as I was told. Stephen examined the man's face. I heard him whisper, 'Oh, my God.' Then in a louder voice, 'You're OK, old boy. Just need a bit of cleaning up. Go with those guys in the ambulance.' He turned away quickly.

I had glanced at the man's face. It seemed to be pitted with spots of blood, but it was only after he was in the ambulance where he could not hear that Stephen spoke to me.

'I had a closer look than you did, Xaviera. Those marks – and there must have been dozens of them – they were glass, from the window or the windscreen that had shattered and was embedded in his face. He needs surgery. And didn't you see how blood had poured out of his left eye and was all congealed? No wonder he couldn't see. I would not be surprised if he never sees again.'

'Blind?' I was horror-struck.

As it turned out, I learned later, that the man did recover the sight of one eye, at least partially. But the other had been totally destroyed. I had seen his broken nose and where a couple of teeth had been knocked out, but had no idea at the time, how serious was his state.

By now, a police car had arrived. The Spaniards who had helped us were allowed to carry on with their journey into Benahavis, since they were not witnesses to the accident and they agreed to give Horst a lift back. The rest of us followed the ambulance back into Marbella.

As the three injured were taken out of the ambulance, I heard the man, calling out to his companions.

'I did say that it was not worth taking that horrible, little car up to Benahavis for a meal. The food isn't that good. But when we get out of here, I'll take you somewhere really fabulous.'

I realized that he was doing his best to put on a show for the girls.

It was while we were waiting in the hospital, that one of the doctors came and told us how serious the damage to the young man's eyes was. In an unemotional voice, he informed us also that one of the girls had indeed broken her ankle and the other had fractured her leg. Then, in the same cold, remote voice, he indicated that there was nothing that we could do to help the injured and that we should go home. What he said was quite right, but he might have shown some feeling.

But Ben was no robot. He sat, huddled, with his face buried in his hands; he looked terrible. The white shirt of which he had been so proud was stained with dirt and blood and his bare arms were scratched and bruised. Some of the slivers of glass had got into his clothes and on to his hands, so that his blood was mingled with that of the unhappy trio from the Citroen.

As I gently pulled his hands from his face, I saw that he was crying.

'God, what a waste! Why do things like that have to happen, Xaviera? That guy was so brave - and now he is blind!'

'Not completely,' the doctor commented. 'Here, you are

pretty badly shaken. I'll get you a tranquillizer.'

'Never mind me, do what you can for the others. They are the ones who need help.'

Stephen took Ben by the arm and led him out. He was suffering from delayed shock, but, as I watched the pair of them, I could not help being proud of them both. They were ordinary guys – but that is the stuff that heroes are made of.

12

The Magician

'He is the true enchanter, whose spell operates, not upon the senses, but upon the imagination and the heart.'

Washington Irving

The remainder of Ben's stay passed without incident. We had experienced adventure enough, and Ben was not his usual, cheerful self. The plight of the half-blinded man and the crippled girls preyed on his mind. I felt the need for some livelier company. Ben was always gentle and affectionate, but he lacked the high spirits and witty brilliance which, I suspected, I could find in Stephen. I was pleased, therefore, when Stephen called me and proposed meeting for dinner. I explained that Ben was with me, but Stephen was in no way discouraged.

'Splendid fellow,' he chortled. 'Bring him along. I am sure that as accomplished a lady as you can cope with two beaux to her string.'

Between Marbella and Estepona, there is a restaurant, called Benemar, run by two Moroccan Jewish brothers, and it was there that we met. I liked their oriental salads with cooked vegetables and the inevitable couscous. Yet, I must admit that the evening was not a great success. In Stephen's presence, Ben became reticent and had little to say for himself, and I was conscious that Stephen would have preferred to be alone with me.

Then a very strange thing happened. I wanted to go to the toilet and freshen up, and I excused myself from the table. I had to go out of the dining room through the bar, and as I walked through, I heard somebody calling my name. I turned around and found myself looking into the smiling face of Merlin Rees-Evans.

'I knew you'd be here,' he said triumphantly. 'I have been waiting to talk to you.'

'How could you have known I was coming to this restaurant?'

'Didn't I tell you, I'm a magician. There are many things I know, but they are hidden, secret.'

I gazed at him, not knowing whether to believe him or not.

'Well,' I said at last, 'I'd love to talk to you, but I am with two men already.'

'I know that too,' Merlin smiled. 'But don't let it worry you. All good things go in threes, Xaviera, and here I am – the Third Man. But, no, I don't want to barge in. Not tonight, anyway.'

There was a mystery about this man, and suddenly, I knew that I had to be with him and penetrate his mask of inscrutability. Ben was going home and Stephen could wait.

'Tomorrow,' I told him, 'I shall be alone.'

'When shall I come?' He had no doubts. He seemed to know what I would be saying or doing before I did.

'Be at my apartment at nine,' I told him and walked away.

Next day, I packed Ben off, back to Churriana. Although he liked being with me, he could not stand the snobbishness and artificiality that is so common in Marbella for long, and he was glad to be getting out of the place.

On the stroke of nine o'clock, Merlin rang my doorbell. In one hand he held a bottle of red wine, in the other a bunch of red roses. He cocked a critical eye over my flat.

'Very comfortable,' was his judgement. 'I particularly like that picture.' He nodded towards a print of a painting by Leonore Fini. It showed three women, obviously quarrelling, one of whom was pushing another in the face.

'It's Franny's favourite,' I told him. 'It has that quality of implied violence.'

Merlin leaned back and regarded me thoughtfully. I had to admire his perfect self-assurance. He had the poise of a man who had everything under control.

'Do you spend much time here?' he asked me.

'A few months every year. And during the spring, before it gets too hot, my mother usually stays with her friends.'

'Just your mother? What became of your father?'

Merlin's tone was not in the least unfriendly, but I felt that he was analysing my every word, getting the measure of me and making up his mind what sort of a woman I really was. He struck me as too wise and level-headed to judge me in terms of my fame or notoriety or to be interested in my public image – my outer self as it were. He was studying the woman within, my true personality.

'My father died about eight years ago, while I was still living in Canada,' I answered him.

'And did your father know about your career in New York and how you got involved in the call girl business?' His voice brought memories of my father flooding back: there was something paternal about Merlin, himself.

'No, thank God! The shock would probably have killed him. It's strange the way things work out. You see, I loved my father more than any other living creature, and yet I left Holland to get away from him.'

'He was cruel to you?' Merlin asked.

'No, nothing like that. He was a dying man – he had a number of strokes and was no longer aware of what was going on around him. I just could not stand by and watch him suffer. There was nothing I could do to help him. I had to get away.'

'So it was in the depths of your misery that you became "The Happy Hooker."'

I nodded.

'But your father must have been a man of great personality to have affected your life so deeply. Beyond your love of your friends and even your most passionate affairs, your memory of him is still the most precious thing in your life. Aren't I right?'

I looked at Merlin in wonder. 'How on earth could you

know all that after so short a time?'

'If you like, you can think of it as my magic. When you speak about your father, your whole appearance changes. Then, I see you, not as the busy, successful writer, surrounded by fans and interviewers, but as a sad, lonely, little girl. So tell me something about the extraordinary man who was your father.'

'He was extraordinary,' I said slowly, 'and you would have appreciated him, for there was something of magic about him, too. He was a doctor and a psychiatrist, but he was very interested in the occult. Perhaps it came from his background. He was Jewish but had lived a lot of his life in the Far East, and I believe that he had some Indonesian blood in his veins. But there was no field of human knowledge or artistic achievement which did not draw him as if by a magnet. He could talk on philosophy, the theatre, music, painting, and not just talk; he could write, paint or play music. The pity is that I was too young to understand the richness of his intellect, the wealth that was there in our home.'

'Regret for the past is futile,' Merlin said gently. 'But I am sure that there is much of your father which lives on in you. Don't you feel that?'

'Sure. There are things which we had in common. For example, neither he nor I could ever tolerate mediocrity.'

'I am sure of that,' Merlin seemed amused. 'But there must be other things. You say your father wrote. And you must have inherited from him something of his love of the arts and music?'

'Yes, that's true. And I can tell you, Merlin, though I would find it difficult to explain to many other people, there is something more. There is a sort of telepathy. It happens often that when I am writing a book, I will describe some event that occurred to a friend with whom I have lost contact. Within half an hour of typing his name, he will call out of the blue. And I will know that it is him, even before I pick up the phone. How do you explain that?'

'Most people will talk about coincidences, but to me,' Merlin's tone was serious, 'it is magic. Your father was a man who had magic – and it is a power – which has been handed on to you. For your father to have achieved so much in his lifetime, he must have been a man of great will-power. And I think that you are a strong woman, too. Aren't you a determined person who won't let things – or people get in her way?'

Again, I was impressed by the acuteness of Merlin's observation. Or maybe Merlin had intuition – but if so, he had that power to a degree which was very rare among men. There is such a thing as a woman's intuition; did Merlin possess it?

'I suppose I have will-power,' I replied to his probing question, 'although some people would call it stubbornness or even bloody mindedness. You see, I can't bother with people whose minds I do not respect. I am a Dracula who feeds on men's brains, not their blood.'

'And not their bodies?' Merlin smiled.

'It used to be like that, but as I have grown up, the merely physical aspect of sex has attracted me less and less. That's why I have turned right away from group sex, for example. To be honest, there are moments when I am simply horny.'

I did not have to finish my sentence. Merlin interrupted me. 'I have read some of your books, and I need no convincing of your sexuality.'

I laughed outright. 'That's enough about me. I know nothing at all about you. Do tell me the story of Merlin the Magician.'

My guest glanced at his watch. 'I'll tell you in the car,' he said. 'I booked us a table for dinner at The Yellow Book, and we ought to get moving. I am afraid that I have been very thoughtless, cross-examining you, when you are probably famished.'

I knew the restaurant. Situated just before Estepona, it

was run by two aging English gay types and had deservedly become known as one of the best tables on the whole of the Coast.

Seated in the car, Merlin picked up his narrative. 'I really am a professional magician,' he assured me. 'Not one of those charlatans who move tables or bend forks, but I have performed tricks in public since I was fifteen.'

'How old are you now?' I asked.

'Forty-three,' he answered. 'So you see I have been in the magic business for quite a time.'

'But surely you were still at school.'

'That's right. But I used to get engagements during my holidays in England, and later all over Europe. Still, I needed to be something more than one of the run of the mill conjurers or sleight of hand performers if I was going to be able to earn a living as a magician. That's how it is that I became an escapologist.'

'You mean one of those types who get themselves tied up, hand and foot, handcuffed, stuck in a strait-jacket, sewn into a sack and then thrown into a tank of water and who, two minutes later, are standing, free, on the stage, not even out of breath?'

'Yes, that's the general idea. Followers of the great, Harry Houdini.'

'That sounds a very unlikely occupation for an English gentleman,' I commented.

'Again, it is something that goes back to my school days,' Merlin continued. 'One day, I asked one of my friends to tie me up and blindfold me. It was just a lark, you understand. I wanted to see if I could get out of the knots. He was a regular boy scout and had me trussed up so tight that I could not budge. Or so he thought. Within four or five minutes, I was free.'

'How did you manage it?'

'I wriggled my feet and twisted my fingers, and I soon knew exactly where to put on the full pressure of my muscles.

Once I had started, I never looked back. I read books on the subject and took proper lessons from an experienced escapologist who had retired. By the time I was thirty, I had put on shows all over England, mainly for private entertainments in the great houses of the aristocracy.'

But it was not all plain sailing. When we arrived at the restaurant and were sitting at our table, awaiting our meal, Merlin told me of a narrow escape in his career as an escapologist.

'I was in Stuttgart,' he told me, 'and the grand finale of my act was to get out of a tank of water, in which I was hung, upside down, after being securely tied up, of course. I would invite somebody from the audience to tie the knots and then call on a second person to come up and check that they were properly tied. Then, as I was being suspended in the water, the trick was to take an enormous breath, the instant before I was put under the surface. I needed that air to keep me alive while I worked my way free.

'Well, that night in Stuttgart, the second man was a tough, cocky fellow, who wasn't going to let me get away with anything. He not only had a look at the knots that the first guy had tied, which would not have presented me with any problems, but this man retied every one, and much too tight. They were cutting into my wrists and hurting like hell. However, I could not protest, without making the whole trick look like a put up job. So, I gritted my teeth. But the pain had confused me for a split second, and I was in the tank, before I had recovered my wits sufficiently to take that all important breath.

'Of course, with no extra air in my lungs, I needed to work my way free quicker than usual, but because of the tightness of my bonds, it took me longer than ever. I worked feverishly, but I could feel the pressure growing every second and I knew it was only a matter of very little time before I would lose consciousness – and I could not rely on the guys outside getting me out of the tank, before I drowned. I was almost desperate, yet I know that if I panicked, I would be lost. With one last great effort of will, I concentrated on the Yoga technique of slowing down my body rhythms, and I made it, literally, at my last gasp. When I got out, my face was purple and the whole world had gone dark. It was a good thing that it was my last trick, for I was so spent, I could not have twitched a muscle.'

As we drove back, I said to Merlin, 'You know, it's a funny thing. You have told me all about how you earned your living, but nothing about your life. What about loves, companions, your home.'

'There's not a lot to tell. I used to travel about from hotel to hotel, without anywhere to call my own. So I bought a caravan - then I had my home. But I still ate out in restaurants because I hate cooking and clearing up.'

'You're dodging the question,' I accused. 'Were you always alone?'

'Not always.' Merlin gave me the impression that he was choosing his words with great care. 'But, I am an emotional man and I lacked a real companion. You don't get much chance to start a long lasting relationship when you are on the move every two or three days. There was just one time—'

He paused, as if recollecting some long lost joy.

'How long did it last?'

'Four years. But I became too jealous. It had to end.'

We had reached my apartment and I invited Merlin to come up for a coffee. He accepted eagerly, and that was the last I heard about his romance.

Once in the house, I excused myself and took a shower and changed into a cool, Balinese batik sarong. Merlin thumbed through some magazines, while a tape of Saint Saens' music played. Magic was still in the air, and I had thought that the Danse Macabre was appropriate.

However, when I emerged, I must have been looking really appetizing, and Merlin asked if there was any significance in the music. I shook my head.

'It's simply that they are now playing that symphonic poem "Omphale's Spinning Wheel". You know it tells of how Hercules, the strongest of men, was enslaved by love of the Queen Omphale and made to work her spinning wheel – degraded to women's work.'

'Now that would have been a real problem for an escapologist,' I laughed.

'Would you think me very rude, if I asked you to let me have a shower, too?' Merlin demanded rather shyly. 'You see, the facilities in a caravan are definitely primitive.'

Within minutes, his freshly towelled body was glowing, and I sprayed him with a sweet smelling cologne. I led the way into my bedroom.

'Now, I am going to explore your innermost secrets,' I warned him.

'I took an oath, when I became a member of The Magic Circle, that I would never divulge to anybody the secrets of our magic,' Merlin informed me.

'There are other secrets which I find more interesting,' I replied, as I pulled his towel off and contemplated his naked body. I leaned across, pulled him on to the bed and started to caress his chest and strong, hairy shoulders. I took each nipple in my mouth and sucked and gently chewed. After all, a man who chose as a career to spend his time in bondage must have some masochistic feeling. His nipples stiffened – and so did his penis – a gorgeous, thick and large circumcised cock, raising its head, straining after me.

As I stroked and kissed his body, he gazed at me curiously, almost doubtingly, and then, gently moved his fingers down my back and, something which I adore, through my hair. Then, he pulled me higher and kissed my face, my forehead, my eyes, my nose, and at last, my mouth. I opened my lips, and for the first time, we kissed with his tongue penetrating me, as if to show his cock the way.

In his excitement, he clutched me to him in an iron grip.

'Gently,' I admonished him, 'I'm no Houdini.'

He was so apologetic, and went back to kissing me all over and biting my back, but, so softly. I felt shivers running up and down my spine and through my pussy. I was more than ready for him.

Merlin made me lie still, on my back, so that he could explore my body more closely. I felt the tip of his tongue trace a path from my head to my toes, lingering lovingly at my breasts and playing with the haze of curly hair that reached down from my navel to my triangle, but he skipped past my vagina, as if he were afraid to approach it. His velvet tongue sucked delicately at each of my toes.

'Please,' I said as I raised my body and pushed his head between my legs. Tentatively, he began to kiss and lick around my vagina. It was ecstasy, but I needed him on my clitoris.

'Merlin, darling, please kiss my clitoris.'

I spread my legs for him and displayed my throbbing, swollen organ. For a quarter of an hour, his loving tongue paid tribute to my clitoris, my vagina and my ass; I eventually managed to swivel my own body around so that I could take his great cock in my mouth, and we worked each other towards the inevitable climax in a 69 position. I felt his cock, trembling between my lips, and knew he was on the verge of coming. This excited me so much that I spurted all over his face my juices in a long, heavy orgasm.

'Now,' I half pleaded, half ordered him, 'penetrate me. Fuck me!'

He mounted me and for another ten minutes, we writhed in delight until, towering above me, crouching on his knees, Merlin came. He moaned and groaned like some great wild animal, yet at the moment of his climax, he burst into a loud peal of laughter. He went on laughing, shaking the bed, until he finally collapsed. Luckily, I had enjoyed my second orgasm moments before, otherwise I would have been disturbed by his strange outburst. I still felt that some explanation was due - and I got it.

'Xaviera,' Merlin said, wiping away tears of mirth, 'you must congratulate me.'

'What on earth for? You're not the first man in my life, you know, Merlin.'

'No, but you're the first woman in mine. You have just deflowered a virgin.'

'A virgin!' I screamed in disbelief. 'You mean to tell me that this is the first time that you have slept with anyone?'

'That's right. At least, my penis has never penetrated any orifice, male or female, so I guess I am a cock virgin. Or I was.'

'Are you like Arthur, into transvestites?'

'No way. But I was a super queen and I can't tell you how many young, gipsy boys have had my ass. And they have robbed me as pitilessly as Arthur's transvestites have fleeced him. But I have never played an active role and fucked anybody, man or woman.'

'Well, if it is any consolation to you, you are an excellent lover. You seem to have enjoyed it, so what's wrong with women?'

'Nothing at all, if they were all like you,' Merlin replied. 'Don't you see, Xaviera, I have not just fucked your body, but I have entered into the whole of your being, your wildness, your energy, your craziness – for a short time they were all mine. It would not be the same with anybody else. Don't you feel that what we have had is something unique?'

'Of course it is,' I assured him.

'That is the way I love you,' he asserted. 'Think of me as your fiancé. Or rather, may I consider you my fiancée? My one and only female fiancée?'

I smiled my assent and added, 'Now, my magician, I think that I have arrived at the heart of your mystery.'

I kissed him.

13

Say it With Diamonds

'Nor shall our love-fits, Chloris, be forgot,
When each the well-look'd linkboy strove to enjoy,
And the best kiss was the deciding lot
Whether the boy fucked you, or I the boy.'
John Wilmot, Earl of Rochester

Ben had stayed a few days with me in my apartment, now it was the turn of Herman to be my guest. Unlike Ben, who never felt at ease in the chic Marbella scene, Herman was overjoyed at the prospect of strutting around the bars and rubbing shoulders with the super-rich. He arrived in a vivid, canary yellow jumpsuit and Gucci shoes of the latest fashion, staggering under the weight of his jewellery. He deposited his matching Louis Vuitton suitcases in his room, had a quick shower and preened his feathers, ready to swoop down on the smart set of Marbella or Puerto Banus.

We discussed which were the 'in' restaurants, who was going where. Then we touched on the subject of prices and Herman suggested that we had a quiet evening, with him cooking a meal at home.

'After all,' he pointed out, in a tone of sweet reasonableness, 'Why waste money eating out when I am a superb cook? We can spend it on other things.'

I had my doubts about this spending spree, but since Herman was an excellent cook, I was quite ready to give him the run of my kitchen. So, as the moon rose over the still sea, we settled down on the balcony to a spicy green pepper salad and hot, aromatic, shish kebabs. I had prepared a big fruit salad to complete the meal and we decided to round off the dinner with a drink in town.

We parked the car not far from the church in the old town of Marbella and strolled through the narrow alleys, looking at the shop windows and the people sitting at the tiny terraces. We had a few drinks at two of my favourite bars.

By now it was well after midnight and the old town of Marbella was beginning to quieten down but Herman and I were still full of life, so we headed to Puerto Banus, where we knew there would still be plenty of action.

In the picturesque port, nestling beneath tall, nodding palm trees and a promenade of white walled shops and apartment blocks, there was a great panorama of boats of all shapes and sizes. In the larger berths, some of the most luxurious yachts in the world were riding at anchor, their sleek outlines, floodlit. The irregular, jagged skyline of the buildings seemed to be crowding around the ships, as if they too wanted to take to the water. In this theatrical setting, hordes of people jostled against each other as they gazed in the windows of the shops or clustered in bars and on the terraces of restaurants. Music blared from loud-speakers in every boutique and singers with the inevitable guitars made their way between the tables, serenading the late diners with romantic ballads, pop songs or fiery flamenco canciones. Pretty girls courteously displayed port-folios of paintings of local views, bullfights or haughty, black eyed, Castilian beauties in black lace mantillas to fat-bellied drinkers at the tables, who were often clearly more interested in the person displaying, than the things dis-played.

Herman was in his element. He loved the glitter and the bustle and he joined in the feverish excitement of the place. He insisted that we look in at the Hollywood, the trendiest gay bar on the Coast. I was prepared to stop and have a drink but Herman, after a quick glance around assured me that there was not sufficient talent on display to justify our halting there. The gay charmers were Herman's scene, not mine, so I was happy enough to accept his judgement.

We had just passed the Hollywood when a nubile, slim-hipped, Adonis emerged from the interior of the bar. Either

Herman had eyes in the back of his head or he somehow caught the scent of the youth with a mysterious sixth sense. He gripped my arm, as he turned his head.

'Gee, Xaviera, just look at that!'

I looked around - and tripped over the feet of a young man who was sitting at a table on the next terrace with two companions. I hastened to apologize and as I regarded the unfortunate, young man whom I had trampled, the contrast with the gazelle who had captivated Herman could not have been more striking.

The gay boy was wearing a gauzy, white robe, very much a Western imitation of an Arab burnous, my victim was wearing the real thing and the brown of his skin was not mere suntan. However, he certainly lacked the sylph-like grace of the boy from the Hollywood. The seated Arab was gross: his loose fitting cloak could not obscure the great rolls of fat which seemed to stretch out in every direction. When he was sitting down, the young man was grotesque, his width exceeded his height by an impressive margin. There was so much of him that perhaps it was not entirely my fault that I had fallen over his feet.

'Please, do excuse me. I'm so sorry,' I mumbled.

'It is nothing.' The young man dismissed the matter with a surprisingly graceful wave of his hand, and continued, 'Since Fate has literally decided that our paths should cross, the least that I can do is to offer your friend and yourself a drink.'

'That is very kind of you—' I started, but with the same lordly wave of the hand, the youth said,

'It is nothing. It is but a shadow, a token of the hospitality which we should offer some stranger who chanced to enter our gates were we at home. Let me introduce myself and my companions.

'You would find my full name too complicated, so you may call me Hamid - it is one of my names. This gentleman is called Abdul. Unfortunately, he speaks no

English but is he not a remarkable person? He is no less than eighty five years old, a true Bedouin. He and his family have served my father and our family for more generations than men can remember. My younger companion is called Omar, who acts as my private secretary and takes care of my personal financial affairs. He is a Persian, as you can probably tell from his name.'

'Oh, yes, indeed,' Herman assented.

Hamid and his friends were a strange assortment. Abdul had the dignity and the self contained solitariness of the very old and the very religious. His withered hands clutched a row of beads and his lips moved incessantly as he offered prayers to his Creator. His eyes were not fixed on us: his gaze was on Eternity. Omar was young, slim with finely chiselled features. I could see from the gleam in Herman's eye that he fancied this aristocratic looking youth, but so did I. Omar was the reason that the two of us accepted Hamid's gracious invitation with such alacrity.

The three of them were drinking fruit juices and I ordered an orange juice. Herman saw no reason to deny himself the delight of alcohol in the presence of a party of ascetics and called for a double whisky and soda.

'Are you here on vacation?' Herman asked Hamid.

'You could put it that way,' he replied solemnly, 'but it is certainly not a pleasure trip. You see, I am staying at a health clinic.'

'You are ill?' Herman tried to sound concerned.

'Not exactly ill. But my family thought that it would be a good idea if I lost a little weight.'

When I regarded his podgy arms and massive belly, I could see their point. However, Hamid spoke with an air of injured innocence.

'So, all day long, I am imprisoned in a place little better than a sanatorium.'

'I have never stayed in one of the Marbella clinics, but I do go sometimes to the Buchinger clinic in Germany to get rid of a few kilos,' I confided sympathetically.

'There is a Buchinger clinic in Marbella, but I am at the Incosol on a five hundred calories a day diet and will soon be reduced to a shadow.' Hamid's expression was mournful, as he considered how he was wasting away. 'I cannot imagine why you should want to go to such a place,' he told me.

I knew both the Incosol and the Buchinger clinics in Marbella. At Buchinger, you can starve in luxury, but Incosol is the most palatial of what have been termed 'the concentration camps of the pampered rich.'

While we chatted, Abdul remained absorbed in his devotions and Omar smiled and nodded but did not say a word, much to the disappointment of Herman and myself.

During a lull in our conversation, Herman excused himself to look at a jeweller's shop next door - the fanciest, best stocked and, of course, the priciest this side of Monte Carlo. He told Hamid that he was in the diamond business and wanted to cast a professional eye over the display. A few minutes later, Herman came back, a changed man. He ignored Omar and concentrated on Hamid. He fell over himself to agree with everything Hamid said. He was all smiles as he fawned upon our gross host. Hamid told Herman that he did not have a regular job.

'Of course not,' Herman laughed heartily.

'I get bored here,' Hamid continued, 'but I go out most evenings, usually to the casino.'

'So you want to lose your money as well as your weight?' I quipped.

Hamid shrugged his shoulders lazily, but Herman gave me a furious glare. So I shut up and, taking advantage of Herman's possessive interest in Hamid, turned to Omar.

'Have you been Hamid's adviser for long?'

A shy smile played over the young man's handsome features.

'Only a few years. Of course, I only deal with the private

business and leave official, as opposed to personal, arrangements to the professionals. You see, my full time job is in opthalmology. I work at the Institute of Opthalmology in London, five days a week and I write articles for the medical press.'

I was beginning to make some progress in thawing out Omar. He was an extremely formal person and had the mannerisms of a middle aged civil servant rather than a youngster, not many years out of university. However, Hamid interrupted us, pointing at Abdul, whose eyes were closed and whose black, wrinkled face was relaxed in sleep.

'I am afraid it is long past the old fellow's bedtime and we must be getting back to our quarters. Omar, be a good chap and go and find a taxi. I do have a couple of cars here, but would you believe it, they both broke down at the same time,' he added for our benefit.

I was on the point of offering them a lift, when Herman dashed in, 'We have a car here and I'm sure that Xaviera would not mind taking you back. It's on our way home, anyway.' As a matter of fact, Incosol was several miles beyond my apartment, but I had no objection to fulfilling Herman's offer of my generosity.

At first, Hamid would not hear of putting us out but Herman insisted and so, somehow we eventually squeezed into the BMW. Five normal sized people can be accommodated with plenty of room to spare in that model, but with Hamid we did have an extraordinary load: fortunately neither Abdul nor Omar had an ounce of spare flesh.

'This really is most kind of you, madam,' Hamid said, as he heaved himself into the seat beside me, 'and you must allow me to reciprocate. It would not be much fun for you to join me for a meal at the clinic and tomorrow, we have other things arranged. But the following day, that's Wednesday isn't it, I would be delighted if you would both be my guests at dinner at a Lebanese restaurant in town. We could make a night of it and go on somewhere. What do you say?'

Herman accepted on my behalf, again before I could open my mouth and so it was arranged. I was pleased to have the opportunity to see more of Omar and Herman obviously relished the prospect of an evening with Hamid. However, I was mystified by Herman's conduct and wanted to get him on his own to hear his explanation.

By the time we arrived at the clinic. Herman had made all the arrangements for our meeting a couple of days later. Hamid took Abdul by the arm and gently led him away. As Herman said goodnight to them, I managed to have a few words with Omar.

'I very much enjoyed meeting you,' I said, 'and I hope that we shall have a chance to see a bit more of each other.'

'Yes, indeed,' he replied eagerly. 'I can usually get a few hours away from Hamid and Abdul and it would be a real pleasure to spend some time with you - if that would please you.'

He was so shy that he needed reassuring but before we could make a definite date, Herman had finished his obsequious farewells and it was my turn to say goodnight to the others.

Back in the car, Herman was jubilant.

'We've got it made, Xaviera. What a stroke of luck!'

'Would you mind telling me what's got you so excited?' I demanded, as we headed back towards Marbella.

'This Hamid, guy,' Herman babbled happily, 'Do you know who he is?'

'He strikes me as some spoilt kid. He's obviously got plenty of money - or at least, his family has. I expect his dad runs a self-drive camel service somewhere in the desert.'

Herman snorted contemptuously.

'His father just happens to be the king of somewhere or other. Young Hamid is really Prince Hamid. I tell you, honey, we've struck oil.'

'Listen, Herman, every Arab on this coast claims to be a prince. This way, they get all the best seats in the casino or the restaurants, the pick of the girls and even the seats in the bullring out of the sun.'

'I tell you, Xaviera, this is the real thing. You know when I went across to look at those diamonds while you stayed on the terrace with them? Well, there were some quite reasonable stones, well cut and nicely mounted. However, one whole showcase was completely empty, so I asked the manager if he had suffered a burglary. He said no, the entire case had been brought by an Arab prince as a wedding present to one of his relatives. It was the choice stuff worth a king's ransom. I said to this guy that I'd like to have the luck to meet the man who could afford to buy that lot. The manager gave me a funny sort of smile and said, "You are sitting with him now. I saw you outside, before you came into the shop: the fat man – he's the one who bought this lot." So, what do you think of that!'

'I had been wondering why you had been licking his ass until your tongue was hanging out,' I replied. 'Anyway, you seem to forget, Herman, you've been out of the diamond business for some time . . .'

'So, I'll find something else to sell him,' Herman exclaimed impatiently. 'Don't you think that he might like some of Momir's paintings? And I know people who make fancy jewellery, or shoes, and another sells electronic gadgets – there must be something.'

'Herman, dear, if this guy is who you say he is, he will have all these things. And if he is going to buy paintings, he'll probably collect Cezannes or Rembrandts rather than Momir's offerings.'

'You've just got no imagination, that's your trouble, Xaviera. You watch, I'll find something to sell him. You know, I'm so excited, I don't feel like going home yet. Why don't we go to Pepe Moreno's and dance till dawn?'

'You can dance as long as you like, dear Herman. I am going home to bed but I'll drop you at Pepe Moreno's or any other discotheque you may fancy. You have your own key and can let yourself in whenever you have had enough.'

So I drove Herman to Pepe Moreno's and left him there, his eyes bright with anticipation and all the jauntiness of a man who had won a sweepstake, in his stride. It was nice to see a friend so happy, but I was headed for bed and pleased to be alone.

I had no idea of what time it was when I was awakened by the sound of Herman trying to get in. I had forgotten to explain to him that the lock was complicated, so I slipped a sarong around my naked body, jumped out of bed and opened up.

There stood Herman, with a smile as wide as the Grand Canyon. Beside him was an angelic looking young man, prettily plump, with long, blond hair which proclaimed its peroxide origin, contrasting black eyelashes which fluttered a welcome to me and sparkling white teeth. He was elegantly dressed, a small handbag dangled from his shoulder, his pants and slicker were spotless white and his shirt was of scarlet silk.

'My God, Herman,' I smiled, 'two princes in one night?'

'Isn't he lovely? He's from the Canary Islands and is helping in a trendy boutique in Puerto Banus. I found him just before closing time: another couple of minutes and I would have been too late,' Herman told me in Dutch.

'Not bad,' I commented 'a bit statuesque, but good luck.'

'You're just jealous' Herman snorted as he led his prize into his bedroom and firmly closed the door.

I had not felt at all horny when I went to bed, but now, with only a paper thin wall between me and the two guys, I could not get back to sleep and I was straining to hear what was going on.

The two men were surprisingly quiet. There were none of

the usual frenzied sound effects, only muted voices talking almost inaudibly. I waited and listened.

Then my bedroom door opened and Herman came into my room.

'Xaviera, I have a slight problem. Could you come and help me sort out this sort of technical hitch?'

I followed him back into his room. There, naked on the bed lay Herman's conquest, spread-eagled and most appealing.

'What's the matter, Herman? Do you need a map and compass to find your way?'

'No, I need you,' Herman hissed in Dutch. 'The trouble with that lovely hunk of manhood is that he is basically straight. He won't let me touch him - and as for a spot of innocent buggery, no chance at all.'

'Looks as if you have been wasting your time, Herman. But how did you persuade him to come back with you?'

'That's where you come in. I told him that I was sharing the flat with a sexy woman, so he trotted along like a good, little boy. I reckoned that when we got here, I could tell him that you were with a boy friend and that he would not be too hard to seduce. But he just lies on his back, waiting for this great woman to appear. I can't do a thing.'

'It serves you right for being so selfish. You might have offered to share him when you came in. But, OK Herman, I guess that I am a real pal to you: I won't let down a buddy in distress.'

I walked across to the bed where Mr Gorgeous, very conscious of his charms, waited expectantly, his hands folded behind his head and a fixed toothpaste smile on his face.

'So, Don Magnifico wishes to be spoilt?' I asked in Spanish.

'Si, si.' He was a bit short on text.

I leaned over and thrust my right breast into his mouth. He was sufficiently excited to unfold his hands and to hold me close while sucking my tit.

I knew that while I lay across the top half of his body, Herman could be relied upon to mount an attack on the targets below the belt. I made sure that I had the Spanish boy's full attention and I glanced over my shoulder to see what progress Herman had made.

Herman was on his knees between the Spaniard's legs, engaged in enthusiastic fellatio while holding his own long, rigid penis between his fingers. In my opinion, our guest's penis was fatter but had less personality than that of Herman but the latter clearly found it an acceptable offering.

I turned back to his face which I kissed and caressed to his evident satisfaction. His body odour was strong and salty but not at all unpleasant. Quite the reverse, I found my nostrils tingling as I savoured the scent of the man. Lowering my body, I started to suck his nipples and lick his sun-tanned chest, covered with a faint fuzz of brownish hair. He squirmed with delight from our joint efforts and I moved down further, exploring his navel with my insistent tongue.

By now, my juices were flowing strongly and I pushed Herman aside impatiently as I took our man's cock in my mouth, coaxing, teasing and fondling it with my lips, tongue and teeth. Herman allowed himself to be diverted to the boy's ass. The boy's beautiful body lay there, open to us to do what we pleased and I could hear his muffled gasps of pleasure. Reclining there, completely passive, he indicated to me that he wanted me to sit on top of him. I needed no oral preparation: my pussy was well lubricated as I pressed down on his desperately seeking cock.

I realized that our visitor was too inactive to give me total satisfaction and Herman was in a frenzy to get his rocks off. Why should Don Magnifico be the only one to get what he wanted? So I proposed to Herman, in Dutch of course, that while I continued to fuck the boy by sitting on top of him, Herman should enter my vagina as well. Since neither of them was built like Hercules, I would have no trouble in accommodating the pair of them, once they had been carefully and slowly eased in.

Herman produced a tube of hairgrease and rubbed it on his penis, masturbating himself into a good, stiff, hard-on. Of course, Don Magnifico was already there and then I felt Herman, crouched behind me on his knees, gently inserting his greasy member into my overflowing vagina and rubbing himself against the cock of his beloved boy.

Even while I was enjoying the sensation of being serviced by two men at the same time, I could not help seeing the humour of the situation. The gay Herman only being able to take his boy inside a woman and the straight Spaniard only getting his sex with a woman in contact with a gay guy's penis.

The strangeness of the encounter must have stimulated both of the men and they shot their loads almost simultaneously in virtually no time at all. My pussy was sopping but, while it had been fun, the experience was too superficial to give me any profound satisfaction.

As soon as he had recovered, Herman thanked me most courteously for my assistance.

'Di nada, señores! Sleep well.' I answered, as I left the pair of them and went back to my own room. It really was time to call it a day.

14

The Simple Life

'Come, live with me and be my love,
And we will all the pleasures prove
Of peace and plenty, bed and board,
That chance employment may afford.'

Cecil Day Lewis

Next day, Herman and I went shopping in the market. As we wandered from grocer to butcher and from baker to fruit stall, Herman dug me in the ribs and pointed, 'Do you know that handsome man, over there?'

I looked at the man who had caught Herman's eye. He was a slender, suntanned man in his mid-thirties, busy buying groceries. What first struck me were his bright, green eyes and the thick black curls which cascaded down over his shoulders, half hiding his face. I watched his full lips, as he argued about the price of something; there was a strong, resolute look to his face due to his sharp, slightly curved nose. I was fascinated by the way the tight curls of his hair, sprouting from his chest, seemed to grow out in all directions. He was wearing a light, white shirt which, unbuttoned, billowed out in the breeze. The rest of his clothes were well chosen and artistic - a small, golden chain around his neck, bell-bottom, Indian style, pants and neat leather sandals. Most striking was a beautifully decorated, hand embroidered belt.

'I think that I have seen him around town,' I answered Herman. 'He certainly is an improvement on the blond baby you brought home last night. This one looks as if he might have some brains as well. That's a good, intelligent face.'

'Well, let's go and talk to him,' Herman said.

'What? Simply walk up, out of the blue and pick him up? You must be joking, Herman.'

'Leave it to me, Xaviera. Watch, I'll show you how it is done.'

Herman pushed his way over to where the stranger was standing and, turning his head to talk to me, bumped into him, as if by accident.

'Oh, I am so sorry. Please excuse me. Do you happen to speak English?'

The man looked too dark for an Englishman and I reckoned that he could well be a Spaniard or even a North African. However, much to Herman's discomfort, he replied in faultless English, though with a pronounced accent.

'Yes, of course, although I am myself, French. What can I do to help you?'

That was the point at which Romeo Herman ran out of lines. He swallowed, searching for words, so I stepped in to rescue him.

'We wanted to know where you got such a lovely belt,' I told him in fluent French. 'We both remarked on it and also your shirt. They have so much more style than the things one normally sees around here.'

'Exactly,' added Herman, 'just what I was about to say. By the way, my name is Herman and this is my friend, Xaviera.'

'Pleased to meet you. My name is Jacques.' He turned back to me and flashed a smile at me which melted my knees. 'I am so glad that you like the belt: here, feel it, if you like.'

Before I could stretch out my hand to touch the belt and judge its quality, Herman had grabbed it and fingered it, making sure that his hand rubbed against the young man's stomach. Then, with his other hand, he felt Jacques' trousers.

'And that's a fine pair of pants that you have there. Though I am sure that you have something even finer underneath.'

I was horribly embarrassed. The young man had a feminine grace about him, yet I was convinced that he was not gay. However Jacques appeared good natured enough not to take offence at Herman's unsubtle advances, but he ignored his remark and addressed me.

'Are you honestly interested in knowing where you can find belts and clothes like those I am wearing?'

'Yes. If there is a shop near here, I would go now and choose things like those to buy. There's something about the style which I find immensely attractive.'

'Do you have a car here?'

I nodded.

'Well, if you don't mind a drive to Ojen, I invite you to follow me home. You see, these things are made by my wife, Jeannine. She supplies clothes and accessories which she makes, to some of the better boutiques, but, as you have noticed, what I am wearing is a little different, but she has a few more belts like this. So, if you really want to—'

'That's very kind of you,' Herman interrupted. 'Xaviera, will you just go and bring the car, while I wait here with Jacques and then we can follow you home.'

I was a bit worried at the prospect of leaving Herman alone with Jacques in his present excited state, but there was no alternative. So I hurried to where the BMW was parked and drove straight back as quickly as I could.

When I rejoined the two men, Jacques had explained to Herman that his family were Sephardic Jews who had settled many years ago in Morocco but who had become French citizens and had quit Morocco to settle in Paris while he was still a child.

'So you must be circumcised,' Herman announced cheerfully and grabbed at Jacques' pants to try to confirm his deduction. I was just in time to prevent my exuberant companion from peering beneath Jacques' waistband, and I led him firmly back to the car. We watched Jacques climb into his open Dune Buggy and we swung in behind him.

'He seems a real nice guy,' I said to Herman. 'I am glad that we picked him up.'

'What do you mean, we picked him up? I saw him first, and I was the one who went over and talked to him. If you want to learn how to pick up a guy, just you watch your old pal, Herman.'

'Yes, you gave me a demonstration last night with Don Magnifico. I had to come to your rescue.'

'This man will be different, Xaviera. You see, the Spaniard last night was straight.'

'And what makes you think that Jacques is gay?'

'It's obvious isn't it. Look at the way he invited me home. You weren't taken in by all that talk about belts and clothes, were you, Xaviera?'

'And what about Jeannine, his wife?'

'A lot of gay guys live with a woman for appearances, but their lovers are men.'

'We'll see, Herman, but take my advice and don't rush your fences.'

About half an hour later we arrived at the sleepy, tiny town of Ojen. Jacques threaded his way easily enough through the maze of narrow streets and winding alleys, but it was all that I could do to manoeuvre my wide, heavy car and follow him to the square, where we parked beside the one and only taxi in the town, after having squeezed my way past a stray donkey who clearly considered that as a resident, he enjoyed the right of way.

'This is my town house,' Jacques informed me with a smile. 'Later, I shall take you to my country estate.' Jacques led us into the house which, though small, had been furnished with skill and taste. Before he could introduce us to his wife, who came to greet us, a pretty, long-legged girl of about twelve leaped into his arms, threw her arms around his neck and joyfully kissed Jacques.

'Meet my daughter,' Jacques laughed, 'Hey, Juliette,

come and say hello.'

The child disengaged herself from her father and smiled a shy welcome to us. She combined grace and awkwardness, like a young foal: she was so full of life that she danced, rather than walked, across the room. I took an instant liking to her, with her big, frank eyes and her long, brown hair, piled up in a knot on top of her head.

Jeannine had been in the kitchen when we entered the house, and she came towards us, drying her hands on a dish cloth.

My first reaction to Jeannine was one of disappointment. She looked rather ordinary, not what I would have expected as a mate for so handsome a man as Jacques. She was of medium height with tiny breasts. Her hair was natural blonde of a very pale hue with greyish streaks, probably from the sun, and she had a small mouth with slightly crooked teeth. However, as I spent more time in her company, I revised my opinion. She was a delightful person, intelligent and sweet natured but an introvert whose qualities were not on the surface.

Jacques recounted briefly how we had met and Jeannine offered to show us some of her clothes and accessories which were in her studio, a couple of minutes away from the house.

'But first,' she said, 'you should sit down for a few minutes and relax while I get some food ready for lunch. Jacques has probably told you something about our little place in the mountains.'

'He did mention his country estate,' Herman replied.

Jeannine laughed. 'I hope that you will accompany us there and then you can judge for yourselves. When we have finished down here, I take some food up there and we have a simple luncheon on the estate. If you don't mind salads and cold meats, it would be a pleasure if you would join us.'

Herman agreed readily but I said that I did not want to

impose on her generosity.

'Nonsense. There's more than enough food, so please do not feel embarrassed. Do come.'

They were such a charming family that I allowed myself to be persuaded. So, while Jeannine prepared a picnic type meal in the kitchen, helped by Juliette, we made ourselves comfortable in Jacques' lounge.

The decor of the room had great character, combining Moorish and Oriental styles. The walls were lined with narrow, Moroccan style banquettes, piled with cushions, but the fabrics were soft batiks and the floor was covered by a thick pile Indian rug. Chinese and Indian vases stood on low tables and in them there were dried flowers and also beautifully made flowers in silk. The whole place, though small, had an air of the exotic, somehow both restrained and opulent at the same time. To complete the ambience, soft sitar music tinkled in the background and there was a sweet scent of some sort of cedar wood incense. Jacques squatted in a lotus position in the middle of the room, while Herman and I reclined among the cushions on the banquettes. It was totally peaceful.

'Would you like a joint, while we wait?' Jacques asked.

I accepted, and soon we were gently inhaling and soaking in the calm atmosphere.

'How did you come to meet Jeannine?' I asked.

'That was way back in the 'sixties, quite a long time after my family had moved out of Morocco and settled in Paris where I went to school and then on to university. I was at the Sorbonne during the student riots and got very involved. You probably don't remember all the turbulence at that time. We occupied the university and kicked out the members of the staff who would not co-operate. When the police tried to restore order, we fought them on the streets. Everybody was an idealist or a latter-day Lenin, making interminable speeches in the Odeon. We really thought that we had a new version of the National Assembly like it was in the days when the French monarchy was abolished and the great Revolution launched. Of course, the communists tried to turn the thing into a Soviet of workers and students - I don't think they knew where to find any peasants to join in, but we all marched down to the big Renault factory where the workers were on strike, to make common cause. Only when we got there, the workers locked the gates on us: they didn't want to have anything to do with the treacherous intellectuals or a gang of school kids. So that was the end of the Revolution. But one of the school kids was Jeannine. She was only fifteen at the time and she was greatly impressed by someone as old and mature as me. After all I was pushing twenty.

'When the riots died down, I never went back to the Sorbonne: a hell of a lot of the students were disillusioned and looked elsewhere for a new society. Being Jewish, I became a fervent Zionist and when the Yom Kippur War broke out, I took off to Israel to fight. Jeannine and I had started living together, but I had no qualms at leaving her behind since we had a fairly loose relationship and when the fighting was over, I stayed on and worked on a Kibbutz.

'After a few months, I realized that the Kibbutz life was not for me. It was not that I was afraid of the hard work or that I stopped believing that Israel was basically a good country. But there was a hell of a lot of organization and precious little freedom to develop a personality outside the group. It's probably a great way to run a country, but I needed a more unrestrained life style where I could do whatever seemed to be a good idea when something new in the way of a challenge turned up. I suppose I have a hippy streak in me, or perhaps I have never outgrown my anarchist youth. Anyway, I came back to Paris and rejoined Jeannine. When she became pregnant with Juliette, we decided to have the child and to marry.'

Jacques was interrupted by Jeannine coming into the room.

'Oh, Jacques, you are not boring our guests with your reminiscences, are you? What a good job I have come in to rescue them before you drove them away. Come along Xaviera and Herman, I'll take you to the studio now. Jacques, you and Juliette can clear up and load the car while we are gone.'

The two of us followed Jeannine out of the house and up a twisting side street until we reached the very small house which Jeannine used as a studio. There I had a lovely time, looking at the different materials with which she worked and I ended up by ordering four sets of pants and blouses to match. As for the belts which had originally aroused our interest, there was only one, similar to that worn by Jacques, in the place and Jeannine insisted on giving it to me as a present. Herman gave the things a cursory glance, but he seemed to have his mind on other things. Perhaps he still had lingering hopes that Jacques would prove to be gay. As soon as we were back at the house, we found Jacques and Juliette waiting for us and we started our journey up to their country estate.

I had thought that the road up to Ojen was difficult, but it was a first class highway in comparison with the track which I followed out of town, on the tail of Jacques' Dune Buggy. Indeed, a couple of hundred yards from his house in the mountains, I had to leave the car and finish the journey by foot. As we trudged up the stony path, Jacques explained the history of his 'estate'.

'This is my retreat, what do you think of the view?'

Beneath us, Ojen lay like a toy panorama, red roofs and white walls, gleaming in the brazen furnace heat of the sun. Here and there were clumps of trees and stunted bushes, their leaves burnt brown on the parched hillside. The barren rock had a harsh majesty and in the midst of this grandeur, a humble, rough-cast stone cottage seemed to cling to the slope as if it were in danger of slipping into the chasm below.

'This place belonged to a man we knew who was killed a few years ago in a big forest fire,' Jacques told us. 'Nobody has claimed the place and so, as it was standing empty, I moved in. Legally, I am a squatter, but I can't imagine that anybody is going to object to this hovel. It has no running water or electricity and it was completely derelict.'

'How do you manage?' asked Herman.

'We do everything down the hill in the town house. Here we are completely cut off from civilization - although we do have a well and we swim in a pool, just below the house.'

The cottage itself certainly merited being termed something better than a hovel. It was quite spacious consisting of two bedrooms, a large one for Jacques and Jeannine separated by a curtain from a smaller room for Juliette. A small lean-to had been constructed against one wall to make an outside kitchen of a sort and Jeannine and her daughter went in there to get the food ready. It was a good job that they were both slender, even skinny, for, if they had been any stouter, they would not have been able to get inside and work together. The bedrooms had been carefully furnished to make the most of the space.

In no time, we were all seated on some simple, wooden garden chairs before a sturdy table on which Jeannine had spread the food, enjoying our meal, country style, on a level piece of ground just outside the cottage. After we had eaten, we sipped red wine and chatted.

'Tell me, Jacques, where do you get the materials for Jeannine and the other things that you sell down in your studio?' I asked. 'You must travel a hell of a lot.'

'Yes, indeed. We have been to India and I have friends there who look after supplies from there. But a great deal of my stuff comes from Morocco. There are a lot of friends of my family in places like Fes and Marrakesh and, of course, it is so easy to get across from this part of Spain to Tangier.

Have you been to Morocco, Xaviera?'

'I have spent a few days in Tangier a few years ago but I didn't like it very much.'

'You should go with somebody who knows the country and, preferably speaks Arabic. Once you are off the beaten tourist tracks, it is a fascinating place, but you have to know your way around,'

'Probably if I had been with someone like you, Jacques, I would have enjoyed it much more.'

'I am sure. You would have a wonderful time in the souks, the native markets, and you could buy exquisite gold, silver and leather work - really lovely things and all hand-crafted, of course.'

'I think we Dutch would find the country terribly uncivilized,' Herman objected.

Jeannine had been listening to everything we said without saying anything but had evidently been reaching her own conclusions. Now she joined in the discussion.

'I don't know whether you would appreciate the place, Herman, but I am sure that with her wide experience of foreign travel, Xaviera would. You talk of civilization: many of us are trying to get away from the strain and the tension of your great cities. The most appealing thing for me in Morocco is its very wildness. In the mountains and in the desert, you can breathe clean air and eat fresh food and the people are simple and good natured.'

'Not the ones I've met,' Herman rejoined. 'As a matter of fact, I have been to Tangier and I bought a few things in the market. I bargained and I thought I had done well, but I tell you, I was swindled.'

'That often happens to inexperienced tourists,' Jacques replied, 'that is why I said to Xaviera that she ought to see the country with somebody like me who knows his way around. But what Jeannine told you is correct, the Berbers in the Rif Mountains, for example, are lovely people and they don't give a damn about a lot of foreigners who dash about, showing off their money.

'And you are very wrong to talk about the place as uncivilized. As Jeannine says, we love the simple life, but in the old imperial cities like Fes and Meknes, there are plenty of reminders of how sophisticated Moorish culture is. Remember, Herman, that the finest buildings in Spain - in Seville, Granada or Cordoba, especially, were built by these Moroccan Arabs before you Dutch even knew how to catch herrings.'

I could see that Jacques was proud of his native land and resented Herman's insensitivity and narrow mindedness. So, again I intervened to smooth things down.

'I'll remember what you say, Jacques and if there is time, I'll make another journey to Morocco, but at the moment, I have not long been back from a trip to Portugal, and I am enjoying being back at home in Spain. But let me know if you are going over some time, and if you don't mind and it is a convenient time, perhaps I shall join you for a few days.'

'I would like it very much and so, I am sure, would Jeannine. You see we always go together.'

'Of course,' Jeannine put in, 'you would be company when Jacques is arguing with the traders in the souks, bargaining to get the lowest possible price. Seriously, you would find it fun. And if you happen to want some things for your flat here - carpets or rugs for instance, you would find Jacques a great help.'

'I'll give you a call when we are next thinking of going across and you can let me know whether you would like to come along,' said Jacques.

'It's not that I object to Arabs,' Herman interposed, in a milder and more reasonable tone. 'I just feel that one can do better than Morocco. Now, for example, I met a charming fellow in Marbella - Xaviera was there and can bear me out. He was young and very overweight, but we should not hold that against him. He was so polite and generous – but then he was a genuine prince.'

'You mean Hamid. I rather thought that I had come across him first. After all, I literally fell over him.' I was getting a bit tired of Herman's arrogance.

'That may be so,' Herman waved his hand at me in an airy gesture of dismissal, 'but I was the one he talked to, while you were making up to his servant.'

'Where is he from?' Jeannine asked.

'He's an Arab.' Herman replied vaguely.

'Of course he is an Arab. But from what country. Is he a Saudi or from one of the Emirates?'

'Yes,' Herman answered uncomfortably. I had no intention of coming to his rescue and left him to flounder in his own ignorance.

'I am glad that you had so happy an experience,' Jacques told him rather formally. 'An awful lot of the Arabs who have descended on Marbella have been pretty uncouth and have behaved badly.'

'But this one is a prince,' Herman objected.

'So are thousands of others,' Jacques told him, 'I heard that there are about three thousand members of the Saudi royal family who are entitled to call themselves princes. And all the little sheikhdoms along the Gulf have princes galore.'

'Well, Hamid is certainly very rich,' Herman pointed out.

'Some of the worst behaviour has been that of the ultra-rich,' Jeannine insisted. 'Down in Marbella, I know a family who let out a beautiful villa to a rich Iraqui for a couple of weeks. When they took the place back, it was a shambles. They had even let the water out of the pool and used it as a garbage pit. They had plenty of money but there was just no breeding, no decency, you understand?'

'A lot of Arabs got rich so quick that they never adjusted. Types like that have no respect for the property of anybody else. They are sure that if they have any problems they can always buy their way out of trouble,' I stated.

'Unfortunately so many Europeans and Americans are so obsessed by their money, that they are right. They can get away with murder as long as they bring their cheque book.' Jacques gave me a grim smile. 'I was told of a prince,' he mentioned his family name, 'who arrived with about a dozen of his family to do some shopping in London - at Harrods, of course. The store closes at six, but this horde descended about a quarter of an hour before the shop was due to close. When one of the staff explained that they would have to leave within a few minutes, the prince sent for the manager and wrote a cheque for an astronomical sum. "That is to pay your staff to stay on until eight," he explained. "I shall not need everybody, but you will leave an assistant in every department just in case we want to buy something there." When the manager saw the figure on the cheque, it was arranged in minutes.'

'And they,' I told Herman, for I had noted the name that Jacques had quoted, 'are the family of your friend, Hamid.'

We had long ago finished eating and drinking, and Jeannine rose from her seat, and with Juliette, cleared the table, going into the improvised kitchen to pack the things to take down to Ojen for washing up.

'Your story reminds me of something else which happened in London,' I told Jacques. 'I was a member of Tramp, the most chic of the West End clubs. One night, a young Arab from one of the Gulf states arrived but was refused admission because he was not wearing a tie. The English are like that. The kid argued and pulled rank and wealth but it was no good. Very politely, he was shown the door. Next day, the rich boy's daddy called round to see the owner of the club and bought it on the spot.'

'And you are telling us that the Moroccans are different?' asked Herman.

'They simply have not been spoilt by having more

money than they know what to do with,' was Jacques' reply. 'Maybe if they were to find huge reserves of oil in the Western Sahara, they would become like the others. But things have not worked out that way, so I can promise you, as I have said, the simple life, if you come over with us.'

'Well, Xaviera might go, but it wouldn't suit me,' Herman dismissed the matter haughtily.

'I am going to have a swim,' announced Jacques, 'would anybody like to join me?'

'You have a pool here?' asked Herman incredulously.

'No, of course not. As I told you, there is a small pond just below the house where we swim. It's a bit overgrown and the bottom is muddy but at least, it's never overcrowded.'

'In that case, I'll give it a miss,' Herman sneered 'Back home, at Torremolinos, I have a very pleasant pool and I've got used to swimming in comfort.'

'It's no Olympic pool,' I retorted, 'I'll come and keep you company, Jacques.'

The two of us walked down a track for about a hundred yards and came upon the pool, surrounded by a clump of trees. I sat on a rock, enjoying the shade while Jacques quickly stripped off his clothes and plunged into the water. He swam about vigorously: he was a powerful swimmer and I admired his graceful yet muscular torso, as he dried himself off on a bath towel.

'That's quite a physique you have there. Tell me, is Jeannine the jealous type?' I asked jokingly.

Jacques' answer was serious. 'I shall be honest with you since I believe you to be a completely honest person, sexually, Xaviera. Jeannine and I have a clear understanding. We love each other very dearly, but after the birth of Juliette, she was changed. I don't know how or why it happened, but Jeannine lost her sex urge. Nobody was to blame: it just happened. For a while, I had a German girl friend and she wished to become a friend of Jeannine. Of course, Jeannine knew all about her and I wanted the two of them to get on well together, to include her in the family as it were. But Jeannine flatly refused to have anything to do with her. She told me that I could have affairs with whoever I chose: she realized that I needed sex. But she didn't want to be involved in any way. I suppose it is a form of jealousy but I respect her and I would never do anything to hurt or humiliate her. So, I go down to the coast and have casual affairs with boutique owners. But my rule is that no woman I sleep with can be a friend of the family.'

Jacques threw aside his towel and looked down at me, almost as if he were challenging me.

'You are an attractive woman and sexually potent,' he told me. 'I am prepared to make love to you, if that is what you want, but in that case, you will never be welcome again in our home. We won't hate you, Jeannine won't resent you, but you will be excluded from our circle of friends. The choice is yours.'

'For me the choice is simple,' I replied. 'I find you attractive and I believe that we could have good sex. But I am not in love with you and I have no intention of falling in love with you. I have my own group of lovers and my own group of friends and I can tell you that the friends are far dearer to me than the lovers. I find Jeannine and Juliette charming and I hope that they will accept my friendship. I certainly would not renounce it for a quick fuck.'

'You have no idea how pleased I am that you think that way.' Then, as if to dismiss the serious tone of our talk, Jacques added 'Anyway, I got the impression that it was Herman who was out to seduce me.'

'It surely looked that way,' I answered, 'but I suspect that he has lost hope now.'

We walked back towards the cottage, and Jacques went on talking as we ascended the path.

'I said that Jeannine was jealous, in a strange way, but that is nothing compared with the possessiveness of Juliette. We have some friends in Ojen who have a daughter of the same age as Juliette and we got used to looking after each other's child when one or other of the couples wanted an evening out or to stay for a few days. Nowadays, Juliette does not mind if we take her friend to stay with us, but she gets quite upset when we want to leave her with them and she cannot keep her eye on me. I'm afraid that she'll grow into a proper dragon and I won't be able to stir a finger without having to account to her.'

'Nonsense,' I smiled, 'wait until she's just a few years older and she begins to have boy friends of her own. Daddy will be pushed into the background.'

'I suppose you are right. I hope so. And yet, I would not want her to lose that warmth and freshness.'

'She's sweet.' I told him.

We had got back to the cottage and the rest of our party were ready and waiting to go down into town. Clearly, Herman thought that Jacques was worth one last attempt.

'Why don't you drive Jeannine in your car, Xaviera, and let me go with Jacques? I haven't had a chance to speak to him and I would like to talk to him about those lovely belts before we leave. You really have monopolized him, you know.'

'Why of course, that's OK with me, Herman,' I assented. 'I remember that it was you who first pointed out Jacques' belt when we saw him shopping this morning. Or at least, you were the first to lay hands on it.'

'I'll come with you, papa,' said Juliette, taking Jacques by the hand. Off they went, Herman, Jacques and his chaperone, Juliette. I was glad of the chance to speak to Jeannine who tended to say little in the presence of her more extrovert husband.

'You must have found Ojen quite a contrast, coming straight from Paris,' I said, as we started off down the hill.

'Oh, but we did not come immediately to Ojen,' Jeannine told me. 'When he got back from Israel, Jacques was not happy in the city and he had fallen in love with the sunshine. We drifted off to the Mediterranean and we settled in Ibiza. Have you been there?'

I nodded.

'Well then, you know what the place is like. Everybody is involved in some sort of village crafts or home potteries or painting – that sort of thing.'

'Why did you move, didn't you like it there?'

'Yes, we were at Formentera, a tiny island just off Ibiza and very picturesque. There were lovely beaches: one could go naked there and it was a fine place to bring up Juliette without all the stupid hangups of the big cities, like Paris. But, you know after a while, Ibiza became very fashionable and a bit too jet set for our taste. Things began to get more expensive and by now, I was making clothes and Jacques was bringing in some nice things from Morocco. But it seemed that everybody else on the island was trying to do the same thing. We thought a great deal and finally decided to move to somewhere close to the Costa del Sol, where we were sure that there would be a market for our things and which would still be convenient for Jacques when he needed to go to Morocco. Ojen seemed the ideal spot, near enough to Marbella, Fuengirola and the whole of that part of the coast and yet peaceful and – as Jacques said, the simple life.'

Back in Ojen, we said goodbye to Jeannine and Juliette who set about taking in the dirty crockery and cutlery for washing up, while Jacques escorted us to my BMW, promising to be in contact soon.

As we drove home, Herman gave vent to his frustration and disappointment.

'What a waste of a day,' he moaned, 'I really thought that they would be interesting, but they were so boring. I suppose it's all one could expect of people who choose to live out in the wilderness.'

'I liked them very much and had a good day,' I retorted 'But cheer up, Herman. Tomorrow, we shall be going out with your favourite Arabs. That should be fun for you.'

'I hope so,' he said, brightening up somewhat, 'I can't stay away from Torremolinos any longer. Momir has an exhibition coming up, and I know that he will need my help. I must get away the day after tomorow.'

'Well, we'll stay in tonight so that you can get your beauty sleep and be in good form tomorrow.'

'You know, Xaviera,' Herman mused, 'I might try to sell some of Jeannine's junk to Hamid. It could make an extra wedding present, don't you think?'

I said nothing. I had heard quite enough from Herman for one day.

15

Forced to Fast

'Outside every fat man, there is a fatter man, trying to get in.'

Kingsley Amis

'You know, Xaviera, there really must be something we can sell your fat friend,' said Herman as he gobbled up the last of the toast and marmalade. At breakfast, Herman had continued on the same topic which had obsessed him even before we had left Ojen the previous day.

I did not bother to reply. The morning was the time of the day when I concentrated on whatever was needed for the apartment, shopping, cleaning, running repairs, paying bills and getting down to my own business correspondence.

Herman's deliberations were interrupted by the phone. I answered it and found that I had a worried Omar on the line.

'Xaviera, you have been around Marbella for several years; perhaps you can help me.'

'I hope so. What seems to be the trouble, Omar?'

'Hamid needs a bathing costume - just a pair of trunks. Have you any idea where I could get some?'

'That's no problem. There are dozens of shops in Marbella and San Pedro. If your cars are still off the road, I'll gladly run you into town.'

'That is very kind of you and we could certainly make use of some transport. But it's no good trying to get the bathing costume in those shops.'

'Why ever not? They have a big selection.'

'Have you forgotten Hamid's vital statistics? No shop has a garment of those proportions in stock and Hamid is far too self conscious to stand about in a shop while he is measured with a lot of people looking on and making fun of him.'

I smiled grimly at Herman and said to Omar, 'Don't worry, my friend. I think that we can deal with the matter for you. When can we come and see Hamid?'

'He is taking a sauna at the moment and then he's due for a massage. Why don't you come at lunch-time?'

'Won't we be a nuisance at meal times?'

'Not at all. You might help to take his mind off his food – or rather, the absence of it. You can join us and we can share a lettuce leaf.'

I promised that we would be there and hung up.

'Herman, your chance has come,' I announced and I related our conversation. Herman was greatly excited.

'Momir knows where we can get hold of some beautiful Chinese silk and we could sew into the trunks a design in diamonds – perhaps an imperial crown or his own personal coat of arms.'

'He'll sink and drown and you will be accused of regicide. I think they still boil criminals in oil where he comes from. Or else, he'll be seized by the Customs.'

'The trouble with you, Xaviera, is that you don't have any artistic flair,' Herman scolded.

'Artistic flair, my ass!' I snorted, 'all you are interested in is seeing how much money you can extract from Hamid.'

'Taking money on that scale requires artistic flair,' Herman explained.

By the time we drove over to Incosol, Herman had planned an entire aquatic wardrobe for Hamid.

We arrived to find the reception of the great hotel-clinic complex in an uproar. At the centre of this outburst were a couple of elderly women in a state of hysterical collapse.

'What's got into them?' I asked a man who was standing near the sobbing women.

'That old man – the one with Prince Hamid—' he answered. 'At the crack of dawn, he fell flat on his face in the lobby and started shouting his prayers. He woke everybody up.'

'He obviously did it to scare us. Must be some sort of exhibitionist. If I had my way, he would be horse-whipped,' snorted a heavily built, bossy Englishwoman.

'It looks as if we missed some fun,' I said to Omar, who had just joined me.

'Poor Abdul!' he replied, 'he simply does not understand that one cannot behave here in the same way as if he were at home.'

'Tell me, Omar, why was he saying his prayers in the lobby? Couldn't he have done it in his own room?'

'At certain hours of every day, the religious Muslim will prostrate himself, facing Mecca, and say his prayers, no matter where he might be. You have seen what a simple soul Abdul is. He never thought for a moment that anybody would take offence at his praying publicly. Mind you, I consider it bad form, one should behave quietly and discreetly, especially in a foreign country.'

There was something old fashioned and very proper about Omar but I found it a refreshing contrast to Herman's brashness.

We found Hamid sitting on the terrace, recovering from his massage. He greeted us with a smile, 'Don't mind if I don't get up to meet you. I don't think that I could get out of this chair if the bloody place caught fire. This treatment is going to kill me.'

I could not help thinking that Hamid had chosen the loveliest setting in which to expire. Incosol stands on a hill which commands a sweeping vista of the coast below. On the other side, there is a magnificent view of rugged mountains, savage and sun-drenched in violent contrast to the luxurious clinic buildings, standing in a blaze of flower beds and neatly tailored lawns around the blue waters of the giant pool. Hamid was starving and being pummelled in paradise.

'How long are you going to stay here?' I asked Hamid.

'Until I have lost twenty kilos or died in the attempt,'

was the gloomy response.

'That might take some time,' Herman ventured. 'Why don't you buy yourself a video?'

'I have to meet a deadline,' was the reply.

Hamid read the question in my look.

'I am getting into shape for my marriage,' he added sadly.

'Congratulations,' I said.

'What for?' Hamid demanded.

'Well, I suppose that you are in love with the girl since you are going to marry her.'

'Don't be ridiculous,' was the terse reply. 'I had nothing to do with it. All the arrangements were made by my father and her dad. She is one of the royal family of a neighbouring state, so she is quite suitable.'

'How old were you when you became engaged?' Herman asked.

'I was six and Rashida was four.'

'Anyway,' I pointed out, 'you must be fond of her, otherwise you wouldn't go to the trouble of shedding twenty kilos. That's quite a sacrifice.'

'It's not my choice.' Hamid was both sulky and aggrieved. 'The old cow of my mother-in-law to be, insisted and what she says, goes.'

'Let's look on the bright side,' Herman soothed the ruffled prince. 'You will have a splendid wedding and you must be looking out for all sorts of gorgeous wedding presents.'

'My father has looked after all that. He bought up most of Harrods.'

'So I heard,' I murmured.

'What about some jewellery for the bride?' Herman did not give up easily.

'We picked up a few things from Cartiers, Asprey's and Tiffany's.'

'I could find you some beautiful shirts?'

'Mine are hand made by Turnbull and Assher in London.'

'You could probably do with a good interior decorator for when you move into your new home.'

'Herman,' Hamid fixed the would-be salesman with a tired glare, 'We shall have our own wing in the palace of my father. It is splendidly decorated in traditional Arab style. As a matter of policy, when we buy houses in other countries in Europe or America, we always use architects and decorators of that country. It makes for good relations. You are Dutch, aren't you?'

Herman nodded.

'I am sorry to inform you that I have no intention of establishing a residence in your country. Can't we talk about swimming trunks?'

'Let me measure you now, and I can get something made for you by a wonderful craftsman,' Herman assured his over-weight and over-wealthy customer.

Hamid grumpily fended off the last despairing efforts of Herman to sell him practically anything but agreed to pay him an inflated price for a simple swimming costume - no diamonds, no gold lamé, not even sequins.

While these negotiations were being concluded, I chatted with Omar. He was a very shy person and it took a bit of time before he loosened up enough to talk without self-consciousness, but before we left, he and I had become good enough friends for him to speak to me without blushing.

Lunch was served on the terrace. It consisted of a plate of clear soup in which floated a sliver of carrot. Omar had summoned Abdul and the three men sat solemnly at the table as if attending a state banquet. I was struck by the absurdity of the situation. Hamid was gross and, forced to fast but Omar was lithe and slender and Abdul, positively emaciated. I asked Hamid why his two companions were undergoing a starvation diet.

'If I cannot eat, neither can they,' he growled.

'It would not be proper for the subjects to indulge themselves while their prince went without,' Omar said gently.

'Do join us,' invited Hamid, 'It's no trouble to get another couple of plates.'

'I think that we shall just watch,' I answered, 'I really don't have much of an appetite.'

'Never mind. You will eat well tonight. Lebanese food is delicious. It will be a pleasure to watch you eat.' Hamid's tone was regretful as he reflected on the delicacies in store for us. 'I, of course, will stick to my diet. And so will these two.' He rewarded Abdul and Omar with a savage glare, as if defying them to partake of the feast.

'Do you think that I could have a quick dip in your pool?' I asked our host. 'I am wearing a bikini and I would appreciate .the opportunity to cool down.'

It was the hottest time of the day and Hamid was sweating like a pig. However, he was still waiting for his hand-tailored trunks but he raised no objection to my having a swim. I had the impression that Omar would have liked to join me but considered it improper since Hamid was not able to bathe.

When I climbed out of the pool, Hamid regarded me critically and said, 'You really ought to do something about your figure, Xaviera. You're a good-looking woman: it's a shame to spoil your appearance and it shows when you wear a bikini.'

I felt indignant that somebody as obese as Hamid should have the nerve to comment on my figure. However, I swallowed my rage and laughed off the remark.

'I'm afraid Incosol is too fancy for me, but I do go sometimes to the Buchinger clinic. I think I told you about it.'

'That makes no sense,' Hamid retorted. 'In these places,

you lose weight. You should be trying to put on a bit more fat. You're far too skinny for Arab taste. I could never fancy you unless you got yourself better covered. Why woman, you are simply skin and bones.'

'I'll see what I can do about it,' I assented weakly, not sure whether to take Hamid's strictures as a compliment or not.

It was time for Abdul to offer more formal prayers to Allah, and Herman and I decided to leave before there was any repetition of the morning's devotional crisis.

Herman and I took it easy during the afternoon since we did not know what sort of an evening we would enjoy with Hamid and his merry band.

We drove over once more to the clinic and picked up the three men. It was the first time that I had been inside the Lebanese restaurant which was doing a flourishing trade in the wake of the Arab invasion of Marbella.

Herman and I were served with mesos, the light appetisers which traditionally opened the meal - hummus-tahinah and falafel as well as some delightful concoction of aubergine and we followed that with a tasty kebab for Herman and mechui, a roast joint of lamb for me. Our hosts moodily picked at salads and rounded off their feast by munching an apple. Herman had a beer - the rest of us stuck to water. The food was tasty but the portions were pitifully small and the conversation was hardly sparkling. I felt all the time that we ate, that Hamid resented his enforced abstinence and Omar rarely opened his mouth in the presence of his employer except to pop in a fragment of a lettuce leaf. Abdul mumbled incessantly but that did nothing to make the evening a feast for the intellect. I was relieved when we had finished and Hamid had called for the bill.

The bill proved to be the high point of the meal. It was astronomical, especially when I considered that only Herman and I had eaten full meals and we had not drunk any wine or spirits. I ventured to tell Hamid what I thought of the rip off: we could have eaten cheaper and far better in one of the most exclusive restaurants in Paris, London or New York. He shrugged his shoulders in resignation, and then, to my astonishment, left a tip as big as the bill. I looked at Omar but he seemed to be embarrassed at my concern, so I shut my mouth. After all, Hamid could afford his extravagance, but I could see that Herman was thinking what a waste it was – all that money and not for him!

'How about dropping in at Régine's for an hour?' Hamid suggested.

It was an idea which won approval from everybody, except Abdul but I thought that he would add an unusual note to the discotheque. We all piled into my car and I drove the short journey to the Puento Romano where Régine had established the smartest spot on the Coast.

I parked my BMW among an untidy assortment of Rolls Royces, monster Mercedes, Cadillacs, Ferraris and Lamborghinis. I am not used to feeling the poor relation but mine was one of the only cars present not bearing Arabic characters on the number plate.

At Régine's, entrance is strictly limited to 'members only'. However, if one was prepared to pay, it was not particularly difficult to become a member. Unaccompanied ladies were not welcomed but there was quite a collection of them, waiting outside the door looking out for a lonely male.

They were not the most appetising display. There were a few busty, big boned girls, probably Germans or Scandinavians, but the majority were dark skinned, heavily painted girls from Morocco or Algeria. Most of them were chain smoking as they eyed the men who arrived. However, a few of the less inhibited were busily chewing either gum or perhaps betel. They scarcely glanced at Abdul but Omar attracted a few approving smiles. They really concentrated their fire on Hamid: one look at him and they scented MONEY!

As I was obviously with this delectable prize, most of the girls regarded me with a combination of envy and downright hatred. A couple of North Africans sidled over to me, and one hissed in French, 'You don't need both of them all the night. Share the fat one and we'll cut you in for a share of whatever we can get out of him.'

I did not feel flattered that she should have taken me for a fellow operator, yet there were aspects of the situation which made me smile. Although I have moved a long way from the world of the prostitute, I have always retained some sympathy for 'working girls'. Omar, on the other hand, was scandalized that I should be insulted by such creatures and he shooed them away. Hamid, like Abdul, simply ignored them.

Once inside, Hamid demanded a table at the front, but was told that they were all taken and we were shown to one tucked away at the back.

'But. I can see that there are several at the front which are empty,' protested the outraged prince.

'Yes, but they have all been reserved,' he was told.

'These bloody Spaniards are such snobs,' Hamid complained to me, as we took our places at the table. 'They feel so superior to the Arabs: at every opportunity they will insult us or make fun of us. We aren't good enough for the best tables at their lousy nightclubs or restaurants. But, they're quick enough to take our money. That's another story.'

A waiter hovered over our table, ready to take our order. A cunning smile came over Hamid's features; he beckoned the waiter to come close and pointed to one of the tables at the edge of the dance floor at which sat a young couple.

'Go over to that table,' he told the waiter, 'and invite the young man and his friend to swap tables with us. Tell him, he will find a magnum of Dom Perignon waiting for him here.'

The waiter rasied one eyebrow but hurried off. A short time later, he returned and said to Hamid.

'The Duke of Sussex sends his compliments but wishes to inform you that he is quite comfortable where he is and both he and his companion have given up alcohol - at least, temporarily.'

'Bloody English!' Hamid stormed. 'They still treat us as if we were their servants, ignorant natives waiting on the white man. Come along, Xaviera, let's dance.'

I followed him on to the floor which, before his arrival, had not been very crowded. Hamid stamped about for a few minutes, sweating profusely, and then staggered back to his seat. The music was pretty good and I was feeling groovy, so I asked Omar to dance with me. He shot an enquiring glance at Hamid, who looked ahead stonily. Hesitantly, Omar joined me on the floor.

'What's the matter?' I asked, 'Don't you want to dance with me?'

'Oh, yes, very much. But Hamid gets jealous.'

'I'm rapidly coming to the conclusion that Hamid is a spoilt brat,' I informed him.

'That is not at all respectful,' Omar complained.

'You know, Omar,' I said as I moved close to him, 'I think that you are a nice guy and I would like to spend a little time with you and get to know you better.'

Omar's big eyes opened wider, 'That would be great,' he whispered, 'ever since we met, I have been hoping to see you alone, but you always seem to have Herman with you.'

'Herman is going home tomorrow. But he's no problem. You don't think that I am sleeping with Herman, do you? In no sense is he a ladies' man.'

Understanding dawned on Omar and he smiled happily.

'I did not know what to think' he admitted. 'When can we meet?'

'Whenever you like,' I replied. 'You are the one who is tied down with your having to dance attendance on Hamid.'

'We'll have to be very discreet,' Omar said seriously. 'There'd be the devil to pay if Hamid found out.'

'That, my friend, is your problem. You know where I live and you have my phone number.'

'I think that we had better be getting back to the table,' Omar muttered unhappily. 'Hamid hasn't taken his eyes off us once.'

When we got back, Hamid called, 'Drink up and let's get out of this morgue. I feel like a little flutter at the Casino and we can have a goodnight drink there before we go home. What do you say?'

'It's OK by me,' I replied.

'I'd like that very much,' Herman added enthusiastically.

So, after a few minutes, we were on the road again, headed for the casino in Puerto Banus.

There was quite a crowd in the casino. However, it did not take me long to be able to distinguish between the different groups in the place. Hanging around the anteroom in which stood row after row of fruit machines were some of the poorer tourists, people who rarely had the chance to patronize a casino and were there for the experience, more to watch others than to bet themselves but pleased to be able to place tiny sums in the machines and feel that they were part of the glamorous world of gambling. There were also Spanish families, having a few days at the seaside, some studying hard the sequence of fruits which came up on each machine, hoping to find an infallible way of predicting the jackpot. For all I know, they are still there since I never saw a jackpot come up while we were in the room.

In the big room, things were very different. There was a handful of serious gamblers, many of them unsmiling

Arabs, placing huge sums and showing no emotion whether they won or, as was more often the case, lost. They were surrounded by onlookers and also by a number of smaller betters.

There were also quite a number of unattached women, strolling from table to table. They congregated around the bigger gamblers, especially those who appeared to be winning. Some of them were hookers, like those who were hanging about outside Régine's and a couple of them cast enquiring glances in the direction of Hamid. However, he remained faithful to his distant fiancée, at least for that night.

'You see,' Hamid grumbled to me, 'all the best seats are taken. Just because I am an Arab, I can't have a decent place at a table.'

This was ridiculous when one counted the number of Arabs who were playing in the casino and I told him so.

Hamid walked over to a blackjack game and stood for a few moments behind the chair of a player. Then, as if in answer to his silent prayer, the man got up from his seat and left the place for Hamid.

I told him, 'You can have as good a place as anybody if you are a little patient.'

Omar pulled me on one side and explained that the guy who had left was probably one of the casino employees who would sit in on a game to help draw a crowd and then give up his place to a potentially big player.

'Just watch, he'll lose all his money in no time,' Omar commented bitterly. I had the impression that the Persian felt strongly that the money which was about to disappear from Hamid's wallet could have been put to better use.

Contrary to expectations, Hamid was winning. He did not seem to have any particular system to his play, but the cards fell luckily for him. One of the painted ladies asked him to give her a chip for luck and Hamid pushed across a couple without bothering to even look at the fair charmer.

'Why don't you quit while you are ahead?' I asked him.

'You are a wise woman, Xaviera. I'll do that. Here, take these chips and cash them in for me.'

I walked over with Omar to the cashier. Until I received Hamid's winnings, I had not realized how big the stakes were for which he had been playing.

When I got back to him, Hamid handed me some notes and said, 'You brought me luck, Xaviera and you gave me the wisdom to call it a day. Here, take this and buy yourself something to remember me by - a little dress or a pair of jeans - whatever you like.'

I thanked him and stuffed the money into my bag. It seemed rude to count it in front of my benefactor. Only when we had left and I examined my trifling present did I find that he had given me five thousand dollars. For that, you can buy quite a good pair of jeans.

It would be nice to recount how we left the casino with our winnings. Only, it would not have been true. While Omar and I took a drink at the bar, Hamid threw all the money he had won plus quite a bit more on a couple of spins of the roulette wheel and by the time we had rejoined him, the casino was that much richer.

Herman was aware that the journey back to Incosol would be his last opportunity to sell Hamid the Brooklyn Bridge, the British Crown Jewels or anything else which came to mind. Consequently, he insisted on sitting at the back of the car with Hamid and Abdul. That suited me fine since I was able to talk quietly to Omar, undisturbed and without our being overheard. However, Herman was wasting his time: Hamid had been cleaned out in the casino and, tired and irritable, his sole objective was to get to bed as soon as possible. As soon as we arrived at the clinic, the three men went off with only the briefest of farewells. I guess that Herman was getting on their nerves: he certainly was on mine.

I drove away and, when we were about a hundred yards

from the clinic, I stopped the car and turned off the lights.

'What's the matter? Why are you stopping here?' Herman asked.

'While you were busy chattering to Hamid, I made certain arrangements with Omar,' I informed him.

'You mean he's coming back now?'

'That's right. As soon as Hamid is safely tucked up in bed and out of harm's way.'

Herman stopped and considered the situation for a moment.

'You told him that I was back at your apartment?'

'Yes. But I explained that you had a room of your own.'

Herman began to laugh.

'Do you really think that he is coming back to be with you, Xaviera? You are so green! Didn't you notice how feminine he looks? That sweet face, that slight figure and those long, slender fingers. He's as gay as they come. He's coming for me, not you, sweetheart. My queen for tonight.'

'We'll see,' I replied.

We waited in silence for about ten minutes. Then a form hurried out of the shadows and Omar sank into the seat beside me.

Back in the apartment, I offered Omar something to eat. I reckoned that he needed some nutrition to keep his strength up; after all, he had been suffering the same starvation diet as Hamid. He declined but asked if he could take a shower. All the time we were talking, Herman favoured Omar with his most winning smile and, as the young Persian went into the bathroom, he called after him, 'Mine is the bedroom next to the bathroom. Don't be long!'

While Herman waited hopefully, I went into the second bathroom which adjoins my bedroom and got ready for bed. Omar emerged from the shower, wearing a towel robe which I had passed him and smelling lovely and fresh. He was slightly flushed from the shower and his hair was tousled and damp. He looked gorgeous and I was good and ready for him.

I turned to Herman.

'Remember Don Magnifico?' I asked.

Herman looked puzzled: he could not see the point of my remark.

'When you had that good looking dude, you took him into your room and shut the door in my face,' I reminded him 'and then you had to ask me to come to your help.'

I took Omar by the hand and led him into my bedroom.

'Tonight, dear Herman, the tables are turned and you might as well go straight to sleep because nobody will be calling to you for assistance. Good night.'

And with that, I shut the door firmly on Herman.

16

The Persian Boy

'Oh, when I was in love with you,
Then I was clean and brave.
And miles around the wonder grew
How well did I behave.

And now the fancy passes by,
And nothing will remain.
And miles around they'll say that I
Am quite myself again.'

A. E. Housman

My first night with Omar was one which I shall remember. The dark, delicate looking boy had appealed to the romantic side of my character and I had been looking forward to exploring his body and feeling him make love to me.

It was a great anti-climax. Omar was miserably unsure of himself. When he should have taken the initiative, he was shy, when he should have been deft, he fumbled. He did not even know of the existence of oral sex and when he kissed, his mouth was taut and his lips tight shut. I had the task of teaching him that one can do more with the tongue than simply talk.

After the uncertain, scampered petting which passed for foreplay, he mounted me fearfully, his body shaking with nervousness.

There was nothing wrong with him physically: I liked the sight and the feel of him and his penis was both longer and thicker than I had expected in surprising and pleasing contrast to the slenderness of his form. However, he was obviously inexperienced and after I had guided him into me, he came so fast that he did absolutely nothing for me.

As he lay back in the bed, I said to him. 'Omar, I enjoy

being with you, but you do seem terribly uptight. Is there something that I have said or done which is upsetting you?'

He shook his head. 'No, Xaviera, you have been most kind and understanding. I know that I have not proved to be a very good lover, please forgive me. But I am nervous. I can't stop thinking about Herman in the next room and what you said about him - being homosexual, you know.'

I felt very let down. 'You mean that you would rather be with him than with me?'

'Good Lord, no!' Omar burst out laughing. 'I can't stand that sort of thing. A few men have propositioned me; I suppose that they think that I look effeminate, but I find the whole idea of sex with another man repulsive. No, the trouble with having Herman so close is that I didn't like the way he made advances towards me and I guess that he is pretty macho. I had the fear that, knowing what we were doing in here, he would break in and do something to me.'

'You mean that he'd fuck you?'

Omar looked uncomfortable. He did not have many four letter words in his vocabulary.

'Yes, you could put it that way. That he would violate me.'

'Don't worry. I promise you that Herman will behave. Why don't we go on where we left off?'

It was no use. The presence of Herman in the apartment raised a psychological barrier which Omar could not surmount. We embraced but his awkwardness got through to me and put me off so that there was nothing for it, but to turn out the light and go to sleep. I kissed him goodnight and whispered, 'Never mind. Herman is going home tomorrow. Perhaps you will feel better when we have the place to ourselves.'

Before we could put the matter to the test, we had a couple of ordeals to undergo. First, there were Herman's farewells. His last words to Omar were a suggestion that any time the Persian boy would care to experience a real, sexual thrill, he should contact Herman and stop bothering with such childish follies as sex with women and a request that Omar would remind Hamid that whatever he might want to purchase, Herman could supply it - at a price.

With a deep sense of relief, we deposited Herman at the bus station and drove on to Incosol where Omar rejoined Hamid and found one hell of a reception awaiting him.

'And where do you think that you have been all the morning?' stormed the peppery potentate, totally ignoring my presence.

Omar tried to evade the issue, 'Have you been looking for me?' he asked innocently, 'Is there something that you want?'

'Yes. I want you to be there when I look for you, not stealing off somewhere without a word of warning. You are paid to be with me and your work is here, in my presence.'

Omar apologized abjectly and I was furious at his humility and at Hamid's jealously - for I was sure that was what was eating him.

Hamid ranted on, 'I don't think that you even slept here last night. Abdul couldn't find you when he got up early. You had better come clean. Where have you been and what are you doing behind my back?'

Omar was so confused by this bullying that he offered no defence to his lord and master, but I had heard enough and weighed into Hamid.

'Since you ask, Hamid, Omar spent the night with me. It was my idea and I don't see what business of yours it is. You say that you pay Omar: that hardly gives you the right to treat him like a slave and dictate his private life.'

'I don't think that anybody had ever answered Hamid back and stood up to him in the whole of his life, and I wondered what his reaction would be. I half expected him to order Omar and me to be boiled in oil or tied to a couple of camels and torn limb from limb but, to my amazement, a broad grin spread over his flabby face.

'So, you were looking after the little boy, were you, Xaviera? Well, I don't see how I can object to his passing his time in your company. You have become almost one of the family and I am sure that you will be a good influence on him. If you want to take him off in the evenings, that's alright with me: only make sure that he is back at breakfast time so that he can attend to his duties.'

And with a paternal chuckle, Hamid slapped Omar on the back. The tension slipped away and all his bad temper was immediately forgotten.

The person who benefited most from Hamid's bout of good humour was me. That night, Omar was a different man. He did not have to fear the distant anger of Hamid or the menace of an all-too-close, Herman. His sexual education got off to a promising start and I found that I had a ready and able pupil on my hands - and in other places.

There was a new sensitiveness and awareness in his lovemaking. My only criticism was that he still came too fast, although there was a distinct improvement on his first attempt, and I was able to respond which both excited and delighted my lover.

'You've certainly made some progress?' I complimented him.

'Well, I'm gaining experience,' he replied. 'You know, Xaviera, before I met you, I had only made love to four or five women in my whole life.'

'And did you satisfy them?'

'They were not the sort of women who would talk about that kind of thing. They were all rather snooty English girls from good families, very correct and well mannered. It took a few months before you could hold hands, let alone touch a girl's breast.' Omar reflected for a moment on his not very dissipated youth and added, 'None of them ever complained: they wouldn't criticize me like you do. But then, none of them ever seemed to enjoy sex the way that you do.'

'Perhaps you never gave any of them an orgasm?'

'I don't know: I never thought about it and they would never mention it. I suppose I ought to have noticed.'

'Dear Omar, you still have quite a few things to learn,' I said and I kissed him gently.

When we were out together, Omar would tend to annoy me with his obsession on formal good manners. He was for ever telling me that one didn't speak like that or one didn't do that sort of thing. In vain, did I explain to him that people were more relaxed in this part of Spain and what he might consider bad taste was nowadays normal behaviour. But when we were alone, all was forgiven and I began to grow genuinely fond of the boy. One of his more endearing features was the speed with which he would recuperate after climaxing. Even after a couple of orgasms, his penis would remain rock hard, I loved the contrast between the duskiness of his skin and the creamy whiteness of his sperm. Often, I would make him come on his belly and I would savour his sperm, feeling its thick stickiness and tasting it. I also enjoyed working him to a climax between my tits and watching the languid river of his come, winding along the valley of white skin between my breasts.

Yet our love affair was not destined to last very long. Our last night started pleasantly enough without any shadow of what was to come. I gazed fondly at Omar as he buried his handsome face between my legs and I felt the warmth of his pink tongue thrusting between my lips. He had come a long way in a short time. I smiled at his almost hairless body - even under his armpits, he had only a few wispy tufts of hair. Yet, despite this and the delicate scent of his body, he was not in any way effeminate, merely tender and sensitive and well taught, I thought.

We had made love early since Omar had got away from Hamid a couple of hours sooner than was usual. For four or five nights in a row, we had made love in my apartment and then gone to sleep and we had not been out anywhere. So, I turned to Omar and suggested that we got dressed and went down to Puerto Banus.

He was ready for a break also and we were in excellent spirits, as we strolled through the crowded promenade.

'Do you want to stop somewhere for a drink?' Omar asked.

'Let's go to one of the piano bars,' I answered.

In fact, we went to two of them. In the first, I was greeted as I walked in by Stephen. I introduced him to Omar who seemed to approve of Stephen's aristocratic Englishness but, at the same time, to be shocked by his uninhibited exhibitionism. For Stephen had been drinking and this was the first time I had the chance to see how wildly happy and unrestrained he became when his alcohol level rose.

The best known piano bar in the Port was The Crescendo, the first of them to open. The pianist was a brilliant Argentinian named Roberto who had a sound conservatoire training and would appear in classical concerts or recitals at some of the big hotels and who had made a number of commercial recordings. Now, Roberto had opened up his own bar together with a highly successful woman folk singer and this was the bar which I had chosen for our quiet drink.

But, of course, I did not know that Stephen would be there and with him about, nobody had a quiet drink. He pranced from table to table, joining in other people's conversations and telling everybody his joke. I say his joke for, although Stephen was one of the most accomplished raconteurs I ever met, when his blood-cognac level reached a high point, Stephen would become obsessed by one funny story. He would tell everybody the same story, repeating it at each table, but like a skilful musician, adding fresh variations with each performance.

Stephen certainly drew a lot of attention and a few

women resented his way of taking Polaroid pictures of them but he did no harm, apart from spilling a few drinks over people's clothes, and he was treated with good humoured tolerance at the worst and in many cases, he was warmly applauded. The one exception to this general approval was Omar. I could see that he was getting more and more on edge but all went well when Stephen staggered over to where Roberto was playing and joined him at the keyboard. To our amusement, Stephen started to play a pretty nimble piano. Roberto watched for a few seconds, and then picked up the tune. The two of them got through unrehearsed and without any major mishap to enthusiastic applause and a couple of free drinks from delighted patrons.

Omar saw that Stephen was coming back to our table and he said hurriedly to me, 'Xaviera, let's move on somewhere else.'

I was a bit irritated since I had been enjoying myself but I was ready to humour Omar. He surely was uncomfortable, so we got up to leave.

'I'm glad you're going too,' Stephen cried as he rejoined us. 'I want to get a breath of fresh air; I'll walk with you.'

This did not please Omar, but it would have been rude to refuse, so the three of us emerged from the bar and started along the promenade.

We had not walked very far before Stephen tugged at my arm and insisted that we follow him into another piano bar.

'This place has only just opened. It's much more fun than the other bars. Let's have one for the road.'

'Thank you, but I think that we have to get back,' Omar replied, and pulled at my other arm.

'Oh, come on! I've hardly got to know you and the night is young. You must let me buy you one drink.' Stephen yanked the arm he was holding and I began to understand what it must feel like to be a rope in a tug of war.

Each time that Stephen offered us hospitality, he would pull at my arm and every time he was answered by Omar who obviously feared what might happen if we went into another bar with this wild Englishman and he emphasized his point by pulling me away. I felt that he was being just a shade too prim: after all, we had not had a night on the town for some time and Stephen was not the type to start a fight or get us into any sort of trouble. So, I steered my reluctant escort towards the bar.

'Come along,' I coaxed, 'we'll stay for one drink and then we'll get back home.'

The new bar was less crowded than Roberto's and Stephen immediately took over. He ordered drinks, trotted around all the tables and enquired if everybody was satisfied before coming back to us.

All might have gone well and, as promised we would have slipped away after a short stay but, while we were sipping our drinks and Omar was cringing in embarrassment, two newcomers entered the bar. I recognized a wealthy American, Porky McGrew, a man as fond of his booze as Stephen and, in his own way, just as extrovert. In every other respect, however, he was completely unlike the Englishman. Porky, as his nickname implied, had a barrel of a belly, heavy jowls and the rich purple colour of an expert alcoholic. He was as modest as a Texan millionare (which he was) and as soft spoken as a drunken sailor (which, as he owned his own yacht, he was also). Porky's companion was a radiant platinum blonde. If she liked money and he liked dames, they were both on to a good thing.

'Why, Xaviera, fancy seeing you here! Gee, this is nice,' Porky lurched towards us and waved a cheery greeting to Stephen and Omar. 'Meet Tootsy.'

The blonde giggled.

'Drinks for everybody,' roared Porky.

'We're just about to go,' Omar murmured apologetically.

Porky smiled through Omar as if he were invisible. 'You're staying for a drink with me,' he informed the world in general.

Stephen produced his Polaroid, knelt before the blonde and took a quick snap, tripping up a waiter as he did so.

'Clumsy sod,' Stephen smiled at the unfortunate waiter.

The blonde giggled.

'I admire your style, boy,' drawled Porky. 'As a technique, it sure beats trotting around with a dog to stimulate a little interest from a lady.'

'That's right,' chortled Stephen, 'and you never have to take a camera out for a pee.'

Porky howled with laughter and slapped Stephen on the back, nearly knocking the amiable dwarf over. Omar coughed nervously: he did not like the way things were going. The blonde giggled.

Somehow, one drink got stretched into two or three - or more. Every time, Omar attempted to make a move, the Anglo-American alliance restrained him and the party got more and more uproarious.

I thought that the climax had come when the two comics linked arms and sang a couple of army ditties. Musically, their effort left something to be desired since Porky was completely tone deaf but they got full marks for enthusiasm and the words left nothing to the imagination.

'Really,' Omar muttered to me, 'gentlemen do not behave like that.'

'Why don't you relax and enjoy yourself,' I demanded. 'It's nice to see people having a good time and they aren't doing any harm. Nobody else seems to mind.'

'Let's get away, soon,' he implored.

Stephen now demonstrated a trick with a glass of water. He showed how you could hold it upside down without spilling a drop. Unfortunately, it didn't quite work out. The glass of water was, in fact, a large gin and tonic which had been ordered for Tootsy. Stephen turned it upside down with a quick flick of his wrist and, as promised, didn't spill a drop. Then he tried to change his grip and poured the whole glassful over Porky.

'Oops, sorry,' Stephen shouted with a broad grin.

Porky was too far gone to object and he went on laughing hysterically. The blonde giggled.

'This is too bad,' Omar told me. 'Horse play!'

It was then that Chuchu arrived. Little is known of Chuchu's past, but much is conjectured. One thing is for sure. If there was a lively party going on, Chuchu would join it and it would get much livelier. When Chuchu was on the scene, singing got louder, dancing wilder, gossip more scandalous and behaviour more free and easy. Chuchu was big, blonde, busty and brassy. She was also very drunk which made her an ideal companion for Stephen and Porky - but not, definitely not, for Omar.

Chuchu had a small, benevolent looking Arab in tow when she swept in but she swiftly parked him on a banqette once he had ordered her a drink and got into an animated conversation with our party.

'Madam,' Stephen gasped admiringly, 'I have seen plunging necklines in my time, but yours would win an Olympic high diving contest.'

'Glad you like it, dear,' Chuchu beamed. 'It's a special treat for these Eastern gentlemen.' She jerked her thumb towards her escort. 'The Arabs can't resist big tits. No offence,' she assured Omar.

I could see that her tits had been fixed but I was not going to say anything which would spoil anybody's pleasure.

'Hold on, I must take a photograph of them. I'll exhibit it as an Alpine landscape.' Stephen goggled at her decolleté, while Chuchu obligingly posed, looking for all the world like an updated Toulouse Lautrec tart. Her Arab friend nodded his approval and Porky let out a long, loud wolf whistle. The blonde giggled.

'God, this place is like a morgue,' screamed Chuchu, 'What do you say we liven it up?'

The men, other than Omar, hooted their assent.

'Let's give them a song,' Chuchu invited, looking at me.

'Xaviera, I absolutely forbid you to make an exhibition of yourself in a public place.' Omar exclaimed.

Up to that instant, I had no intention of singing, but I was not going to be dictated to by somebody as afraid of his shadow as Omar.

And that's how it was that Chuchu and I ended up, singing in Hebrew and dancing a hora on the piano, in honour of our Arab friends. Porky jumped around, clapping his hands in time with the music, Stephen took countless snapshots, the Arab joined in a chorus of Hatikvah and Omar - Omar disappeared. When I climbed down from the piano, breathless but happy, my boy friend had vanished.

I realized that I was not sorry that he had gone. It had been nice while it lasted but there was no way that I could stay any length of time with a man who was so inhibited himself and who tried to restrain my own natural high spirits.

Porky led off his giggling blonde. Throughout the evening, she had not opened her mouth.

'She's not my regular girl friend,' Porky explained, 'just company for tonight.' Chuchu had secured her Arab: she was not going to share her sugar daddy.

As I got up to go, Stephen squeezed my hand, 'Going my way?' he enquired, pleadingly.

'No, You're coming mine,' I answered.

17

Penthouse Pet

'We can do without butter, but despite all our love of peace, not without arms. One cannot shoot with butter, but with guns.'

Paul Joseph Goebbels

And so, at last, Stephen and I got together. The very first time that I had set eyes on him, I had taken a liking to him and I had always felt that, sooner or later, we would become lovers.

Stephen was full of surprises. I knew, from the way he had been clowning in the bars, that he had drunk enough to sink a battleship and I feared that he would pass out on me before we got home. It had been so much fun and I had so enjoyed his company that I told myself that it would not matter even if I had to pour him through the front door. As it turned out, I found that Stephen was both an alert and affectionate bedmate. As long as I was to know him, Stephen would never have an erection problem - unless he was actually unconscious.

'I have been hoping to get you to myself for so long,' Stephen confessed, as we walked into my apartment, 'but you always seemed to be with some other guy. I had practically given up hope.'

'All good things come to those who wait,' I assured him. 'But as a matter of fact, I have been looking forward to having you, too.'

He took me in his arms and pressed his lips against mine but I pushed him away.

'Get yourself into the bathroom,' I ordered, 'and whatever else you may do, make sure that you clean your teeth after the amount that you have drunk tonight. I keep a guest's tooth brush especially for occasions like this.'

While Stephen showered and cleaned himself up, I

busied myself, making the place appetizing - arranging the lights, putting on some sexy music and tidying up in the bedroom.

'Got something to drink, love?' Stephen called out.

'You have had enough,' I retorted, 'Maybe later, if you deserve it.'

'God, I'll die of thirst,' he threatened.

Stephen joined me on the bed and kissed me passionately. I felt his hot tongue, thrusting into my mouth and at the same moment, his hands were roaming over my body, caressing my breasts, stroking my belly with velvet soft finger tips. This was a new Stephen, not the light hearted, witty clown whom I had known, but a considerate, masterful and experienced lover. I squeezed his heavy balls and ran my fingers over his strong, insistent cock.

'Slow and easy,' I breathed. 'Kiss my titties.'

But Stephen did things his way in his own time. He moved up over my body and pushed his proud penis into my mouth. I sucked him and rippled my teeth up the shaft, all the time licking him until his cock was sopping wet and slippery. Stephen closed his eyes and gasped in bliss. I could feel his excitement mounting and his member growing ever more rigid. In a moment, I had slipped him out of my mouth and with my finger, I pressed behind his balls, checking his climax.

'You wait for me,' I told him.

Then, he took my breasts in his mouth, first one then the other. I could feel that my crotch was sopping wet and I was hot for him. His hand had found my clit and as he rubbed, I heard all the music and saw all the colours.

'Come on, fuck me,' I called.

But Stephen had other ideas. Before I knew what was happening, he had turned me on my belly and was lubricating my ass with my own juices from my aching cunt. I shrieked, as he forced his way into my ass, all the time playing with one hand on my throbbing clitoris. First gently, then ever harder and faster, as I grew used to the feel of him within me, he thrust inside me. I felt myself pinned down and helpless and, as Stephen shot his load up into me, I came in a shattering orgasm.

'Don't tell me,' I said, when I had got my breath back and we were lying side by side, 'it must have been at one of your English boarding schools that you learnt that way of making love.'

Stephen shook his head, 'No. I have spent quite a time in the Middle East and among the Arabs, its not only with the boys that the back door is favoured.'

I knew that no matter how long I had stayed with Omar, he would never have become as free and adventurous a lover as Stephen. Before we went to sleep, he had hardened up again and he came in my vagina and I had a wonderful glow of satisfaction as we settled down in each other's arm for our well earned rest. To his credit, Stephen never asked for that drink again.

Next morning, we had a leisurely breakfast and Stephen told me that he would have to get back to his own place.

'I have not told many people, so it's not general knowledge yet,' he said, 'but I shall be leaving Spain in a few weeks. I have already made arrangements to dispose of my apartment at La Pacheca, but I need to sell the furniture and there is a hell of lot to do before I can get away.'

'Are you leaving for good?'

Stephen nodded. 'It's time for me to move on. I have a great opportunity waiting for me in the UK.'

'In London?'

'No. Running a bus company in the Channel Islands.'

'That doesn't sound much fun.'

'My mother owns the company,' Stephen said apologetically. 'Things are in a bit of a mess and there is a big job for me to try and pull it around.'

'It's not the sort of thing that I would have expected of

you,' I said. 'Tell me, what do you do for a living, when you are not retrieving the family fortunes?'

'I've done a lot of things,' he replied with a mysterious grin. 'Some of them have been more shady than others. Among other jobs, I have been a sort of financial adviser.'

'Was that in the Middle East?'

Stephen nodded.

'And what about the shady things?'

'That's a secret. I expect that I'll tell you about it some time, Xaviera, but not yet.'

'Well, you couldn't have been a bootlegger. You'd have drunk all the stock.'

I had some shopping to do, and we were about to leave when Stephen said, 'Hang on a moment. I must go and strangle a darkie.'

I hadn't the faintest idea what he was talking about so he laughed as he explained, 'It's a phrase I picked up from the lads in the Congo. It means that I must go to the shithouse.'

'And what were you doing in the Congo?'

'Strangling darkies,' Stephen replied.

I had the feeling that he was not completely joking and I wondered what else Stephen had got up to before he had descended on Spain.

As we left the flat, there was one of those chance encounters which can change one's life quite unexpectedly. I wanted to have a word with Matteo, the porter, but when I found him, sitting at his desk, one of my neighbours was in conversation with him. I recognized her as the occupant of the penthouse: I knew that she was a somewhat obscure princess, but we were only on nodding terms. The princess was telling the porter that he should let in to her flat a representative from the firm which managed the block.

'I am selling my apartment,' she told me, 'it's such a nuisance. I'm not used to business and I just want to get away as soon as possible so I am offering it very cheap. But it means people visiting and God knows what legal formalities. I wish that one of my friends wanted the place; it would be so much easier dealing with somebody whom I knew.'

'Why don't you let me see it?' I said, as an idea flashed into my mind. 'I could do with a larger place myself and I like the block.'

'That would be marvellous,' she said. 'Come up now.'

'Do you mind?' I asked Stephen.

'Not at all,' he smiled, 'I'll come with you, if I may. My business can wait for a few minutes.'

It was all so sudden and so fast. We went upstairs and looked at the flat which was double the size of mine. The price was attractive and, on the spot, I agreed to buy the penthouse. Of course, we would have to meet again to thrash out details but, the more I reflected, the more I liked the idea of moving into a bigger and more comfortable flat in my own block. It would mean selling my present flat, but I was sure that I could dispose of it for a good price if I took my time. As for the Princess, she was delighted to get through all the sale of her apartment with the least possible fuss and bother.

'That's a nice place,' Stephen commented, as we left, 'and I think that you have a bargain. But I've never seen anybody clinch a deal so fast. I wish I could find it as easy to get rid of my things.'

'You might just be lucky,' I replied. 'Listen, Stephen, this new flat is twice as big as mine. I need a lot of furniture and household goods. I liked the look of your home when I was there, why don't we go over together and see what is for sale? Maybe I'll take what you want to sell.'

And so, an hour after I had bought a flat, I had also acquired practically all the furniture and fittings which I would need.

For the next few days, I saw a lot of two men, and both of them were Stephen Noble. Stephen by day, that is to say, Stephen sober, was a model of correctness and courtesy. His behaviour was all that one would expect of an English aristocrat and his conduct before members of the opposite sex would have won the approval of Queen Victoria. But, when the serious business of the day was over, Stephen would relax with a glass of cognac which he would refill with breath-taking frequency. He must have had a blotting paper stomach and a sponge of a liver for he was able to absorb alcohol in staggering quantities and without seeming to pause for breath. Stephen by night played Mr Hyde to the Doctor Jekyll of the daylight hours. Not that he was in any way dangerous or objectionable. Stephen drunk was as good company as Stephen sober - provided you did not get easily embarrassed. He became a puckish, scintillating sprite, as mischievous as a kitten, a lecherous leprachaun. I found that his fun and games with Porky and Chuchu were normal for Stephen in his cups. On a number of occasions, I had to take him, more or less, by the scruff of his neck and carry him out of some bar of club where his liveliness was not being appreciated by more conventional souls. Back at home, his vivacity would gradually melt into a tender and sentimental sweetness. For there was a third man in my life - Stephen in bed and, for my money, he was the best of the bunch.

A few days after my decision to buy the penthouse, Stephen and I were at home when the phone rang. It was Jacques.

'Xaviera, Jeannine and I are going to Morocco for a few days next week. I promised to let you know before our next trip in case you would like to come along.'

'I'd love to,' I said, 'but I don't think that I can spare the time. You see, I am in the process of buying a much larger flat, and there's a hell of a lot to do.'

'I understand,' Jacques replied, 'but it might not be a bad idea for you to come. You could buy some carpets and all sorts of things for the house. We could go to Fes, for example: you'd be surprised what you can find in the markets. Anyway, think it over and if you change your mind, call me. We'll be taking the car and plan to leave next Monday. There'll be room for you if you want to come: you could even bring a friend.'

We spent a few more minutes, chatting and I promised Jacques I would call him a day before they left. I related the conversation to Stephen and he said, 'I really don't know why you don't take advantage of Jacques' offer and have a few days off. You have been getting through quite a bit of writing during the days and buying the penthouse and getting your place here ready to sell has meant a lot of work. Why not have a break?'

'Would you come along, if I go?' I asked.

'If that would make you happy, I'd be delighted to have a few days in Africa again. I don't know these people, Jacques and Jeannine, but they sound decent types. It could be fun.'

Stephen was right and I rather hoped that I would find some lovely things for the new flat, as Jacques had suggested. So, that evening, I called him back and asked if he wa. serious about bringing a friend.

'Why not,' Jacques laughed. Then his voice changed. 'It's not that Herman, is it?'

'Don't worry. He would not be interested in the trip,' I reassured him. 'No, this is a much nicer guy.'

Jacques sounded very pleased and when I spoke to Jeannine, she told me how much she was looking forward to seeing me again. By the time we had finished speaking, I was quite excited at the prospect of our excursion.

The day before our departure for Morocco, Stephen and I were lunching at the Marbella Club Hotel. Somehow, with all the changes which have taken place in Marbella, the sedate hotel remains the Number One place which sets the tone for the whole of the Coast. Stephen had played a game of paddle tennis with a Canadian, Mannie, who was one of my oldest acquaintances in that part of the world. Indeed, I had originally met Mannie in Canada about seven or eight years previously and it was with the idea of seeing him again that I had first come to Marbella. Like so many of my friends, Mannie had been in real estate – and in many other businesses as well. He had a natural tendency to sell any piece of property which he came across. I suppose he owned those things he sold, or if not, he, he begged, borrowed, stole or bought.

Mannie had always made a point of keeping himself in good shape and his paddle tennis was a by-word. My recollection of Stephen as a sportsman was his hobbling around the tennis court and wilting under the fusillade of drives and volleys from Franny. I was thrilled therefore when Stephen gave a very creditible account of himself. Indeed, after a strenuous match, he snatched victory from a swearing, sweating Mannie. The two men went to shower, and Mannie agreed to join us for lunch. I went to our reserved table on the terrace and languidly sipped an orange juice while I waited. Looking up, I found myself gazing into the eyes of Omar. He nodded at me coldly and would have passed on without a word, but Hamid and Abdul followed him on to the terrace and, when they saw me, came over to my table.

'Are you alone?' Hamid asked.

'No. I am waiting for friends,' I replied.

'What a pity! You could have lunched with us. However, you have practically finished that orange juice: have a drink with us until they arrive.'

I agreed, and when Stephen and Mannie came out, they found the three men sitting with me, drinks in their hands. Omar recognized Stephen and frowned. I went to make the necessary introductions but somehow, everybody seemed to be acquainted.

One thing was obvious. Mannie had a clear idea of Hamid's wealth and set about trying to sell him a video. The Arab assured Mannie that he was too late: only a couple of days ago he had bought some expensive equipment. Mannie persisted with his hard sell.

Hamid listened patiently and then interrupted: 'I don't want to buy anything today thank you Mr Mannie,' he said. 'Wherever we Arabs go, people try to sell us something. We do get tired of it, you know. The guys who pull off the real sales are the ones who make least fuss. You don't see young Stephen here rushing about with a catalogue in his hand, but he must have done more business with we Arabs than all your high pressure salesmen put together.'

I blinked. This was a new aspect of my cheerful comrade.

'Well,' Stephen murmured softly, 'I had something to sell which they wanted.'

'You didn't sell those videos before I could get in, did you?' Mannie asked anxiously.

'No, nothing like that. It was a few years ago in Oman and I didn't know that Hamid knew about it.'

'The Sultan is a personal friend. If you are still in the business, it is always possible that we could use your services one day,' Hamid replied seriously.

'So, what did you sell in Oman?' I had become curious and I could see that Mannie wanted to know more about these mysterious transactions.

'There were a few tanks and missile launchers, but mostly small arms – automatic rifles and ammunition. All very boring.'

'You were a gun-runner!' Mannie gasped.

'Let's say I was a freelance in the armaments business,' was the smooth reply. 'You see, Mannie, men can say no to videos or even blue movies, but there is no state or revolutionary movement which will turn down the offer of guns. That's the one commodity for which there is always a market.'

'What did you say you were doing in Oman?' I asked.

'I was financial adviser to the Ruler.'

'So you sold the guns to him?'

'I'd rather not comment on who bought my wares. In this business, you have to be discreet. Those arms dealers who are not discreet have a tendency to be dead.'

'How did you get into the business?' I wanted to know.

'Oh, that was easy. You see I was a mercenary in the Congo. As a matter of fact, I was Paymaster General to Tshombe's army, so I knew where to go when I decided to start off in trade on my own account. But that's quite enough about my murky past. Have you told our friends that we are going to Morocco tomorrow, Xaviera? Perhaps they would like us to bring back something for them. I understand that you can buy videos and blue movies very cheap in Ceuta.'

Everybody laughed except Mannie. I found out later that the duty free port of Ceuta had been where Mannie had bought his equipment and he had smuggled the goods into Spain. This was, he believed, a well kept secret, but Stephen had known about it for some time.

'Morocco is an unpleasant place and you will be robbed,' Omar told me pompously. 'In the Gulf States and Saudi Arabia - even in Oman,' with a condescending nod at Stephen, 'you will find the true Arabs. Morocco has been westernized. The people have no breeding: they are simply a mob of merchants.'

'I am going with some friends who know the country well,' I told him, 'and they have led me to understand the reverse to be the truth.'

'Omar, you exaggerate and you are a snob,' Hamid said. 'Thanks for the offer to do some shopping for us but there is nothing that we need. Be careful yourself, Xaviera, if you decide to buy some hash. You could get into trouble.'

I thanked Hamid and then the three men left Stephen,

Mannie and me to get on with our meal. I wondered what sort of trouble we could possibly get into in Morocco. I was soon to find out.

18

The Road To Morocco

'We should consider every day lost on which we have not danced, at least once.'

Nietzsche

The following day, Jacques and Jeannine presented themselves at my front door just as Stephen and I were finishing breakfast. They had already eaten but they joined us for a coffee before we hit the road.

I gladly followed Jacques' suggestion and left my car behind, all four of us travelling in a rugged and rather worn station wagon which Jacques always took for long journeys in preference to his Dune Buggy. We would have plenty of room, Jacques explained for everything that we might purchase and the Moroccan roads would have wrought havoc on my sophisticated BMW. We followed the coast road to Algeciras and took the car ferry across the narrow straits to Tangier. As we passed under the towering mass of Gibraltar, I could not help thinking how absurd it was that to get to the Rock from Spain, visitors were obliged to go to Africa first because of the squabble between the British and the Spaniards. We could see the barbed wire between La Linea and the causeway leading to Gibraltar.

We entered the great sweep of the Bay of Tangier and Jacques pointed to the gleaming white hotels which fringed the golden sands of the beach.

'We'll drive straight to one of those hotels as soon as we have changed some money and reserve a couple of rooms for tonight,' he said.

'Are we going to spend the whole day here?' asked Stephen.

'By no means. I want to get into the Rif Mountains, to Chechaouen actually, but accommodation can prove a bit primitive so I thought that, if you don't mind rather a lot of driving, heading back to Tangier for the night.'

'You're the boss,' I told him.

Passing through the customs was a wearisome business. However, Jeannine told me that coming back would be a hundred times worse, so we waited patiently while officials busied themselves with passports, car registration and insurance papers and a thorough search of the vehicle. At last, the final rubber stamp was affixed to our documents and we rolled through the docks, past the armed guard and into the town.

'First, we must change some money into dirrhem,' said Jacques.

'We'll come with you into the bank,' Stephen told him, 'we have to change some money too.'

'The bank,' Jacques laughed. 'There, that's my bank.'

He pointed to a delapidated cafe on the waterfront. Outside were three or four tables at which several disreputable looking men were sipping mint tea and smoking a mixture of cheap tobacco and local hash. Jacques informed us that the locals always promised that they would give the most favourable rate of exchange for pesetas since they had so many visitors from Spain, but he found that it paid to change dollars despite what they said. So Stephen and I handed him a few hundred dollars and entrusted him with the task of changing them.

Without a moment's hesitation, Jacques walked over to the dirtiest and most dishonest looking of the tea party. The old Berber, dressed in a greasy, brown jellaba favoured us with a smile which exhibited his matching brown tooth to perfection. After several minutes of haggling, a bargain was struck.

The Berber banker then insisted that we take a mint tea with him and, although we wanted to get on the road, it seemed too rude to leave without accepting his hospitality.

As we tasted the stickly, sweet concoction, served in elaborately chipped cups, our host leaned over and asked in a confidential tone whether we would like to buy some hash.

'Yes,' I said.

'No' Jacques exclaimed with great emphasis. Before we left, the Berber whispered something to Stephen, but I could not hear what he said. Stephen laughed, shook his head and slapped the old villain on the back. We got up to leave but after we had walked a few paces, the owner of the cafe ran after us and demanded that we pay for the mint tea.

'It was a present from our friend' Jacques replied, turning to point to the Berber. But the Berber had disappeared so we handed over a few coins to the outraged cafe owner.

We climbed into the car but before we could drive off, a stout, white robed man walked over to us and said, 'Did you buy any hash or kif from that old Berber?'

We shook our heads.

'Good,' said the newcomer, 'now you can buy some from me.'

'Not now,' Jacques called out, as he let out the clutch and we moved away.

'So what did the old fellow have to say to you in the cafe?' I asked Stephen.

'When he whisperd in my ear? Oh, he was asking if I wanted a little boy.'

'What did you tell him?' Jeannine asked.

'I told him that I preferred girls. He seemed to think that I had a perverted taste but volunteered to find a girl for me since I was kinky that way.'

'Why won't you let me buy any dope?' I asked Jacques.

'Not here, Xaviera. These boys are looking out for tourists and they will all overcharge. One guy I know bought a big bag of hash from some of the wide boys and when he came to smoke it, he found that under a thin layer of real hash, he had been supplied with some first class henna. Wait till we get out into the country.'

The Serralio was a brand new five storey hotel on the beach with its name misspelt in huge neon letters. We went inside and waited at the reception desk until a worried looking young man came to attend to us.

We asked for a couple of double rooms. The man regarded us in dismay. Very reluctantly, he opened the register and studied the list of rooms. I looked around me. A dog sleeping in a corner was the only sign of life.

'What's the matter?' I asked the receptionist. 'You can't pretend that you are full.'

It turned out that the hotel was actually empty and our arrival would mean that there would have to be a change in the staff's routine. That is to say they would have to do some work. The receptionist clearly felt that we were acting anti-socially in disturbing their untroubled existence. However, we insisted and we got our rooms. We dropped off our luggage and went out of the hotel, leaving the overworked receptionist, gently sleeping.

There was very little traffic, as we drove out of Tangier towards Tetuan where we stopped to eat some brochettes at a roadside restaurant and then heading into the hills towards Chechaouen. The heat became oppressive as we left the coast and the hills seemed to retain and magnify the intensity of the sunshine. We crossed a tiny, dried-up river and the little town came into view in the folds of the hills. Its white walls, red tiled roofs and the bizarre outline of its octagonal mosque had a dreamlike quality.

I enjoyed walking in the winding streets of the strange, mysterious town. The place had a haunting quietness, not a bit like what I had expected of an Arab town.

'No, this place is exceptional' Jacques assured me. 'Here, you live in the past. Can't you feel the spell of the ancient town? It's magic!'

Jacques had business to do in Chechaouen. We entered a low, white walled building. All the front doors were painted sky blue and the street consisted of a steep stairway, impassible, except by foot. It was quite unlike anywhere I had ever been. The owner of the house was a tall, clean shaven man who surprised me by speaking fluent Spanish to Jacques.

'I thought Moroccans spoke French?' I said.

'This part of the country was occupied by the Spaniards: very few of the locals speak French,' Jacques told me.

He bought a number of hand made clothes, brightly coloured and with a lot of glittering gold embroidery. Stephen and I looked at the various garments but there was nothing which took our fancy.

'Wait till tomorrow,' Jacques assured us, 'you should find something in Fes.'

Before we left Chechaouen, Jacques did take us to another of his acquaintances, and there we bought some kif, which I realized, when I smoked some, certainly was not henna. The wrinkled old man who sold us the stuff informed me that Moroccans were exceptionally healthy because they smoked kif from an early age.

'How many Moroccans do you know with stomach ulcers or cancer?' he asked.

'Perhaps that is because you do not have the same strains and tensions as we do in Europe or the States,' I suggested.

The old man snorted contemptuously, 'It is the kif that gives us long life and good health. All the rest is just an excuse: your doctors are too prejudiced to admit it.'

After we had smoked a little of the weed, we did not feel like arguing with the sage of Chechaouen.

It was a long drive back to Tangier and we got to the hotel, tired, hungry and badly needing a shower. After we had freshened up, Jacques led us into town for a meal. We had rejected the idea of the sandwich shop, next to the hotel, where one could buy half a loaf, stuffed with meat balls, salad, boiled eggs and the shopkeeper's finger for about half a dollar. Instead we decided to patronize the

Mintzah Palace, an old hotel in the centre of what used to be the International zone of Tangier. Not so many years ago, everybody had concessions in Tangier and the French, Spanish, British and even the Belgians, Americans, German and Dutch have left behind stately buildings which housed their diplomats and their staffs. The hotel belonged to that epoch - a world which had passed away for ever.

Inside the stone wall of the hotel was a lush garden with flowers, shrubs and playing fountains. I was reminded that paradise is an Arab word. We found a table in the restaurant, looking out on this peaceful enclosure. Even the roar of the traffic could not penetrate the thick, stone walls and we dined to the accompaniment of the songs of the birds and the gentle humming of the insects. Of course, we ate couscous but also chicken cooked in juicy plums and wonderful aromatic spices and herbs. It was all very beautiful and formal, but not lively enough for the likes of Stephen. With our meal, we had a couple of bottles of Moroccan wine, rather heavy and on the sweet side, Stephen informed me.

'And rather stronger than you might imagine,' Jacques warned.

I don't think that Stephen took this seriously. Everybody was thirsty and the wine disappeared rapidly. I noticed that Stephen became a trifle flushed and he began to liven up. I recognized the signs.

We strolled out of the hotel refreshed and full of food. We needed a walk to settle our stomachs and, naturally, we turned down a stony path which led into the old town - the medina of Tangier. The quarter of the souk, the market place where food was sold was quiet and deserted but the other stalls and shops were still open. One sold hand made perfumes and cosmetics and I bought a couple of jars of a body oil which had a fragrance of fresh herbs and essences quite unlike the synthetic smells offered by the glamorous names of fashion in the West.

Jeannine suggested that we took a coffee on the terrace of one of those cafes which seem to stay open for twenty four hours a day, but Stephen was in search of something stronger, so we emerged into the modern town where night clubs stood side by side with banks and offices in the area on the other side of the broad boulevard.

We found a spot, misleadingly named 'Night and Day.' It was strictly a night establishment. There were three or four bar girls wearing rather old-fashioned western clothes. They looked hopefully at the men, but glared resentfully at Jeannine and myself. Women coming into bars were bad news for their business.

A gang of musicians arrived and proceeded to get everybody good and groovy with a racket which sounded like rock arranged for an orchestra of road drills, motor horns and double bass. There was a raised dancing floor and on it a group of girls jumped up and down, more or less in time with the music. They wore broad grins and lacy knickers, which they showed by lifting their skirts as they performed.

'Do you want to dance?' I asked Jacques.

He shook his head and added, 'No, thank you, and neither do you. It is understood that the girls who are on the floor are all prostitutes and are available. It would definitely not be a good idea to join in.'

We had a few drinks and Stephen tried singing some lewd words to the music, but the noise level was so loud that his efforts passed mercifully unnoticed.

Suddenly, the music stopped and the girls scurried off the floor. There was an air of expectancy and a man who acted as MC and chucker-out combined, made an announcement in Arabic. It sounded as if it were of earth shattering importance and it was greeted with rapturous applause.

'It is a dancer,' Jacques told us. 'She is very famous and has performed in Cairo and Tripoli before coming here. Afterwards, she has a contract to appear in a well-known

Arabic restaurant and night club in Paris.'

We settled down for the show: even Stephen behaved himself, as the orchestra reassembled and broke into a lively dance. A plump, muscular but good-looking woman whirled on to the stage, dressed in a wispy, long skirt and a sequinned bra. She danced barefoot and around her feet and her wrists, she wore tinkling bangles. Her movements were sinuous and her footwork dazzlingly fast. Her act was punctuated with cheers and rounds of clapping as she executed some particularly difficult movement.

Then the music slowed down, and her movements became more seductive. She stretched her arms out to the onlookers and moved down to dance around the individual tables and the men, sitting at the bar. As she hovered over the men, they took money from their wallets and stuffed banknotes, sometimes of very high value, into her bra or her girdle until she began to look like a well-stocked christmas tree.

Then, she got to us. Jacques placed his donation just below the lady's navel. During this manoeuvre, she swayed her hips rhythmically but the rest of her body was immobile. Her body flowed like a river: it was an impressive display, graceful and well controlled. That was, until Stephen intervened.

'I know this tune,' he announced triumphantly, 'it's "Knees Up Mother Brown".'

And with that, he leaped to his feet and attempted to join the lady in a somewhat unorthodox pas de deux.

His efforts were not appreciated by the locals, who shouted to him to sit down. Stephen took their cries as encouragement, and started to do a dance which resembled Groucho Marx doing a twist, as he circled the unfortunate artiste. She too, was not pleased at his unsolicited assistance and she hissed something to him which might well have been an invitation to drop dead. 'Sit down, you idiot,' I called to Stephen but his artistic inspiration rendered him deaf to all comments and suggestions.

To this day, I do not know how we managed to get out of the joint without bloodshed. I saw the MC-bouncer, striding over to Stephen and he was joined by some enthusiastic member of the public who resented Stephen's interference with the act of their idol. Jacques was on his feet in a flash and I saw him thrust some money into the bouncer's paw with one hand, and seize Stephen with the other. Between us, we hustled him out of the place, still singing and oblivious to the fuss he had caused.

Outside, Stephen suggested that we went on to somewhere a bit more lively.

'I think that it is late enough,' Jeannine told him in a soothing tone. 'Tomorrow we want to make an early start. We have a long journey in front of us. Let's get back to the hotel.'

The cool night air had an effect on our boisterous companion and he agreed meekly to being led home and put to bed.

As we settled ourselves in the car, a ragged man slipped out of the shadows and put his hand on Stephen's arm through the open window.

'Would you like a young boy?' he offered, 'beautiful skin, a virgin, very cheap. Tomorrow he is being given to the King so it is your last chance.'

Stephen giggled and was about to say something but Jacques swiftly slammed the car into gear and drove off. By the time we reached the hotel, Stephen was slumbering like a baby. I think that he even got upstairs and into bed without opening his eyes.

19

Have You Anything To Declare?

'Rich gifts wax poor when givers prove unkind.'
Shakespeare

Stephen complained that I was unsympathetic when he crawled out of bed the next morning. His hangover was horrible to behold: that was his way of describing it. Jacques and Jeannine had risen early and were busily preparing for our departure. At the prospect of breakfast, Stephen's complexion turned a most unattractive shade of green but, with an effort, we managed to decant him into the car although he protested that we had left his head upstairs.

'Look here,' Jacques said, 'you are in no condition for a long ride on Moroccan highways. Before we get going, I'll take you to one of the public baths and get you a massage. It'll make a new man of you.'

Stephen objected, but Jacques was adamant and we descended on the 'Old Town', where there were a number of shabby buildings proclaiming to the world that they were 'Spanish Bath' or 'German Bath', but, in fact they were all Arab baths. Jeannine and I decided that we would look around the shops and stalls when we found that the baths were strictly segregated. Before we departed, we overheard the following conversation:

Jacques: 'How much is a bath?'

Attendant: 'Five dirrhem for one person, twenty for two.'

Jacques: 'That's ridiculous. My friend, here, needs a hot bath and a massage. Alone! And you can't ask for more than a couple of dirrhem.'

Attendant: 'But for that money he gets as much hot water as he wants and soap and the use of a towel. For another five dirrhem, I'll bring him a lovely boy. Bathing alone is not good for a man: it makes him feel lonely.'

Jacques: 'Two dirrhem. And you can find somebody to give him a good body massage.'

Attendant (brightening up) 'Three dirrhem as a special favour since today is my birthday. and I can get you a wonderful masseuse - it'll cost another twenty dirrhem and for that you can have the little boy thrown in for nothing. Now that's really a bargain!'

Eventually, the miserable Stephen got his bath for three dirrhem and the massage for another ten, without the benefit of a little boy.

'You're certain that this is going to do me good?' he asked

'Sure! Now we have the terms agreed, I'll join you, myself' answered Jacques.

The attendant wailed that he was being swindled and tried to go back to his original price but, on being given a firm undertaking that there would be no intercourse between the two men, he resigned himself to the fact that the poor, benighted Europeans did not know what baths were for and he hurried off to get hold of a stocky, good humoured man of about forty who administered massage.

Three quarters of an hour later, we were on the road, heading inland with Stephen transformed into a bright, sprightly creature - quite his old self.

'There were a sequence of steam rooms,' he told us, 'getting hotter as you went further in - not unlike a normal Turkish bath except that you sat on the floor and threw buckets of hot water over yourself. Then this type came along and pulled every muscle of your body out of their sockets. But the amazing thing was the way he slithered his own body against yours and used his body to get enormous leverage in his pulling and pushing until you were completely toned up. Remarkable!'

'Did you like frolicking naked with another man?' I asked.

'Oh, but you don't bath naked,' Stephen assured me.

'That's the strange thing. The Moroccans are not shy about sex as you may have noticed and they are for ever offering ass. Yet, in the baths, men are expected to keep on their underpants. You pour buckets of water into your trunks like in a Laurel and Hardy film but nobody shows a bare butt.'

Despite his stay in Oman, Stephen admitted that he had never before been to a 'Haamman', an Arab bath: it had certainly acted as a tonic on him.

It was late in the afternoon when we drove into the old city of Fes. We found a hotel without difficulty and spent the evening and part of the following morning in the great souk, perhaps the most exciting market place in the whole of the country. Jacques and Jeannine dealt with their shopping skilfully and purposefully. They showed me the row after row of shops specializing in carpets, ceramics and all sorts of metal wares - the things which could be useful in fitting out my new flat. I bought a few items but most of the wares were traditional in design and my taste is more in favour of a modern style.

It was a different story when I saw the work of the gold and silversmiths. There were brooches, rings, bangles and every conceivable kind of decoration, all exquisitely worked into elaborate and complicated designs. I bought a beautiful locket in rich, glowing gold; I was intrigued by the maze-like design. Later, I found that I was wearing the name of the Prophet around my partly Jewish neck.

'We'll have a quiet evening tonight,' Jacques stated with a pointed look at Stephen. 'Fes is a holy city and the sort of thing which happened in Tangier would land us all in jail here.'

'That's alright' smiled Stephen, 'Let's go and have a drink.'

'Alcoholic drinks are not sold in Fes.' Jacques told him. 'As I said, it is a holy city.'

Stephen reeled under the shock and docilely allowed

himself to be led away to dinner – with water and orange juice. Afterwards, we walked around the ancient city – 'the naval of Morocco' as it has been called. It had been a long day and after a short time, we took ourselves off to bed.

I had no reason to complain about Fes by night. Dear Stephen was stone cold sober. Our lovemaking was relaxed and leisurely and we fell into an untroubled sleep. I awoke to find that Stephen was taking me in his arms, nibbling gently my ear and I could feel his hot, straining penis pushing against my skin. I love that languid, muzzy sex which belongs to the moments before I am fully awake. Stephen had eased my legs open without my realizing what had happened and he slipped inside me without any fuss. Happily, I savoured his 'morning glory'.

Suddenly, I was completely awake and scared out of my wits. The room seemed to be filled by a shrill howling. At first, it was just one voice, but within seconds, more and more unearthly screams joined in.

'It's all right,' Stephen comforted me, 'it's only the muezzins calling the Faithful to prayer. At dawn, they cry out from every minaret. And Fes is a holy city!'

'It's put me right off,' I told my lover.

'Nonsense! You'll find as they go on, it'll get to you.'

Strangely enough, he was right. There was something unworldly about the call of the muezzins, almost frightening which stirred the depths of my being. I did not like the noise, but it did something to me and I found myself fucking with a sort of barbarous intensity. I gripped Stephen fiercely and, as those eerie voices grew louder and more intense, our excitement mounted. I came in a wild, uncontrollable orgasm and let out a piercing scream, just at the moment that the muezzins outside, as one man, fell silent. A few seconds later, Stephen pumped his load of sperm into me, but he had the good manners to keep quiet about it.

'Were you disturbed by the morning prayers?' Jeannine

asked us at breakfast.

'Not really,' Stephen lied fluently, 'we went straight back to sleep.'

'That's strange' purred Jacques, 'I could swear that I heard Xaviera joining in.'

After the morning tour of the souk, we took to the road and made for Tangier at full speed, since we wanted to get one of the evening boats back to Spain. We made good time and we stopped at Tetuan, about three quarters of an hour's drive from Tangier, where Jacques and Jeannine wanted to buy some fresh herbs, mint and marjoram, cumin and coriander, all wonderfully fragrant.

While they were occupied with the shopkeeper, Stephen and I were standing next to the car when a chubby man with twinkling eyes and a bushy moustache approached us.

'Hello,' he chortled gaily, 'Are you English? Francais? Deutsch? Italiano?'

He would have gone through the roll call of the United Nations but I stopped him and said that my friend was English and that I was Dutch.

'That's wonderful!' He spoke in French with a strong guttural accent 'You are tourists. They are always so friendly. If there were more tourists there would be no wars.' He patted my arm.

Our new buddy babbled on. He wanted us to promise to write to him when we got home and 'inshe Allah' he would come and visit us in London or Amsterdam or anywhere else, one day. It was Fate that had decided that we should meet and he was fortunate enough to be standing where we had parked the car at the right moment to meet his destiny. We would always be welcome at his home - 'Number One, Next to the Bus Station Tetuan.'

To seal our friendship, we were invited to smoke a little hash with the stranger and he rummaged in his pocket and produced a fair sized lump.

'What, smoke here?' I asked.

'But, of course, why not?'

'Not just now, thank you,' Stephen told him.

'What's the matter? Am I not good enough to smoke with you? Are you too high and mighty to even talk with a poor Moroccan?'

'Don't be silly,' I told the enraged little man. 'We know that smoking hash is illegal in your country and, as foreigners, we are not going to take the risk of smoking in public.'

My remarks was greeted with hoots of laughter.

'That's absurd. Everbody smokes. Here I'll make us a joint.'

I shook my head. 'Maybe everybody does smoke but there are posters all over town threatening the most horrible punishments for anyone caught smoking or taking drugs in any form. Since we are foreigners, we'd rather not take the risk.'

The friend of the human race smiled and shrugged his shoulders.

'Very well,' He assented smugly, 'if that is what you want, but, I tell you, that you are being very foolish. However, we are friends, so I will give you this little lump of hash to take home and smoke in your own place. When you smoke it, think of me.'

He went to hand the hash to Stephen, but was met with another refusal.

'Now, what's the matter?'

'Listen, our good friend,' Stephen said, 'we are on our way to Spain. In an hour or two we'll have to pass through Moroccan customs at Tangier and then, when we get to Algeciras, Spanish customs. There is no way that my girl friend or I are going to try carrying drugs through those controls.'

'You don't understand', the Moroccan insisted. 'Of course, if you were to try to take a great, big parcel of hash through the customs you would have a problem. But a little piece, like this! Nobody cares about a tiny piece just for you to smoke. I guarantee, everybody takes a tiny piece like that as a souvenir of their stay in our country. The police, the customs, neither of them are interested. Here, take it.'

I felt that there was something wrong and nudged Stephen, 'Let's get back into the car' I whispered.

'Thanks a lot, old man, but we'd rather not,' said Stephen, as he sidled towards the car.

'Very well. Go in peace - and don't forget to write,' Our over-friendly acquaintance leaned over and kissed Stephen on the cheek, dropping his hands swiftly from Stephen's shoulders before turning on his heel and striding away. In a second, he was lost in the crowd.

'Hello, you two, who was your friend?' Jacques had emerged just on time to see our parting. 'You seemed to have made quite a hit with him, Stephen.'

We got into the car and told Jacques and Jeannine what had happened in their absence. As he heard our story, Jacques began to look serious.

'I saw him run his hands down your shirt front,' he told Stephen, 'check to see that he didn't lift your wallet without your noticing.'

'He didn't strike me as a pickpocket,' Stephen replied, 'but I'll certainly check to see if anything is missing.'

He examined the contents of his pockets.

'Did he take anything?' I asked.

'Quite the reverse,' Stephen answered with a smile. 'He left me a present!' And, between his thumb and forefinger, he held out that dark brown chunk of hash.

'Very kind of him' I muttered,

'Very suspicious,' Jeannine observed.

We had driven off during this conversation but Jacques now braked. We had stopped just outside the town, and he turned to me and said, 'Xaviera, do you feel like having a quiet smoke?'

'Sure, but I thought that we were in a hurry.'

'Do me a favour. Make a few joints. Use up all that hash: but do it now.'

It didn't seem to be a bad idea and for the next half hour, we smoked our heads off. We kept all the windows open and when we had finished, Jeannine sprayed the inside of the car with some pretty strong perfume.

I felt good and Stephen was positively light-headed.

'It's been great fun,' I said to Jacques and Jeannine, as we rolled gently through the dock gates at Tangier. 'Thank you for inviting us to come along.'

'We're not back yet,' Jacques said grimly.

I was encouraged to see that the cars in front of us were moving quickly through the customs shed. Obviously, they were only receiving a cursory glance. The customs men were having an easy day. Or were they?

When it came to our turn, one of the customs men stepped out and checked the registration number of our car. Then he called out something to some of his colleagues and two more officials walked over to us.

'Have you anything to declare?'

'A few things we have bought in the market.'

'May I have a look, please?'

Jeannine and I opened the back of the car and displayed our treasures. The official cast his eye over the things without any show of interest.

'Tell me,' he said, 'do you, by any chance happen to have any hashish?'

We exchanged glances.

'No' answered Jacques.

The custom man put the same question to each of us in turn and received the same negative response.

'Not even a tiny piece?' he asked. There was an unpleasant, supercilious tone to his voice.

Again, each of us had to give an answer.

'Not a trace of hashish?' This time there was no mistaking the menace in his voice.

Very emphatically each of us denied having a trace of the drug.

'Very well, we'll see about that.'

Our interrogator nodded to his two companions.

'Drive over there,' he pointed to a shed. Jacques obeyed.

'Outside' he ordered. All the early politeness had vanished. 'Get those cases over on to the tables!'

We followed the three customs men inside the shed and put our cases on the tables behind which they had taken their places. They knew exactly what they were looking for and they wasted no time with non-essentials. One of them went over our pockets while the other two made an unholy mess of our clothes.

'Excuse me,' Jacques asked, 'but are you going to be long? We particularly want to catch the next boat.'

'You'll go when we have finished with you,' he was told. 'And if the boat goes before we're through with you, then you'll miss it.'

'You boys must be a great help to the tourist trade,' I flared up.

'Don't be impertinent,' ordered the first customs man.

We decided to ignore them and chatted among ourselves. This seemed to put the officials off. They had expected us to be terror-stricken and our casualness quite spoilt their pleasure. The minutes ticked by and their self-confidence began to seep away. They ferreted about with ever growing desperation, but they could see from our unconcern that they were on to a loser.

'We're only doing our job' one of the Moroccans apologized.

'Once you guys have a uniform, you think that you can bully everybody,' I told him. 'Why don't you get on and finish? I don't care if you waste your time, but I do object to your wasting ours.'

'We shan't be long,' mumbled the second man, as he fumbled with some of Jeannine's underwear.

'You make me sick,' I told him. There was an icy edge to my voice and I could see that my words were getting through. 'I don't want to stay in the same building as you. I am going to stand outside and get a bit of fresh air. You can call me when you want to see me or when you are through.'

I glared right through the miserable creatures and flounced out of the shed. Nobody said a word or lifted a finger to prevent me.

A few minutes, later, I was joined by my companions, still grappling with their cases as they tried to close them on their rumpled possessions.

While we had been away, there had been a check on our car but now we were able to drive through the control and on to the dockside, where the ferry was waiting.

As we steamed away, I stood by the rail, looking my last at Morocco.

'That poisonous little man at Number One next to the Bus Station, Tetuan. I wonder how much he would have copped from the customs boys if they had found what he had planted.'

'We'd have been heavily fined,', Jacques said, 'and, I believe that he would have got about ten per cent for his trouble.'

'Must be one of the country's sources of revenue,' Stephen observed.

'They're a poor country and a lot of them consider any foreigner as fair game for plunder,' Jacques replied, 'Still, it was not without its funny side, standing there while those idiots searched high and low, knowing that we were absolutely clean and not carrying anything.'

'You speak for yourself,' I rejoined.

'What do you mean, Xaviera? We had smoked all the hash that was planted on Stephen by that slimy bastard in Tetuan, hadn't we?'

'Oh sure,' I answered, 'But have you forgotten the kif I bought at Chechaouen?'

'That had all gone, hadn't it?'

I shook my head.

Jacques' expression was one of a man in shock.

'You mean that you were standing in there with kif on you?'

'That's right.'

'Where were you carrying it?'

'Well Jacques, let me put it this way. You should be too much of a gentleman to ask and I am too much of a lady to tell you . . . But that's why I had to get out of that damned shed. It was slipping and I needed to make some rapid adjustments.'

My luck held. There was no body check at the customs at Algeciras.

20

Men of War

'A good soldier has his heart and soul in it. When he receives an order, he gets a hard-on and when he sends his lance into the enemy's guts, he comes.'

Bertolt Brecht

Back in Spain, Jacques and Jeannine left us, but first made me promise that Stephen and I would come up to Ojen the following week-end for the annual feria - a sort of combination of a fair and a carnival.

Both Stephen and I had plenty to do, what with the legal formalities for my purchase of the penthouse and then arranging to have Stephen's furniture transported to my new home. I was delighted that the princess allowed me access to the apartment before the end of the complicated ritual which accompanies the buying of a property on Spain. As Stephen was now bereft of his furniture, he was obliged to stay with me - an arrangement to which neither of us took exception . . . For his part, Stephen had to clear up his affairs preparatory to his quitting Spain.

We were sitting in my lounge, relaxing one evening. For a change, neither of us felt like talking a lot: in both our minds was the thought that very soon we would be heading for Northern Europe. For me, my Spanish summer was drawing to a close and I was getting ready to say goodbye to Spain for another year. As for Stephen, his adieus had more finality to them. Heaven alone knew when, if ever, he would be returning to Spain and there was inevitably a tinge of melancholy which toned down his normal exuberance.

'I'll tell you what, Stephen. Why don't you come back with me when I leave? It would be company for me in the car and you could take a turn with driving.'

'But, love, I am going to England, home and beauty, not the Low Countries.'

'You don't have to make the place sound like a depressed area! Anyway, if you are not in too great a hurry, you could stay a few days in Amsterdam. Be my guest; I promise you won't be bored.'

'I'm sure of that.' Stephen grinned. 'But I can't hang on here for weeks while you finish the buying of the penthouse.'

'Don't worry. I need to get back, too. I don't have to stay. My lawyer can complete the deal for me. I want to leave as soon as we get back from Ojen.'

'Well, that would suit me very well,' Stephen said diffidently. 'I'll come along if you promise me that you will drive nice and quietly and not try to burn up the road and put your car into orbit.'

'I promise I shall drive like a lady.'

'I don't believe you, but I'll take a chance.'

Our conversation was interrupted by the phone. It was Porky McGrew.

'Oh, Xaviera, you're back! I tried to get hold of you a few days ago.'

'I've just got back from a trip to Morocco.'

'Glad to catch you . . . Listen, honey, I am going up north next week to pick up a new boat which has been built for me. I'd like to say ciaou to you and your limey boy friend before I leave. How about the two of you coming over here for a drink and a bite to eat tomorrow night?'

I consulted Stephen and as he had no objection, I agreed.

That evening, we went to dinner at La Consuela, a pretty restaurant in the Old Town managed by a sensitive, gay Englishman whom I had always liked as much for his amusing small talk as for his culinary inventiveness. Stephen had a few things to clear up with somebody in La

Pacheca and we arranged that he would join me at the restaurant.

'Good evening, Xaviera,' Gary, the manager greeted me, as I walked into the dining room. 'I don't often see you alone. A quiet table for one, dear?'

'No, I have a friend who will be joining me shortly. Don't worry, Gary I'm not on the shelf yet!'

'I wouldn't have thought so for a moment. Would it happen to be my cousin that you are dining with, by any chance?'

'Your cousin?'

'Stephen Noble?'

I nodded. 'I had no idea that he was your cousin.'

Gary laughed. 'There's no reason why you should: we don't look alike and we don't see a lot of each other. It's not many aristocratic, old families which can boast two black sheep.'

Gary had led me to a table which gave a view of the narrow footpath on which the restaurant fronted, through a screen of verdant greenery. A red shaded lamp stood on the red gingham tablecloth, stiffly starched and spotlessly clean . . .

'You know,' I said, 'Stephen has never told me anything about his family and life back in England. Tell me, Gary, is Noble his real name?'

Gary stared at me and then a sly smile spread across his face.

'Now, tell me, Xaviera, why on earth do you ask me that?'

'I honestly don't know. The idea just came into my head.'

'Well, you must be psychic, darling,' Gary was amused and astonished. 'No, Noble is not his real name. As a matter of fact, his family is one of the oldest and most illustrious in the country. He chose the name Noble as a sort of joke, because the family is noble, you see.'

'So why is he living incognito?'

Gary shrugged his shoulders.

'There have been episodes in the life of my dear cousin which are regarded as rather shocking by our highly respectable relatives. In fact, come to think of it, there were precious few episodes which did not shock them.'

'Tell me more,' I urged Gary.

'Not me, love. I don't see a lot of Stephen but I respect him and I am not going to be a party to Marbella gossip. But you could get him to tell you some of the things which he got involved in when he was in the Congo. It should appeal to a writer – Stephen's secret life, I mean. Get him to talk and you will have material for a half a dozen books.'

'But he doesn't talk. He's full of this English stiff upper lip, no chattering in the mess, baloney.'

Gary nodded with a smile. 'He keeps up the upper class tradition of tact and understatement even if he does not always behave like the perfect gent. Catch him with a glass in his hand when he has had a few.'

Our discussion was cut short by the arrival of Stephen himself and I carefully avoided the subject during dinner. However, it was never far from the surface of my mind and my opportunity came far quicker than I had expected.

The following evening we went, as promised, over to Porky's villa. It was a splendid place, perched in the hills with a great, sweeping view across the sea as far as the looming mass of Gibraltar in the far distance. Although it was still summer, there was a hint of autumn in the air and there was too much of a breeze for us to stay in comfort on the terrace. There was a mild disorder about the place, reflecting the temporary absence of Porky's regular girl friend. He and Stephen sprawled in deep, comfortable easy chairs, swapping yarns . . . I had wandered into the kitchen to get a fresh bottle of orange juice. On the way back, I stopped to look at an old, framed photograph of a slim, young man in uniform, standing in front of a fighting plane of the propeller era.

'Good God, Porky, was that handsome hunk of manhood you, before you put on that belly?'

'That's right, Xaviera. Way back in World War Two, I was a Navy pilot. That's how I got into the flying business.'

'What did you fly?' Stephen enquired.

'Fighters. Carrier based. You Brits called them Corsairs.'

Stephen nodded . . . 'I remember them.'

Porky burst out laughing. 'How could you remember them? You're too young. When we were winning the Battle of the Atlantic for you fine, old, English gentlemen, you were still in your cradle.'

I was amazed when Stephen reeled off a mass of technical data about the aircraft. Porky gazed at him, open mouthed. Then he recovered himself and exclaimed, 'Oh, I get it. You're one of those plane enthusiasts. Learnt all about them from books: probably made models of the damned things when you were a school kid.'

'Not at all, ancient warrior. I dare say I've flown more of those crates than you have.'

There was nothing boastful about Stephen's remark: just a plain, factual statement.

'Now, how can that be?' Porky's eyes were popping out of his head in bewilderment and indignation.

Stephen smiled. 'What do you think happened to all those aircraft at the end of the war? They didn't simply vanish, you know.'

'Sure thing!' Porky beamed at both of us. 'That's how I got going. You could buy them all . . . fighters, bombers, transports, you name it, for next to nothing. I laid my hands on a couple of old B-25s, took out the bomb bays and had them running as freighters, supplying the American army in Germany. Eventually, I had my own airline. Of course, I've sold it now.'

'And where did you buy your planes?' Stephen asked.

'From the US Army in Germany – indirectly.'

'You mean that you made your money by flying supplies for the US Army, using their own planes?' I demanded.

'That's right. I had a little help, if you follow me. Before I took the planes, I had a charter agreement and I got them real cheap. Hardly anything down, and the rest on deferred terms.'

'B-25s were not the only planes to be traded. There were a few of your carrier based wrecks which passed through my hands.' Stephen said.

'But they couldn't carry anything. They'd have no payload.'

'Porky, old fruit, my customers weren't going into the airline business.'

There was a pause as the implications of Stephen's statement percolated into Porky's consciousness.

'So, you were an arms dealer?'

'Among other things. Just think, Porky, I might have sold your plane.'

Porky shook his head. 'Not a chance. What's left of Mary Lou is rusting away at the bottom of the Bay of Biscay.'

'Mary Lou?' I queried.

'I named my plane after a kid who used to be a cheer leader for our local football team.'

'You were shot down?'

Porky needed no more encouragement. He described in graphic detail how he had been shot down in 1943. He would have lost his life but for the chivalry of the German pilot.

While Porky talked, I was watching Stephen. He was drinking quite heavily but the light-hearted prankishness which normally accompanied alcohol was absent that evening.

'Does Porky's war story bring back memories?' I asked him.

'Yes,' his voice was subdued. 'I suppose that there is a quality about war which makes the deepest impressions on us. Once you have seen the fighting and the brutality that goes with it, you can never forget it, like a scar in your mind that will be with you as long as you live.'

'But you were too young for the World War and I don't suppose you got caught up in Viet Nam,' Porky observed.

'War is a business and those of us who are professionals will always find a war somewhere to give employment for our talents.'

'Stephen, I know that you have traded arms, but the way you speak, one would think that you were a mercenary.'

'Oh, but I was, Xaviera. I have not been paid merely to provide weapons but also to make sure that they were used with the maximum effect - and that meant often using them ourselves.'

'Where was that, pal?'

'Here and there, Porky. Notably in what used to be the Belgian Congo and the province of Katanga.'

'Yes,' I said, 'I remember now, you told me that you were Paymaster to Tshombe. And then, later you were in Oman.'

'Oman? Didn't the sheikh of that place die under rather mysterious circumstances some years ago?' Porky's face was wrinkled as he delved into his memory.

'The father of the present Sultan Qaboos was assassinated.' Stephen's tone was terse, almost like a lawyer dealing with a piece of evidence in court.

'I heard that the whole thing was put up and paid for by the British,' Porky breathed.

Stephen said nothing and I recollected how reticent he had been with me when the subject of Oman had come up in our conversation with Hamid.

'What about the Congo?' I asked. 'Was that as messy as people say?'

Stephen nodded. 'Yes, there was nothing of Porky's old world chivalry. We had no gallant Gunthers. There was bestial behaviour on both sides. It was a dirty war and we fought dirtier, so we won.'

'I remember hearing about a lot of raped nuns,' Porky said.

Stephen snorted. 'There's a story of raped nuns in every war. I think they were Belgian nuns at the beginning of the First World War. Perhaps they were the grandmothers of the ones in the Congo.'

'You mean that there weren't any nuns?'

'There were women - maybe some were nuns. I saw them alive and - afterwards. In fact, I suppose we were instrumental in getting the creatures raped and in what followed!'

Both Porky and I were curious to hear Stephen's story and Porky encouraged him by refilling his glass.

'Maybe you recall that the Belgians were chucked out of the Congo by black nationalists who set up their own government with Lumumba as prime minister. But the wealth of the country - and believe me, it has everything you can imagine in the way of minerals were in the province of Katanga. There were some boys in the Union Minière, that was the company which virtually ran the country when it was a colony, who were mates of mine, never mind how. They'd set this guy Tshombe up to head a breakaway state of Katanga and they got me to recruit a batch of well-trained European, Australian and South African mercenaries to pull off the coup. They rather hoped, as they put it to me, that Lumumba's troops could be shown up as the barbarians that they were.

'Well, the uprising was carried out without too much difficulty and there was a bit of sporadic fighting but nothing to hit the headlines. If anything, world opinion tended to be on the side of Lumumba since he was the constitutional head of the state and he was approved of by the UN Secretary General, Dag Hammerskjold. Our Belgian buddies were not put off by that: one more air crash and the United Nations had to find a new Secretary General. However, I had nothing to do with that.

'The Belgians had shipped out money to pay the troops. They were not too bothered about the natives, Tshombe's boys, but they knew very well that the mercenaries would only fight as long as they were paid and without the mercenaries, the whole uprising would collapse. Of course, they were not the only people who knew that - so did Lumumba and his ill-equipped, half-starved and underpaid soldiers . . . If they could lay their hands on that bullion, it was a fair bet that they would win the war. If not, sooner or later they would be cut to pieces. So they were pretty desperate, and we knew it.

'We had the stuff safe and sound in a missionary station - a solid, stone built place which could be defended. There were detachments of Lumumba's troops outside in the hills but they could not attack while we were in the station with a few old Bren carriers and some half-tracks and armed to the teeth.

'Both sides made their plans and it was a game of cat and mouse - but it wasn't clear which of us was the cat and which the mouse. Their chance came when they ambushed one of Tshombe's patrols about twenty kilometres away. A straggler got away and came to the station to beg us to send reinforcements before it was too late. Lumumba's boys were no fools: they'd let this lad get away so as to lure us out into the open.

'We decided to take the bait but before we drove out to relieve the Katangan patrol, we warned the missionaries to get the hell out of the place.

'"But we have to stay and look after the sick" an elderly Flemish doctor cum priest told us.

'"You'd better get them out as well or else they'll be worse than sick" we told him. "If you are still here in a couple of hours, you'll look like a jigsaw puzzle."

'The missionaries pleaded with us to leave a few of our men behind to protect them but mercenaries are investments. They cost money and you don't squander them. Like I told you, war is a business and mercenaries have a market value: missionaries don't. When we hit the trail, some of the sick had been loaded into an old truck and the Belgians were fussing about, trying to get themselves organized.'

'You expected that the Congolese soldiers, Lumumba's boys, would attempt a raid on the missionary station to get their hands on the boodle?' Porky asked.

'Of course. We had a couple of American journalists with us but we thought that it was better that they should not have the facts of life spelt out for them. After all, our boys were the rebels, even if you disapproved of Lumumba and his politics and a few martyrs would go a long way to win our men international support - above all from the Americans. As far as the journalists were concerned, we were rushing to support one of our patrols which was under fire against overwhelming odds. It was a good enough story and they got quite excited, like a troop of boy scouts.'

'And did you get to the patrol in time?'

Stephen laughed grimly. 'Oh, yes, Xaviera. There was never any doubt that we should get to them. They were pinned down on the highway between a couple of hills. There were about twenty of them, crouching in the ditch beside the road. They were scared shit stiff and in their panic even fired a few rounds at us, as we came to their aid. Three of them were dead. They had been riddled when they first ran into the ambush. Some of the others were wounded. One way or another, there was quite a bit of blood about. However, when we got there, there was precious little gunfire.

'We drove up to our position. The only shots were those of our panicky lads as we swung round the bend of the road. Their aim was so wild that even the reporters weren't scared.

'It was not very difficult to see the tactics of the Lumumba boys. As long as we stayed in our ditch, they left us in peace but the moment we tried to break out and head back the way we had come, they fired everything they had at us. That woke the journalists up and they were scribbling away like mad, with their heads well down. Those of us who were experienced saw at once that we were not under very intense fire, but we were not going to spoil the story for the great American public. So we hung about for a couple of hours before we decided that the farce had gone far enough.

'Half a dozen of us mercenaries slipped into the bush beside the road and made towards the enemy. We had grenades and automatics and we were covered by fire from the rest of the lads on the road. It didn't take long. There were just three of them, lying in a hollow and armed with rifles which they must have got from a museum. They were concentrating on the boys who had fanned out from the half tracks and Bren carriers and were keeping up a steady fire on them. One of our men, he used to be a gamekeeper in South Africa, crawled close enough to lob a grenade. We ducked down. There was a big bang and then – silence.

'We rushed the position. One of the black soldiers was definitely dead. A fragment of the grenade had severed the artery in his neck and blood was still gushing out. The other two were pretty badly hurt and shaken. They threw down their guns and raised their hands. We cut them to pieces with fire from the automatics. Prisoners would simply be a nuisance – and the reporters were out of sight with their heads down at the roadside.

'We got back to the road and loaded up the trucks. But before we drove off, we stopped to take a meal. It was after midday and we took our time.'

'Weren't you afraid that there might be more Congolese soldiers?' Porky wanted to know.

'Obviously, there had been more than three men who had ambushed our patrol but we knew well enough that the rest of them would be fully occupied and would leave us in peace while we ate. The reporters were eager to get moving but we didn't want to get back too soon.

'By the time we got on the road, it was hellishly hot and the stink of the corpses, covered with a horde of huge, black flies made my stomach turn, but it was all good copy.

'We had got to within a mile of the crumbling walls of the missionary station when we ran into trouble. We had expected it and we knew exactly what to do. Four of us, me included, together with the reporters in a half track made for the station like a bat out of hell while the rest of the boys got down to some serious fighting.

'I must admit, I had a nervous moment as we rushed through the gates in case some of Lumumba's troups had stayed there as a reception committee but the place was as still as the tomb.

'And, in a sense, it had become a tomb. Everywhere, there were signs of disorder - windows broken, doors shattered and woodwork splintered. The only living creature to meet our eyes in the courtyard of the station was a frightened, half starved black dog which was whimpering in a corner. It was eerie. The deadly quiet in the blazing sunlight.

'Then, we saw the first of the Belgians. At first, it looked as though he had been killed by the blast of some explosive; his hair was singed and there was dried blood from a score of jagged wounds. The reporters stared, unable to take in what had happened. Then we showed them the bayonet stab marks. Again and again, the Belgian's body had been savaged. The slashing cuts in the testicles could only have been inflicted by bayonets and we made sure that the journalists got the point.

'Soon we found the others . . . One of them had been deliberately dismembered. The guy from the "News" threw up on the spot. Some boys must have worked him over with heavy hunting knives: the power of their blows had cut even through bones and I don't think that I have ever seen anything so horrible as those shattered and mangled limbs, lying in pools of congealed blood.

'They had massacred the bedridden sick also. All the men had been mutilated before being despatched. There had only been one woman in the building and her state was worse than any of them. Maybe she had been raped but there was no way of telling from what was left of her body. Her agony must have been excruciating: the bayonets had been thrust through to her womb. Have you ever seen anybody, disembowelled? Literally turned inside out. Well, you can imagine the impression that made on the naïve young reporters straight out from the East Coast of the States!'

'Were there no survivers?' I asked.

'Just one. One of the sick had managed to crawl under his bed. He had been stuck like a pig on a bayonet and left for dead. As a matter of fact, he didn't last much longer, but he was able to gasp out a few words, so the lads even had an eyewitness account.

'Of course, what had happened was that the main body of Lumumba's men, after they had ambushed the Katangan patrol, had made for the missionary station. They watched first to make sure that we had quit the place and gone to where they had left three of them to keep the patrol pinned down. They reckoned that we would not be so stupid as to carry our treasure with us into the jungle and that they could storm the station before we got back. We had purposely made it easy for them by not leaving anybody behind and they broke in, shouting and firing into the air.

'The doctor who tried to stop them was grabbed and interrogated. Where was the money? When he said that he didn't know anything about money, they bayonetted him to help to stimulate the memory of the rest. It didn't take them very long to discover the big, tin box which we had left behind.

'We didn't bother to translate for the journalists the account of how they had tried to open the booby trapped box and how four of the soldiers had been blown to pieces. The ones who had escaped went berserk and murdered and mutilated everybody they could find. That was the message which got into the papers.'

'Was this the truth about the raped nuns?'

'Xaviera, I have no idea whether there were any nuns or not, but it seems that you cannot have a decent atrocity without nuns being raped, so that was the way it crept into the story.'

'But you knew that would happen. It was a put-up job,' Porky gasped.

Stephen stared at him coldly. 'From that time on, there was no sympathy with the Congo Government. They were barbarous savages, murderers! As I told you, our war didn't have your chivalry. It was no place for men with weak stomachs. And, of course, they had murdered and mutilated – just like the boys on our side did whenever they got the chance but we were paid to fight, not to read sermons.'

'What happened to the soldiers who had captured the station after they had opened the tin box?'

'They guessed that we had the bullion with us and that we would be making tracks back to the station as soon as we had relieved the patrol so they waited for us outside. The rest of the mercenaries mopped them up after a bit of a fight. After all, we had been expecting them so there was no element of surprise and they didn't have our training or our equipment.'

'Did they ever get a chance to tell their version of what had happened?'

'No, Porky, we didn't want people confused by too many different accounts. We had our eyewitness story in the American papers and that was sufficient . . . We captured the black soldiers who had survived the skirmish – none of them got away.'

'But you didn't maim and massacre like they did?' I couldn't help shuddering as I put the question to Stephen.

'No, we were more civilized than that. We hanged them from the trees outside the missionary station. After that, the war rather fizzled out and once Lumumba himself had been disposed of – but that's another story.'

'I think that I've had quite enough of the reminiscences of you heroes for one night,' I told Stephen.

'You're quite right,' he agreed. 'Anyway, it's late and we ought to be making a move if we are going out for dinner. I don't know about you two, but all this talking has given me an appetite. I could eat a horse – or a black man.'

'You're a cold-blooded bastard,' Porky grunted, 'I don't know how you can even think about food after all that.'

But, when we got to the restaurant, he ate as hearty a meal as Stephen and me.

21

Fiesta in Ojen

'He that is of a merry heart hath a continual feast.'
Bible: Proverbs

I was in high spirits when, accompanied by the faithful Stephen, I drove up the long, winding road to Ojen. During the summer, there seemed to be a feria somewhere or other every few days. Down on the Coast, at such spots as Marbella or Fuengirola, they were noisy fairs with side shows, food stalls and unbelievable din. Tourists roamed, cameras at the ready to record what they thought were typical scenes of Spaniards enjoying themselves - all very typical and picturesque. But, up in the hills, in such villages as Benaharvis or Ojen, things are very different. With hardly any tourists, these local ferias are truly for the men and woman of the village. And for the children - above all, the children. The tiniest strut about, dressed in the most ornate finery of brilliant colours. Little boys in black velvet suits and silk foulards ogle six and seven year old belles who flaunt their lace petticoats and silk, scarlet, flouncy skirts. It could be a production of Carmen in Lilliput. Their parents stroll around the village, swapping yarns, eating, drinking and dancing and eyeing with amusement the odd foreigner, who had stumbled across the fiesta. By foreigner (estranjeiro), they would include anybody who came from further than the next village. The man from the next village was labelled a 'forastero', merely a stranger. These ferias were almost family affairs and although I was a mad foreigner (all foreigners are by definition mad) I was accepted with the amused tolerance that the good natured Andalucian shows to mortals not fortunate enough to have been born Spanish.

I know Ojen as a quiet, sleepy, miniature town but that

night there was noise and confusion everywhere. The local police were out in force and a very burly guardian of the law waved wildly, as I attempted to park in a tiny space. I was obliged to reverse up a narrow street and, avoiding a couple of trees and some other vehicles, stop the car a foot or two from a break in some railings and a sheer drop immediately beyond. Stephen offered to take over, but as he was not sure which was the position of reverse on my automatic gearbox, he almost gave me a heart attack before I chucked him out of the driving seat and finished parking the car myself, to hoots of applause, derision and encouragement from the highly amused bystanders.

The narrow streets were hung with lanterns and electric lights and music blared from loudspeakers placed in trees and dangled from walls. Somehow, I reflected, the Spaniards are impervious to noise. Cars roar down main streets with no mufflers; kids rev screeching bikes; neighbours shriek at each other across busy streets; radios and TVs are left on at maximum volume, completely unnoticed. I suppose the reason the people gesticulate so much in conversation is that they cannot hear what is being said in the general hubbub.

We had not made any arrangement to meet Jacques and Jeannine in any specific place but since everybody in Ojen knew them, we had no difficulty in getting directions. We made our way across the main square near which we had parked to a bar where the noise level was even higher than elsewhere. The place was foggy with cigarette smoke which blended with the natural reek of garlic from the snacks which were served at the counter. The place was so crowded that you would have thought that every man, woman and child in Ojen were in the bar – together with the odd sociable cat and dog. However, we had no trouble spotting Jacques. Spaniards tend to be short, stocky people, and Jaques' black, curly hair floated above all the other heads and hats around. We fought our way across the floor. Jacques clasped me in his arms and hugged me. Stephen struggled to the bar and brought drinks, but we were so pushed and jostled that quite a lot of what should have gone down our throats got spilled.

'Where's Jeannine?' asked Stephen.

'She and Juliette are in another bar. Finish your drinks and we'll go over and join them. I slipped in here to see a couple of friends.'

'We certainly can't talk here. Christ, what a racket!'

'You won't find it much quieter anywhere tonight, Xaviera.'

In fact, I did not find the noise, overpowering though it was, troublesome, but the kids were a confounded nuisance. They were everywhere, scurrying about like mice in a pastry shop, tripping over my feet, pushing, shoving, squealing and generally getting in the way. Spaniards are among the world's most indulgent parents. Having dressed their children up like dolls, they let them run riot with just the occasional mild rebuke or half-hearted slap when things got too much out of hand. Each proud papa grabbed his daughters by the hand, patted their raven black ringlets while pointing to his own grizzled grey mane, plastered down for the great night with foul smelling brilliantine, to let the world know just how much his adorable daughters, surely the loveliest in all Spain, took after him.

Jacques made his fond farewells to his friends. They were all exceptionally pretty women.

'Boutique owners,' Jacques explained with an airy wave of his hand. 'I have to keep them sweet, you know. Good for business.'

'Good for a hell of a lot of other things, too,' Stephen snorted, as we edged our way to the door.

Out in the street, we passed a group of teenagers, arms

linked, who were marching along the street, singing at the top of their voices. Jacques led us into another bar where the atmosphere, though festive, was a lot quieter. There were a number of young boys and girls but virtually no children. This was less of a family dive than the first bar. Jeannine and her daughter were sitting at a long table and they pulled up chairs for us.

'Weren't you enjoying yourself over there, dear?' Jeannine asked Jacques with a light, mocking tone.

'Oh, you know how it is with business contacts,' her husband replied. 'We have to keep them sweet.'

Jeannine nodded and then suggested to him that he wipe the lipstick off his collar. They both laughed good naturedly: at feria time, anything goes.

I looked around me. Everybody seemed to be having a good time. I particularly liked the look of a party of half a dozen older men, shirts unbuttoned, caps pushed to the back of their heads, sitting at a nearby table, intent on a thrilling game of dominoes. Dominoes is a game which intrigues me and I peered over at the friendly battle which was in progress but before I could make out how things were going, I received a hearty slap on the back and turning my head, found myself looking up at the grinning face of David Cradle.

'Hi, Xaviera, I was told that you were coming over to Ojen for the festivities. I was thinking of looking in myself and I wanted to see you again before you go off to Holland.'

'Yes, for me Spain is nearly over for another year. And all I have to show for the time I've spent here, is this,' pointing at Stephen.

'You could have caught a bigger fish than that,' David laughed, 'Better luck, next year.'

'I would have you know,' Stephen interposed with mock dignity, 'that, although a miniature, I am perfect in all respects.'

'Come and dance, Xaviera,' Jacques invited.

'What, out in the street?'

'No, not yet. Behind the bar, there's a sort of cross between a garden and a patio where the kids are dancing. Can't you hear the music?'

'There's so much noise, I can't tell what comes from where.'

Jacques took my hand and led me to a door at the back of the bar which led out to an enclosed space. The moment we opened the door, I was hit by the noise of a small but wildly enthusiastic rock band who were seated at the back of the garden. The dance floor was crowded, mostly with teenagers, casually dressed in blue jeans and check shirts in marked contrast to their rather overdressed parents and resplendent younger brothers and sisters. We joined in the dance for about ten or fifteen minutes. It was fun for a short time but the music went on without a break and without any contrast of tempo. It was hot and stuffy and after our short session, I felt like a drink, so we made our way back into the bar.

We found that plates full of tapas had been placed on the table - shrimps, mussels, chicken livers, chopped tomatoes and onions, olives, little sausages and practically everything soaked in the most pungent garlic.

'What do you plan on doing afterwards?' David asked Jacques.

'I thought that we might go up to that little gipsy place. They'll have some flamenco tonight for sure. I've brought a little hash with me, and we could have a quiet smoke up there.'

'What about Sylvie?' Jeannine asked.

She turned to a tall, dark girl who had joined our table while Jacques and I had been outside, dancing. She had been abandoned by her escort, a conceited French sculptor.

'I'd rather like to come along with you, that is if you

don't mind,' she answered.

I was pleased. Sylvie looked as if she might be fun. She was vivacious and there was a sparkle in her eye which took my fancy.

Another woman joined us. I recognized her as one of the admiring throng who had surrounded Jacques in the first bar.

'Hello, Antoinette, glad you found us,' Jacques cast a sheepish glance at his wife, 'Jeannine, this is—'

'I know - a boutique owner.'

I decided that the time had come for me to seek a change of scenery. The game of dominoes was still in progress, with the same earnest crew. I walked over and sat at their table.

'Mind if I sit and watch?'

'Suit yourself, but what would a woman know of so subtle a game as dominoes?'

'Enough to enjoy watching and even sometimes playing.'

The men all laughed. Obviously, I was a foreigner. Foreigners were nice, friendly people but without exception insane. And, of course, foreigners could not play dominoes like true Spaniards. Especially foreign women.

They were coming to the end of a game. They played very fast as if each of them knew exactly what all the others were going to do. Grunts of satisfaction, terse comments and exclamations of annoyance punctuated the game. The winner told the others just how badly they had played and they, in turn, congratulated him on his extraordinary good luck which had more than compensated for his lack of skill.

'Will you allow me to buy you all a drink?' I asked meekly.

The men looked at me with a fresh appreciation. They were not accustomed to being stood a drink by a woman. Still, I was a mad foreigner and they decided to humour me. If it gave me pleasure, they would graciously accept a glass of red wine. I called to Stephen to go the bar and fetch the drinks and I turned to the leader of the aged domino fanatics:

'Please, deal me in.' I pleaded, as the drinks arrived.

'Willingly, lady, but we back our skill with our wallets.'

'What sort of stakes are you playing for?'

Their spokesman rolled his eyes impressively and all of the men assumed grave and solemn expressions. They wanted to convey to me that heavy money was involved.

'How would it be if I agreed to buy another round of drinks if I lost?'

Their eyes twinkled. Their luck was in: the last of the big spenders had hit town.

They dealt: we played: I lost. It was almost as quick as that. The old men concentrated on the game with the purposefulness of rural Napoleons and they each seemed to be endowed with a photographic memory. Half way through the game, they recollected who had played what and had an accurate assessment of what pieces remained in each hand. I had to admit it. I was outclassed.

'How about another game?' I urged as the second round of drinks arrived.

'Lady, you have already been sufficiently generous. We shall play another round - but this time, not for money or wine.'

I thought that this was a high minded gesture, but Fate was on the side of the senior citizens. I had extraordinary luck in the pieces I picked up and my most dangerous adversary was put off his game when a youth tripped over a chair and spilled wine over him. By a combination of luck and some skill, I was the winner, to the amusement and amazement of the men. I decided not to put my reputation at risk and to quit while I was ahead. After all, I had avenged the honour of the foreign women. So I thanked them for the game and sauntered back to my table.

It was getting late. Jeannine had taken Juliette home and David Cradle had left. But there was a newcomer.

'Peter,' I cried, 'Peter from Poona. How have you been getting along?'

Peter still wore orange - his colour after his session with Bagwan. He greeted me with all his old tenderness. I had forgotten that his place in the mountains was not very far from Ojen and I had not expected to see him. Jacques was fully engaged in animated conversation with his attractive boutique owner. They did not seem to be discussing business. Sylvie was telling Stephen the story of her life - or at least that part of it which she cared to repeat. She was French and a fashion photographer. She had come to Spain with a boy friend for a holiday but they had split up. Not feeling like going home, she stayed on for a while on her own and had met the sculptor at his exhibition. Both of them were strong, extrovert characters; I had the feeling that they would not stay together for long.

'How about that flamenco show?' I called to Jacques.

'Oh, I'd love to join in the dancing in the square. Please, Jacques.' Sylvie tugged at Jacques' arm.

Jacques laughed. 'Alright, you two. We can go into the square and dance and then go on to the gipsy house.'

'House? I thought we were going to another bar.'

'You'll see, Xaviera. It really is a private house, but at fiesta time, they sell a murderous sangria and do a bit of singing and dancing. It's all very informal and friendly.'

'Come on, Jacques, let's go and dance.'

Sylvie was so insistent that Jacques called a waiter, settled the bill and we prepared to leave.

The square was seething with people. What might have been the town band was playing with great gusto for short spells and then recorded rock and roll took over. The dancing was joyful rather than stylish but almost everybody seemed to join in. A lot of the children were still up, prancing and imitating their elders in the dance area. Despite the lateness of the hour, several old women were sitting outside their houses, nodding to the rhythm of the music, while they bent over their knitting or rocked babies in their arms. They all wore sober black dresses, in contrast to the bright colours of the young girls and their grey hair was drawn together in a tight bun. They talked to each other and I got the impression that, in their own way, they were enjoying themselves as much as the more active participants.

Several young, Spanish boys grabbed my hand and danced with me, stamping their feet and clapping their hands and occasionally bursting into song. Then I found myself opposite Peter, who seemed to have become a livelier person than the meditative hermit I had previously met. I caught a glimpse of Sylvie who had pulled off a flimsy waistcoat which she had been wearing and, using it as a cape, was making mock passes at a big, burly boy who pretended to be a bull.

On one side of the square, some stalls had been erected and people sat about, sipping soft drinks or eating hot, sticky, scented pastries. Some of the local lads were lining up to try their hand at a rifle range, blazing away with more swagger than expertise at a row of clay pipes as they attempted to win a doll in traditional dress for their girls or a box of cheap sweets for patient wife or girl friend.

After about twenty minutes street dancing, we were ready for a rest and quiet drink, and Jacques led the way, past the stalls up a steep alley. I plodded behind him, up the worn, irregular steps between ancient houses. All was still and there were no street lamps or lanterns. In place of the smell of boiling oil from the food shops or stale cigarette smoke, the air was fragrant with the heavy scent of jasmine. We might have been in another village, indeed in another province but for the distant sounds from the square, drifting faintly on the breeze.

As we approached the end of the alley, I heard a woman singing to the accompaniment of a couple of guitars. The music came from a slightly ramshackle house, the front door of which was standing half open, casting a shaft of bright light into the pitch black through which we were climbing. We pushed our way in and found ourselves in a large room, lit by candles and oil lamps. About twenty people were sitting around the walls, a few on chairs, most sprawling on the floor. The atmosphere was heavy with smoke, not all of it from tobacco, and an older woman was dispensing drinks, including the notorious sangria. The price of the drink was really an entrance fee, so my glass of Coke looked a bit expensive.

The woman performer had just finished a song and she strode into the centre of the room, holding her skirts up almost to knee height, and began to dance. Her black, patent leather shoes crashed down, setting the room echoing as she stamped with the savagery and the precision of a machine gun. All around, the audience began to clap, rhythmically and ever louder until the whole place seemed to be exploding, while the dancer set a pair of castanets throbbing and clicking, as she waved her hands over her head. She was a tall, dark, arrogant woman. A true gipsy and proud of it.

However I was fascinated by one of the boys who was playing the guitar. He swayed with the music and seemed to be part of it. His instrument moaned and wailed like a soul in the torments of a tragic love. The boy could not have been more than sixteen or seventeen. His black hair was tousled and I could see the stains where sweat had streaked his swarthy face. What gripped my attention were his eyes, black and glowing. I decided that this young boy could be a passionate lover: he had that smouldering look.

When the dance was over, I leaned over and offered the

boy a joint which we had prepared. He inhaled deeply and gratefully before passing it back.

'What's your name?' I asked.

'I am called Juanito.'

'You play very well.'

'Thank you. I have played ever since I was a tiny child. I cannot remember a time when I could not play the guitar. You know, we gipsies have a hard life: we are a poor people, but we always have music.'

Our conversation was interrupted by the resumption of the flamenco. Under the influence of the music and the joint, everybody began to get mellow and when Peter suggested that at the end of the entertainment, we all go up to his house and end the night 'in sweetness, love and tenderness,' as he put it, we were all in agreement.

'I would like to ask Juanito, as well,' I suggested. 'He could bring his guitar and help set the mood.'

'He could probably do a lot more than that,' Jacques smiled.

At the next break in the music, I asked Juanito whether he would come with us.

'Yes, indeed, I would like to, if you are prepared to wait till we have ended our last song in about a quarter of an hour.' So, when the music came to a close, we made our way down to the square to wait for the boy who had to pack his guitar and collect his pay before joining us.

By now, the band had gone home and things had quietened down. Just beyond the square, on the way to where we had parked, another, miniature version of the main square had become the meeting place of a group of teenagers, now that the organized entertainment was over. It was a charming spot. A low, stone wall and several orange trees screened it from the road and in the centre stood a diminutive fountain and two wrought iron benches. The walls of the houses around the tiny plaza were lavishly decorated with coloured ceramic tiles in a style as traditional and ageless as the architecture of the simple, single-storey buildings. Pots of begonias and geraniums, hanging from the walls on curly, iron frames and brackets, gave a bright and festive air to the place.

The kids, three boys and a couple of girls, were seated on one of the benches. Showing off, they were perched on the back of the bench, dangling their feet on the seat. The boys, in tight T-shirts and jeans puffed cigarettes with the same display of self assertion as their elders, the same macho gestures, the same natural, almost insolently proud, grace in all their movements, as though the flamenco lived in their veins. The girls giggled excitedly and flirted and coquetted, revelling in their new independence.

Suddenly, as we watched, the players in this pantomime froze. Strolling up the street came the village policeman, his face bored and unconcerned. Then, he saw the teenagers and his expression changed from dreamy amiability to stern alertness to duty and consciousness of the respect which was due to a guardian of the law.

'Take your feet off that seat and comport yourself like human beings.'

The kids climbed down and sheepishly and silently settled down on the bench like good children, but made sulky grimaces the moment that the uniformed, majestic presence turned his back to resume his dignified progress and no sooner had he turned the corner, than they were back once more in their original, arrogant position.

Juanito came clattering down the street, his guitar slung over his back and we walked to my car which, as it happened, was only a few feet from Peter's. We drove off, Peter leading the way and Juanito bringing up the rear on a noisy spluttering motor bike.

Peter's house was small but elegant. We went inside and collected a few drinks and then brought them out into the garden to where Peter set light to a fire which had been prepared earlier, perhaps for some projected barbecue. We lay on mattresses or on the soft, spongy grass beside the pool, under the shade of a stately cypress. The fire threw flickering shadows and the garden seemed the most peaceful, the most tranquil place in the world. We sipped our drinks and passed a joint which I had rolled. The mood was relaxed and sentimental, and then the boy, Juanito, began to sing softly and sweetly, an old gipsy song of forlorn love and the sadness which follows passion. His long, black hair fell over his face and, crouched over his guitar as if over a lover, he was a romantic figure with the firelight playing over his handsome features.

I think that we were all in a tender, loving mood by the time the music faded away. From the corner of my eye, I could see Jacques stretched on the grass beside Antoinette, gently stroking her breast. I motioned to Juanito to come and join me, and as he laid down, I ran my hand through that fascinating hair.

Juanito was not a subtle, sophisticated lover: indeed, he was a bit clumsy and a bit intimidated at the idea of doing anything in the presence of possible onlookers.

'Don't worry,' I murmured, 'nobody's paying any attention to us.'

Slowly and deliberately, I unzipped his jeans and gently took his throbbing cock in my hand. It was not that big but good and firm and I placed it between my lips and let my tongue play gently down the shaft. Juanito quivered and gasped. Then, grabbing my shoulders, he pulled me up so that he could plunge his hand into my crotch. Foreplay was not his forte but I was ready for a simple, uncomplicated fuck, and that is exactly what I got from Juanito. He was a young animal. His breath came in irregular, panting gulps as he thrust into me with all his might.

'Take it nice and easy' I urged but he kept up his piston

blows. He did not hurt me and he came pretty quickly but I was far from satisfied. At his climax, he let out a short, sharp cry, half a shout, half a shriek and then fell back in my arms with a muffled moan. I disengaged him, the strong, raunchy tang of his sweat acrid in my nostrils and I felt his juice trickling down my thighs.

Over on my left, I saw that Jacques was busy supplying his boutique owner with something which she really favoured. They were side by side and Antoinette was pressing big, wet open mouth kisses on his lips. Their rhythm was easy and unhurried, like waves rippling on the sea. Behind me, Stephen and Sylvie were petting rather than making love: nearby, Peter sat quietly, watching the scene. There must be some sort of telepathic rapport between us for, as I remembered that evening when Peter and I had laid together and been united in every sense except the physical, he smiled at me and came to my side.

Juanito recovered with the resilience of youth and I looked forward to a session with him and Peter, who, I was sure could show him how to soften his lovemaking. But when Peter kissed me and slipped his arms around me, Juanito shrank away. I called him to join us, but he shook his head and nervously took up his guitar as Peter nibbled my ear and stroked my tits.

Making love to Peter was, for me, the completion of our earlier evening together: it was as if we went on where we had last left off and the intervening time had never existed. For a fleeting moment, I had a twinge of conscience over Stephen, but I convinced myself that he was not the jealous type and that anyway, he should by now be fully occupied with Sylvie. A short break would bring us back together more closely and with greater passion than before. Or so I told myself. I knew at that time I wanted Peter and that I had always wanted to complete what we had started before I even knew of Stephen's existence.

In fact, neither Stephen nor Sylvie wanted to fuck. They were content to fondle each other. They had drunk and smoked quite a lot and both were in a cheerful but passive frame of mind, enjoying touching each other and watching the rest of the mini-orgy.

Juanito was not at all sure of how he ought to react, and he sat back by the fire and plucked a plaintive tune on his instrument. He kept sneaking a look at Jacques, who was now sitting up and, holding Antoinette's legs over his shoulders, was diving deep into her. Probably, Juanito did not realize that there was more than one position in which a couple could perform. Peter and I set about furthering his education. I had Peter on his back, and I sat astride him, kneading and pinching the flesh on his shoulders and his chest.

There was a gorgeous moon and the combination of the bright moonlight, the brilliance of the stars and the glowing embers of the fire was magical. The only sounds were the sad tones of the guitar and the busy chatter of insects – and a certain amount of heavy breathing and murmured words of endearment or encouragement.

Then, in Stephen's unmistakeable English accent:

'Christ, I must go and bleed the lizard.'

'I do not understand, Stephen.' Sylvie was understandably mystified. Stephen had obviously not got round to telling her of his days in the Congo and his racy army slang. 'I see no lizard. Are you not comfortable with me? And, then what do you do with the bleeding lizard when you have bled him?'

I burst out laughing. Trust Stephen to destroy a romantic mood! The little man blundered off to have a pee. Perhaps he intended to make it back to the house and find the lavatory and 'bleed his lizard' formally and privately like a true, blue-blooded British aristocrat. Maybe, he only wanted to make it to the nearest clump of bushes where he would be out of everybody's way and relieve his feelings there in a manner more becoming to an ex-mercenary and soldier of fortune. I never got around to asking him. What actually happened was that Stephen, possibly still a bit befuddled by alcohol and hash, was just a trifle unsteady on his feet and at the psychological moment, a passing cloud obscured the moon. In the sudden darkness, Stephen tripped over Juanito's foot – the boy was sprawling on the ground – lost his balance and staggered a couple of paces before overbalancing and falling headlong into the pool.

I suppose I must be one of the luckiest ladies in matters of love and sex. Only seconds before Stephen's show-stopping performance, Peter and I had enjoyed a great, shattering orgasm together. I think that he had been ready to come and had held back until he felt me arriving at my climax. It was a lovely long, throbbing finale to our love-making which swelled into a wonderful sense of triumphant fulfilment.

Then came Stephen, and romance gave way to farce.

'Don't bother to bleed your lizard, drown it!' I called to him.

Stephen struggled out of the pool, dripping and swearing. Peter bought him a towel from the house and Stephen took no active part in the rest of the night's festivities.

Antoinette had disengaged from Jacques and she walked over to me and asked me if I had a cigarette. I told her that I did not smoke, but instead of moving off to one of the other people, she squatted down beside me, in what had been Peter's place. I suspected that she was bisexual and still unsatisfied. I stroked her hair. She responded immediately and enthusiastically. When she saw what was developing with the two of us, Sylvie came over to join us.

Feeling mischievous, I called to Juanito to enter our erotic group, but that was expecting too much from him.

Blushing and confused, the gipsy shook his head, still clutching his guitar. Women making love to women - that was a depth of depravity to his way of thinking which was too unnatural to bear thinking about.

'It is late: I must leave.' Juanito called - and made a desperate dash to where he had left his motor bike. I heard him call a few words of thanks to his host and then, with an ear-splitting roar, he disappeared into what was left of the night.

We made a lovely daisy chain, Antoinette, Sylvie and myself. There is something about the way women make love to each other which is gentler, sweeter and more tender than straight me-Jane, you-Tarzan, sex. Peter sat back and watched contentedly and was soon joined by drip-dry Stephen.

When we finished, dawn was already streaking the horizon, and Peter brought us back to earth with a breakfast of ham and eggs. As we left, I wondered just how Jacques would explain to Jeannine the intimate nature of his business chat with the boutique owner. Perhaps, she was well accustomed to the occasional lapse. As far as Stephen and I were concerned, it was back home to catch up with our sleep.

'You didn't mind my enjoying myself with Peter, did you darling?' I asked Stephen.

'No, of course, not. After all, we're not married. You do what you please and so do I.'

I glanced at him. I was not sure that there was not a trace of jealousy there. He gazed back at me and then grinned.

'Well, let's say I didn't mind too much. I kept telling myself that when the night was over, you would be coming back to me and then nothing else mattered.'

I squeezed Stephen's hand. I knew that he would never become the love of my life, but he could be good fun, good company and above all good humoured.

22

Highway Robbery

'God hates violence. He has ordained that all men Fairly possess their property, not seize it.'

Euripides

The days were getting shorter and, like some migrating bird which had lost its inner calendar and consequently mistimed its homing instinct, I knew that I must head north, back to Amsterdam.

The days and nights after our return from Ojen were fully occupied with frenzied preparations for our departure. There were so many things to do, both for Stephen and myself that we were too exhausted to hit the town and we passed our evenings at home. Until the last evening.

The last suitcase had been closed - and reopened three times as some forgotten item came to light, business letters had been signed, the car had been serviced, housemaid and porter tipped. I felt that I badly needed a holiday.

'Xaviera, sweetheart,' Stephen's tone was apologetic, almost sheepish, 'we've been so cooped up in this flat that I've not had the chance to say goodbye to some of the boys. How about our slipping out for a farewell drink?'

'Not me, darling. I've had it. You go if you want to, but remember that we want to make an early start tomorrow, so don't make a night of it, will you.'

'I'll be an hour, that's all. Or maybe two,' Stephen added, and with a reassuring smile and a quick kiss on my cheek, for all the world like a suburban husband running out to the local pub or the neighbourhood deli, he took his leave.

I noticed that Stephen had left his key to my car behind, (he had sold his own), so I knew that he would not be going far but I decided not to wait up for him. He had his own key to the apartment and I had a long day's driving ahead of me the next day.

I was awakened by what at first sounded like a revolution breaking out just outside my front door. As I staggered out of bed, I realized that, in fact, somebody was knocking urgently and energetically. When I opened the door, there stood Jaime, a large, swarthy man from northern Spain who had opened a bar at the end of the road. Jaime was supporting the limp form of Stephen whose face was wreathed in a seraphic smile.

'Have to get back,' Stephen's voice was slurred but his tone was contented. 'Got to start early. Mustn't wake up Xavi—' He gently lapsed into unconsciousness. Jaime picked up the little man and deposited him on his bed. I glanced at the clock. It was just before five o'clock.

'Thank you for seeing him home, Jaime.' It was chilly and I pulled my flimsy robe tighter around me. Jaime stared at me as if his eyes were fitted with X-rays. 'He had his keys in his pocket. You could have got him inside without knocking.'

'But then I would not have seen you.' Jaime made it clear that he was in no hurry to depart and sat himself down on the sofa.

'Jaime, it's lovely to see you and you were very kind in looking after my bottled beau. But, as you heard, we are leaving early in the morning, in a couple of hours in fact. So, please don't think me inhospitable if I don't invite you to stay.'

Jaime was unco-operative. 'You have never asked me home, Xaviera and now you are leaving Spain and heaven knows when we shall meet again. Business has been bad and I may not be here when you come back next year. I'm thinking of selling the bar.'

'I'm sorry. I do hope that things get better for you.' And I moved towards the front door. Jaime continued to sit on the sofa.

'I am not leaving until you give me a proper farewell.' Jaime's obstinacy was evident in his voice and the truculent jut of his jaw. In case I was in any doubt of what he wanted, he unzipped his fly.

'Oh, no, Jaime, not now!'

'What's the matter, Xaviera? Have you become a prude?'

One look at the wolfish lustfulness in Jaime's eyes was enough to convince me that there was no way that I could be rid of his company except by fucking him. I was furious at Stephen. To think that I had to pay for the delivery of my bombed boy friend with my fanny! I was in a hurry to get what little rest was left for me that night, so I led the unappetizing specimen of male chauvinism into my bedroom. He wanted fucking: he would get it so fast and fierce that he would come before he realized what had struck him.

Jaime had no difficulty in getting an erection. His penis led the way into the bedroom but my body could raise no enthusiasm. I grabbed a bottle of body lotion and splashed it between my thighs and over Jaime's straining member. I rubbed it good and hard to hurry him on his way. He smelt of stale sweat and alcohol. Jaime must rank high among the world's most unromantic studs. I slithered him into me and bucked wildly. I could feel Jaime trying to hold back. Although he was not paying, he wanted his money's worth but I was ready for him. I gave him no respite and as he squirmed, I pressed a finger up his ass and squeezed the semen out of his prick.

'Wait' Jaime gasped weakly, his knees buckling.

'That's it,' I called, and before he could recover, I had pushed him off the bed, across the room and through the front door. He was still on the doorstep, getting his breath back when I opened the door again and thrust his trousers into his hand.

'Good night and goodbye.' I called and slammed the door.

Before going back to bed, I looked in at Stephen. He lay, crumpled on his bed, snoring noisily but with an expression as carefree as that of a new born babe. With difficulty, I resisted the temptation to pour a bucket of cold water over him and tell him just what I thought of him. The morning would exact its own revenge on the drunk, I mused.

The sun rose a couple of hours before I did and I scowled at its brightness. Having lecherous bar owners interrupting my sleep does not put me in the best of spirits next day. With grim determination I set about rousing Stephen from his coma. I think that Jesus had a somewhat easier task when he raised Lazarus from the dead, but I stuck at it and eventually my man had resumed a vertical position and was helping to stow cases away in the car. He worked like an automaton, his unfocussed eyes, parched lips and croaking voice were all calculated to increase drastically the premium on his life assurance.

'Do you feel as horrible as you look?' I asked.

By way of reply, Stephen tottered into the bathroom and was sick.

'What do you want for breakfast?' I called cheerfully.

Before we left, I had some orange juice, scrambled eggs and tea. Stephen had gazed unsympathetically at a piece of dry toast. However, as we drove, the breeze seemed to revive him and after about half an hour, it became apparent that he had survived. I stopped at Malaga to fill the car's tank and the power of speech returned to my companion.

'Before we hit the road again please can we stop for a cup of coffee?' he pleaded.

I was misguided enough to give way to compassion. He had deserved to suffer but, by God, he had suffered.

Furthermore, I wanted more lively company than the pale, mute Stephen could provide without being stimulated by strong, hot coffee. The problem was that it was too early for the cafes in the business area to be open. They really got going after nine and it was about half past eight. So, I drove into the dock area, thinking that there we might find some all night cafe – a pull up for truck drivers or a spot for sailors.

The streets grew shabbier and shabbier and the neighbourhood more and more run down. We passed derelict sheds as we headed towards the gaunt, tall cranes which lined the waterfront. There were not a lot of people about; a few knots of seamen at one corner, some North African teenagers strolling along a side street. The place was dreary and depressing.

'There's nothing here,' I remarked, 'we'd better turn around. We'll find somewhere further along the road a bit later.'

'Try a little further,' Stephen implored. 'Once we get out of town, there's nowhere for miles. There's sure to be something near here.'

He was right. A few hundred yards along the street, we found a dirty, miserable apology for a cafe – and it was open.

'You coming in?' Stephen asked, as he climbed out of the car.

'No way,' I replied. 'I wouldn't be seen dead in a dive like that. You go and get your cafe au lait: you'll probably pick up some unmentionable disease just sitting on the chair. I'll stay in the car. There's all this luggage. I wouldn't like to leave it with nobody to look after it in a place like this.'

So, Stephen went into the cafe. I was parked on the other side of the road, and I could see him through the grimy window, as he relaxed at a table and waited for his life saving brew.

Although it was still early, the car was hot and stuffy. I wound down the windows and resigned myself to sitting patiently until Stephen returned. There was nothing in the seedy street to maintain my interest, a few empty shops and old warehouses. Tattered remnants of sun bleached posters advertising long past corridas hung forlornly from lamp posts and a few political slogans were chalked on the flaking plaster of the walls of the cafe and the neighbouring buildings. The road was littered with garbage and a few stray, half-starved dogs sniffed among the debris. The scene was deserted apart from a handful of youths, loafing on a corner. They were shouting, laughing, and pushing each other about like young puppies at play and I never spared them a second glance.

Turning in my seat, I pulled my shoulder bag from the back seat and dumped it down on Stephen's seat. I unzipped the bag and took out a book which I was half-way through. I found my place and started to read.

After a couple of minutes, I heard the sound of approaching footsteps and the heavy metallic clunk of the car door opening.

'That was quick, Stephen', I said approvingly. I finished reading the sentence and then looked up.

It was not Stephen. One of the young boys had opened the car door and now had his hand on my bag. For a split second I was too shocked to move. Then, I crashed my hand down to save my bag. The kid glared at me like some wild animal which had been startled. In that instant, I registered the coarse black stubble on his chin, the streaks of dried sweat, the grim, cruel jut of his jaw. Then his fist smashed into my face. My head snapped back and he tore my bag from my hand, whipped it out of the car and was running at top speed down the road.

I was stunned by the blow. He had punched me in the

eye and for a moment, I could see nothing. There was blood in my mouth from where I had bitten my tongue. It all happened so quickly that I could hardly credit that I had been robbed in broad daylight in the middle of a busy city.

I screamed. Then I shouted to Stephen to come and chase the thief. He had seen nothing of what had occurred and, on hearing my voice, he pointed contentedly at his cup as if to tell me that his coffee was too hot and that he had not yet finished.

In less time than it takes to tell, I had leaped from the car, crossed the road and run into the cafe.

'Quick, Stephen, I've been robbed. Come on, we can catch the kid. I've left the engine running.'

In a flash, Stephen was on his feet. He threw down a hundred peseta note and together we galloped out of the cafe.

Our quarry had disappeared around the corner. My left eye hurt and my vision was still blurred, but I could see well enough to drive.

For a few minutes, I was hopeful that we would corner the thief. There was not a lot of traffic and, once we were round the corner, we caught sight of him, sprinting, my bag clutched under one arm. He glanced over his shoulder and saw the BMW rushing after him like the chariot of some avenging angel. Ducking past a little knot of men who were gossiping on the sidewalk, he darted off into a narrow alley, too narrow for the car to follow.

I screeched to a halt and Stephen and I jumped out and started running down the alley.

Here, it was even dirtier and dingier than the street. We had gained on the kid while we drove but, on foot, he had the advantage. There were more people about and the thief was as agile as an eel, as quick as a deer, as cunning as a fox. We plunged on. My only hope was that the alley would lead to a dead end but I had the sickening realization that he was on home ground and knew where he was leading us.

The boy was hidden from view by a bunch of really tough looking men, probably dockers. They made no attempt to get out of our way and we could feel the waves of hostility arising from these heavily built, surly men. There was no way we could catch our man in this mob.

'Hold it, Xaviera,' Stephen panted, 'the natives appear distinctly unfriendly. We had better get back to the car. This lot will pick a fight so as to rob you.'

'Dammit, I've been robbed.' I shouted bitterly.

'Don't tell me. Tell the local lads and try and convince them. Seriously, you're wearing a valuable watch and they look as if they are ready to have a go.'

He was right. Three or four of the men were sidling up towards us. Big, bearded muscular men with an air that was mean and menacing.

'Christ!' I cried, 'and I've left the car unlocked. God knows how many of these thugs are helping themselves to what's left of our valuables.'

We turned tail and fled. I could hear some of the men giving chase but as soon as we were back in the street, they gave up. Fortunately, when we got back to the car, nobody had taken advantage of my foolishness in leaving it unlocked and unattended.

'Has he taken much?'

'A few thousand pesetas in cash, some travellers' cheques and, worst of all, credit cards,' I answered Stephen. 'Lucky I took out my passport or we'd never have got out of the country. What now?'

'We'd better find the police.'

That proved more difficult than we had imagined. We went back into the cafe and explained what had taken place. Nobody was interested. We asked where we could find the police and the atmosphere became even more chilly. Finally, we found one man who reluctantly gave us directions to the nearest station of the Garda Civil.

It took us a quarter of an hour to follow his instructions and find the station. When we burst in, I had the sickening sensation that we were following a cold trail.

'I've been robbed' I told the desk sergeant.

He looked bored and picked up a long, official form.

'If we hurry, you can probably catch the kid,' I added.

'What's your name?'

I told him.

'Let me see your passport.'

'Can we deal with the formalities later. I can take you in my car to where the kids are hiding.'

'Hand me your passport.' His tone was bleak and I realized that he was more concerned with getting rid of the troublesome foreigner than tracking down one of the local lads.

Three quarters of an hour later, we had completed the form and listed, as far as I could recollect them, all the items which had been stolen. On learning that I was on my way back to Holland, the policeman told me that he would write to me as soon as something turned up. That was one fan letter which has still to be delivered.

By now, the traffic was very thick in the seaport and it was some time before we had found our way back to the highway. I glared at Stephen.

'You and your bloody coffee! If you hadn't drunk yourself paralytic last night, none of this would have happened.'

'Come on, honey, don't overreact,' Stephen protested. You've lost your money, you've lost time, don't now lose your temper.'

I swallowed my rage and shut up. After all, I couldn't push all the blame on the hapless Stephen. The way I had left the car unlocked and displayed my bag so temptingly on the seat had been asking for trouble. But I took out my irritation in my driving. I normally drive fast but this time, I cut in on slower vehicles, slashed the car around corners and behaved in a thoroughly selfish, bad mannered way.

'Gently, Xaviera,' Stephen murmured, 'you're scaring the living daylights out of me.'

I shot a glance at him. His complexion was a most unbecoming shade of green. He looked as if he might be sick at any moment. I pressed harder on the gas.

It was late that evening when we checked into one of the best hotels in Barcelona. Stephen had survived my savage driving but it would be a gross distortion of the truth to suggest that he had enjoyed the experience.

However, the little man had great powers of recuperation and he was eager to get out and do Barcelona by night, largely to take my mind off the bad time I had suffered. Luckily, I had avoided getting a black eye, although it was still painful.

'Come on, Xaviera. Hose yourself down and put on your glad rags. Uncle Stephen has had a few words with the All-Knowing Hall Porter of the hotel and I am able to promise you a super evening – a fitting farewell to Spain.'

'To hell with Spain,' I growled. 'Hoodlums, crazy, brutal kids, parasitic cops! I've had enough.'

Even as I was saying these words, I knew that I was over-reacting. There were plenty of good, friendly, helpful Spaniards and I loved them and their country, but I just didn't want to think about them in my present bout of bad temper. Nevertheless, I allowed myself to be soothed and placated by Stephen and after a hot tub, I began to feel better. After an expensive and beautifully prepared dinner which Stephen had chosen for me, I was sufficiently recovered to consent to go on living. Stephen smiled as he noticed that I was thawing.

'And now, my dear, we are going to take in a show,' he told me. 'I've got it all worked out. All you have to do is to sit back, take it easy and enjoy yourself.'

I was prepared to do just that and leave all the arrangements to my escort. I had no idea what sort of entertainment he had in store for me.

We took a taxi. Stephen told the driver where to go and the destination was obviously somewhere well known to him. We drove through the town for less than ten minutes. When I saw where we had stopped, all my annoyance returned.

'Good God, Stephen, do you think that I need to be taken to a sex-club? Don't you think that I have seen all there is to be seen in these lousy, stale dumps? I'd rather go back to bed.'

'Now, wait a minute, Xaviera,' Stephen replied, patting my hand. 'Give the place a try. I'm told that it is quite new and really good. If you don't like it, we can always leave.'

Grumpily, I allowed Stephen to buy a couple of high priced tickets and followed him into the building.

What we were offered was a complete programme of movies and a couple of live shows. I followed Stephen along the narrow, scarlet painted corridor and up a flight of steep stairs into a little cinema with seats for about fifty people. The place was fairly full and although there was a sprinkling of tourists or foreign businessmen, most of the audience were Spaniards, the men looking excited and sometimes even a little embarrassed and the girls, of whom there were markedly fewer, attentive as if they were about to hear a serious lecture.

A well-dressed man walked on to a small raised stage and quietened the audience down. Then, he told us that we were about to see three short porno-movies, especially imported from Germany and Denmark and never before shown in Spain. He hoped that we would find them entertaining and that they would put us in a happy frame of mind to go on to the live shows. With a cheery wave of his hand, he signalled for the lights to be lowered and the show to commence.

The movies conformed to certain well-established patterns and the sight of the wild nymphomaniacs raping the would-be burglar made me giggle: it was so corny.

All around me, I heard sounds of disapproval at my lack of respect for the sublimity of the Art of the Film. The more they tutted and shushed me, the more I felt the ridiculousness of the situation. Pornography is a humourous business: without humour, it becomes dull and pompous.

'Stick your finger up his bum!' I called out to the girl on the screen who was busy working up the overpowered male victim.

'Silence.'

'Behave yourself.'

'Show a little restraint.'

'Don't spoil the film for the rest of us.'

The whole auditorium echoed with protests at my irreverence. I could feel that Stephen was ill at ease but I was still working out my annoyance and spite from the earlier part of the day. When the first film was over and the lights went up, Stephen suggested that we moved on to the live show and I was quite prepared to forego the other films. To the relief of the rest of the rest of the audience, we hurried out, and they settled back to watch an up to date version of 'What the Butler Saw' with all the seriousness of devoted church-goers at a funeral service.

After the movies, the live shows were a welcome surprise. In the first, there was a small stage on which a series of girls, some naked, others scantily but provocatively dressed, performed short dance sequences and mimes.

What impressed me was .that the girls, all young and pretty were obviously enjoying themselves. They were exuberant and enthusiastic, not like the bored routine acts which so often are paraded in Northern Europe. There was fluffy blonde girl, possibly Dutch or Scandinavian, who danced with a puppet. It was an amusing act and when we applauded, the girl burst out laughing. Here there was good humour and a real bond of sympathy between the performers and the audience. A dark girl who played the part of a French maid had the laciest knickers I have ever seen, but she slipped them off before the end of her turn and snuggled seductively on the lap of a middle aged Spaniard who had been watching the show in silence up to then. He was so confused that he did not know how to react, but he sure got plenty of good advice.

From then on, all the girls played up to one or more men in the seats near the stage. Everything went well until there was a turn by a vivacious black girl. She was African, very dark with frizzy hair done in Bo Derrick ringlets, and a snub nose. The way she moved her limbs and shook her breasts, as if in some tribal dance, revealed the natural grace and poise of a jaguar. Her expression was defiant. The eyes of the men were riveted on her. I found other girls prettier, but without doubt, she was the sultriest, sexiest performer in the cast. She slunk off the stage, stared at each of the men in turn and dismissed them with a haughty toss of her head. Then, suddenly, she wheeled around and threw herself on to Stephen's lap.

His reaction was instantaneous. He leaped to his feet, hurling the girl off him with all his force.

'Get away from me, you filthy, black bitch!' he shrieked, completely out of control.

From all around, there were hisses of disapproval. The girl gazed at him in contempt and sauntered away. Stephen had pushed her away as if she were contaminated and he was brushing at his suit, which as it happened was white, as if to remove any trace of where she had touched him.

'What the hell's the matter with you?' I demanded. 'She didn't do anything to you.'

'I saw so many like her in the Congo,' he growled. 'I might even have shot her father for all I know. Can't stand them.'

This time, it was my turn to hustle him out of the room. He had irritated me with his extreme reaction and I told him just what I thought of his racism but he was unrepentant.

We stalked into the other live show, where a lanky but very fit American boy quietly and methodically fucked a handful of girls. He was so relaxed and so self-assured that he chatted happily with the audience, while keeping his erection and working effortlessly at his troop of lovelies.

'Do you keep this up all night?' I called.

'Lady, it's no sweat. I can keep this up all night. Just nice and easy. And the girls, they know just how it goes. Isn't that just sweet?'

He beamed at me. Everybody seemed to be enjoying themselves and the whole show was under control.

He moved off a redhead and a tall, dark girl took him in her mouth. With a happy expression, he leaned back, tucking his hands behind his head.

'Christ, anybody could do that,' Stephen fumed. 'And to think he gets paid for it.'

He was clearly still in a black mood after his brush with his black lady. Also, Stephen had had a few drinks, during dinner, after dinner and now between shows. I knew that sometimes his response to alcohol was wild, almost childish, abandon but there were other occasions when he became stubborn and aggressive. I spotted the signs.

'Sit back and enjoy the show,' I urged.

The guy on the stage waved cheerfully to us, and this was for some reason, the last straw for Stephen.

He lurched to his feet and clambered on to the stage, struggling to unzip his flies at the same time.

'Move over and make way for a real man. I'll show you how it should be done.'

'Now, sport, just you climb down from the stage nice and quietly. This show is not one for audience participation.' The American was quiet and conciliatory but Stephen was not in a reasonable mood.

'Get your ass down here,' I hissed.

The girls made it clear that they had no need for his assistance and they tried to shoo him away. However, Stephen's retreat was expedited by two burly bouncers. I caught up with him on the doorstep.

'Thank you for an eventful evening.' I told him coldly.

'Oh, come on, Xaviera, that was nothing. Let's go on somewhere where there is some real action.'

'I am going straight back to the hotel to get some sleep. If you want some fun, you go on your own. But don't think that I am going to wait for you in the morning. In fact, Stephen,' I added, 'are you sure that you want to drive on with me to Amsterdam? You didn't seem to enjoy today very much and when you are hung over, you are lousy company for me.'

'Well, the way you drove today scared the daylight out of me. If you're going to be in the same mood tomorrow, I'd rather not be beside you.'

'That's fine, Stephen. I know that you are on your way to London, so why don't you have a good time tonight in your own peculiar way and then get yourself a plane direct to London? No hard feelings: we stay good friends but we each go our own separate way.'

'No, I can get a plane to Amsterdam.'

'Don't bother. It's not worth it. Give me a call some time.'

With that, I hailed a passing taxi and left Stephen to do what ever the fancy took him for the rest of the night. To tell the truth, the incident in the show had made me realize that while I found him amusing and often good company, I had no really deep feeling for Stephen. I was not involved with any man - or for that matter any woman - and beneath the gloss of friendships, I was truly lonely. To continue with Stephen would have been a sham and it would not have deceived him for long, since there was no way that I could deceive myself into thinking that our relationship was anything more than a pleasant way of passing time.

Next day, I drove out of Spain, alone.

Three weeks had passed. I was lying in bed with a Dutch boy friend. He was a big, strong guy and a fantastic lover. We were recovering from an energetic session and Ces was asking me about my experiences in Spain. He was intelligent, but something of a stay-at-home.

'So, you got beaten up and robbed. Sounds a great country. Why the hell do you want to go back there again next year, Xaviera?'

'Spain's not really like that, Ces. Of course, I enjoy the sun and the sea, but I could find as good or even better conditions in a dozen other countries. No, I genuinely like the people. The violence comes almost always from the kids, often very young indeed, twelve and thirteen year olds.

'Spain has brought in a lot of the comforts and the ideas of our so called advanced countries of Western Europe and the States. It's only natural that they should have imported some of the bad things as well as the good. But in the little towns and the villages of Andalucia, the old ways and the old values survive.'

'You mean that they loll about in the sun and don't get down to a decent day's work?'

'God, Ces, you are so dour, drab and Dutch! No, that's not what I mean. And, as a matter of fact, it is not a true picture. The Spaniard has only the vaguest notion of time – we all know about manaña. But when the plumber who promised by all that he held holy that he would come to do some work in your house on Monday at ten, eventually turns up at two or three on Thursday, apologizing for his early arrival, he gets down to work with a seriousness as great as anything that you will find here. Don't kid yourself, Ces, Spaniards are hard workers, but they refuse to be organized into great, faceless crowds. They are shameless individualists.'

'Like you, Xaviera?' Ces grinned.

'Yes, like me. And, I suppose that is the basic reason I like them so much and feel so much at home there. When I go on my journeys, I am taking on the world. I find friends wherever I go, yet the whole thing is a great adventure – Xaviera versus the rest. And that is a pecularly Spanish way of looking at life. I can give you an example. You know how crazy Spaniards are on bull-fighting. Every now and then, some wildly enthusiastic, young man will leap into the arena and take on the bull himself, using his T-shirt as a cape. If he is lucky, he will win the applause of the crowd and spend the night in jail. If he is unlucky, he will be dead. El Cordobes, the great torero, started his career in this way and not so long ago, he stood aside and watched as some unknown kid, attempting an espontaneo, as it is termed was gored to death, trying to emulate him and win recognition by his reckless bravery.'

'Oh, come on, Xaviera. I know that successful bullfighters are as overpaid and as pampered as pop stars. How else can an impoverished kid break into the show biz world of the bull fight?'

'No, Ces, you are being too cynical. What you say is true, but it is only part of the truth. What you are missing is the pride, even arrogance, and exhibitionism of the Spaniard. He is a swaggering man of honour, your

Spaniard, certainly in Andalucia, and as jealous as the devil.'

We were interrupted by the phone. It was Stephen.

'Hello, Xaviera, did you have a good trip back. No little differences with the police, no more highway robberies?'

'Thanks, Stephen, no everything went smoothly. Where are you calling from?'

'I'm in London. In bed, actually - like you, I expect.'

'Sure. I'm with a divine man. If you like, I'll put him on the phone and introduce you.'

If I thought that I could discomfort Stephen, I was due for a disappointment.

'Don't bother, dear. I am in bed with two very pretty chicks and I thought that you might have a word with them. You see, I have explained that you are the accepted authority on blow jobs and I would like you to give them a quick lesson over the phone. You'd like them - big boobs, built for Polaroid shots. You see, I am a faithful lover - I always come back to the same type.'

'I'll give your bedmates a crash course over the phone when we get a video system. For the present, they must just use their imaginations. Good night, Stephen, sleep well.'

And I hung up

Why did I feel a pang of jealousy? I was not in love with Stephen and I was in bed with an attractive, young stud. So, what the hell should I care, if Stephen was entertaining a couple of amateurs? Maybe I had become even more Spanish than I had realized.

Next trip to Spain, I could undertake my own espontaneo, but I had yet to find who would be playing the part of the intrepid bull. Could fearless Xaviera find a worthy adversary?